Endc

"Don Collett has written a gripping and powerful story of a dramatic adventure and an all-American boyhood. Compelling and highly entertaining."

Michael Levin
Author of 40 books

"Collett teed up a masterpiece."

Billy Casper, Professional Golfer
1970 Masters Champion

"…a chilling, action-packed survival story about life in rural America. You won't be able to put the book down once you start reading it."

Rear Admiral Bill Harris
U.S. Navy (Retired)

"The pro who taught me the fine points of golf has surprised me with a suspenseful tale drawn from his youth. Don Collett brings to his storytelling the same passion and craft he practiced on the course."

Logan Jenkins, Columnist
San Diego Union-Tribune

"It's just not fair one individual can be as superb a writer as he is a golf professional. Don Collett commands a word processor with the same grace that he uses with an 8-iron."

Frank Williams, CPO
U.S. Navy retired

"You don't have to love golf to thoroughly enjoy Don Collett's nonfiction account of good and evil on a Nevada ranch. Don can drive a golf ball as well as he can power a story."

Dick Harmon, Columnist
Salt Lake Deseret Morning News

"A 300-yard smash off the tee. An awesome story. You'll love it."

Rear Admiral William Thompson
U.S. Navy Retired

THE WELL

"Collett teed up a masterpiece."

—Billy Casper, Professional Golfer
1970 Masters Champion

THE WELL

Surviving A Summer Of Terror In The Western Nevada Desert

A Novel Based On True Events

Don Collett (signature)

DON COLLETT

The names have been changed to protect the innocent.
Any resemblance to actual persons, living or deceased, is purely coincidental.

iUniverse, Inc.
New York Lincoln Shanghai

THE WELL

Surviving A Summer Of Terror In The Western Nevada Desert

Copyright © 2005 by DON COLLETT

All rights reserved. No part of this book may be used or reproduced by any means, graphic, electronic, or mechanical, including photocopying, recording, taping or by any information storage retrieval system without the written permission of the publisher except in the case of brief quotations embodied in critical articles and reviews.

iUniverse books may be ordered through booksellers or by contacting:

iUniverse
2021 Pine Lake Road, Suite 100
Lincoln, NE 68512
www.iuniverse.com
1-800-Authors (1-800-288-4677)

ISBN-13: 978-0-595-36260-8 (pbk)
ISBN-13: 978-0-595-80705-5 (ebk)
ISBN-10: 0-595-36260-5 (pbk)
ISBN-10: 0-595-80705-4 (ebk)

Printed in the United States of America

Contents

Acknowledgements ix
Author's Note xi
Prologue xiii
Chapter 1 1
Chapter 2 6
Chapter 3 11
Chapter 4 19
Chapter 5 26
Chapter 6 32
Chapter 7 37
Chapter 8 44
Chapter 9 51
Chapter 10 57
Chapter 11 65
Chapter 12 73
Chapter 13 80
Chapter 14 88
Chapter 15 93
Chapter 16 99
Chapter 17 105
Chapter 18 113
Chapter 19 120
Chapter 20 127
Chapter 21 133
Chapter 22 140

Chapter 23	144
Chapter 24	150
Chapter 25	157
Chapter 26	163
Chapter 27	171
Chapter 28	177
Chapter 29	182
Chapter 30	187
Chapter 31	193
Chapter 32	199
Chapter 33	205
Chapter 34	211
Chapter 35	218
Chapter 36	226
Chapter 37	232
Chapter 38	236
Chapter 39	240
Chapter 40	246
Chapter 41	254
Chapter 42	258
Chapter 43	265
Chapter 44	270
Chapter 45	277
Epilogue	281

Acknowledgements

TO VERLA, RANDY, CRAIG, PAUL & BRIAN

&

ROD IN MEMORIAM

A grateful thanks for your love and support over the years.

It's been a wonderful journey.

And to

MICHAEL LEVIN AND BRIAN COLLETT

A special "thank you" for your assistance and comments

while editing this novel.

Author's Note

In the process of assembling my memoirs, I realized when I was writing about my teenage years, a story could be told that would be of interest to both young and old alike.

As I thought about that fateful time in my life, years of suppressed memories suddenly came flooding back to me and I began recalling the frightful events that had taken place in the summer of 1939 when I was a 13-year-old boy.

Thus inspired, I temporarily put aside my memoirs and began writing about those events that I had virtually forgotten about. It was no easy task, but still, I remembered some of the things of that long ago summer as if they had happened yesterday.

The effort started out to be a short story; yet, as I thought about the actual people and a faithful little sheep dog who played a prominent role in that real life drama, I felt a strong need to expand it into a book length, non-fiction novel. Other lesser characters and events were added to bring a meaningful purpose to the book.

I then wove the story around life and actual events that took place on and around a large working ranch in western Nevada, including a tragic day when my two cousins and I were abandoned and left to die in the desert by two ex-convicts from the Nevada state prison. Only when it was too late did we realize that we had been led astray by those two renegades.

That terrible experience, along with some others recounted herein, so traumatized me that in the intervening years I seldom thought or talked about that difficult period in my life.

Perhaps that is why I waited so long to write this book.

Don Collett
San Diego, California
December 1, 2005

Prologue

The Summer of 1939
In the Western Nevada Desert

We began our journey right after the break of dawn. In the early morning light, the barren desert was eerily beautiful; quietly beckoning, even luring us onto its dusty plain, but quite unwilling to reveal what lay ahead of us.

If we had only known of the dangers we were about to face, my cousins, 15-year-old Bob Banfield; his brother, Jimmy, 13, and myself, Danny Collins, also 13, would have never volunteered to herd a flock of sheep from my uncle Jesse Banfield's 1,275 acre ranch southeast of Fallon to a 1,100 acre spread he was leasing further to the north.

If all went well, it would take us a full day to make the trip. If we didn't finish the drive before nightfall, we would camp out under the stars and bring the herd in the next morning. The Banfield's faithful sheep dog, a border collie named Nellie, was helping us to drive the herd along a well-marked trail that was supposed to have led us to the North ranch by nightfall.

At Bob's invitation, I had come over from my home in Midvale, Utah, in late June to spend the rest of the summer with him and his brother, Jimmy. Bob said it would be a working vacation, but I knew better having lived on a farm most of my life.

Still, I liked the idea of spending time with my two favorite cousins. Even though I was only six months older than Jimmy, I was used to the rigors of farm life and could hold my own as far as a heavy work load was concerned.

Just prior to leaving on the sheep drive, uncle Jesse, Bob and Jimmy's father, had given us some last minute advice:

"You boys need to watch the herd closely and if any of the sheep start bleeding from the nose or frothing at the mouth, make sure you put 'em down an' rest 'em for awhile."

Jesse's crusty old ranch foreman, Hank Johnson, also warned us about becoming dehydrated:

"It's a nine mile trek, laddies, and it's going to be hot as hell out there today, so drink plenty of water, and if you get tired, get up on Charley's wagon and ride for a ways."

Charley Hartwell was the Banfield's salty old sheepherder and he told us he would join us at mid-morning after he finished his chores and inspected his remaining flock, mostly young lambs, in the southeast pasture.

Charley had never married and his nomadic lifestyle was always a subject of humorous comments among other ranch hands; mostly because he always referred to the sheep in his flock as "my little sweethearts."

Providing direction to the north ranch was eight milestone markers that would direct us to our destination. Having Charley join us meant that we would be well provisioned, but Johnson still cautioned us to make sure we followed the well marked trail since neither Bob, Jimmy or myself had been to the north ranch before. His advice was simple enough:

"Just follow the markers," he said. "Charley knows the trail and he'll hook up with you shortly so you won't get lost. He had some more advice:

"We've stashed some food and water for you inside four milk cans at the second, fourth, sixth and eighth milestone markers so you'll have plenty to eat and drink along the way."

He also informed us that some feed, hay and troughs of water for the sheep were in place at those markers. With Charley and his chuck wagon following us, we knew we wouldn't be hungry or thirsty as he promised to feed us whenever we got hungry.

It didn't turn out that way!

* * * *

A cool, quiet morning had gradually given way to blistering heat and swirling wind gusts. As the sun glared down upon us, the only sounds breaking the still desert air were the tinkling of the Bell Sheep and the constant bleating and baaing from our stricken herd that had been without food and water for hours.

When Charley failed to arrive by mid-day and no one had come out to check on us, we knew something had gone terribly wrong. We had consumed all of the meager provisions that we were carrying with us by early morning and when we discovered that some of the milestone markers directing us to our destination had been purposely relocated, our anxiety level mounted with each passing hour.

Instead of taking us on a more direct route to the ranch, as Hank Johnson had indicated, the mis-directed markers had sent us on a tortuous, zig-zag journey that was far off the path we should have been taking.

Our extra life-sustaining food and water supplies had also been destroyed at the milestone markers. The more we anguished over our plight, the more we came to realize it was the cruel antics of two newly-hired ranch hands, Jake Dalton and Bernie McCoy, that were the cause of our dilemma.

Johnson had hastily hired the two trouble makers when he found himself short of help at the Banfield ranch. They had passed themselves off as experienced ranch hands, when in fact, they were ex-convicts. Their records were as long as their arms and both had served time in the Nevada state prison in Carson City for bank robbery and attempted murder.

Dalton had been released in late June after serving nine years of a 10-year sentence. McCoy had been paroled four years earlier on lesser charges and had been biding his time and doing odd jobs until his running mate was released.

We learned of their criminal pasts shortly after Johnson had put them on the ranch payroll. We overheard the ex-cons talking one evening about some of the dirty deeds they had committed before being sent to prison; including tossing some drunks down a well after robbing them of their gambling winnings.

When Dalton and McCoy found out that we had eves-dropped on them and we now knew of their criminal pasts, they threatened to do the same thing to us if we didn't keep quiet. Their threats scared us into silence and the frequent confrontations we had with them during the summer simply served as prelude to a final, disastrous encounter that left us fighting for our very lives in the desert wastelands of western Nevada.

Chapter 1

Midvale, Utah
Saturday, 8:10 a.m.
June 24, 1939

The phone rang three quick times before I could answer it. My cousin, Bob Banfield, was on the line extending an invitation to spend the summer with him and his brother, Jimmy, at their father's ranch near Fallon, Nevada. I knew where Reno and Las Vegas were located, but Fallon?

"Where's Fallon—and why are you calling me so early?" I grumped.

"It's over by Reno, Danny. I've got to know right away, 'cause we're leaving early Monday morning."

By now, I was half-awake, and half mad, at Bob for waking me up so early.

"I'll have to think about it, Bob. I'm working for my dad now and I don't think he'll be too happy if I take the rest of the Summer off."

"Ah, he'll let ya' go, sleepy head. Get back to me as soon as possible. We've already started packin' the car."

Bob sounded too cheery to me. Maybe it was the early morning call and the fact that my enthusiasm for anything was always at its lowest level early in the morning.

School had been out for a month and my job as a carpenter's helper on my dad's construction crew was earning me a small fortune! At least, given my prior circumstances, it felt like a fortune. I had even gotten a raise since last year, from 25 to 35 cents an hour, and I was feeling so rich after earning $56 for my first month's work that I could hardly stand my new-found prosperity.

I had even managed to save $27.35, which was nearly half of what I had earned to date. That little treasure trove was stashed inside an old tin canister under my bed for safe keeping. It wasn't drawing interest like I would be getting if it was in a bank, but at least it was in a safe place where I could count it and touch it every day.

I had big plans for the rest of the money I would earn during the summer. Now that I was working, my parents, Roland and Luella Collins, fully expected me to buy my own clothes for the upcoming school year.

No one knew that I was planning to replace my battered, old Wilson tennis racquet with a brand new Slazenger, which was, at a cost of $24.95, the most expensive racquet on the planet.

"After all," I reasoned, "why shouldn't the Utah Valley Boy's Singles Champion have the best equipment?"

I had surprised everyone last year, including myself, when I won the 10-12 year-old age division title in Provo, a small university town about 33 miles South of Salt Lake City.

I had exacted a promise from my dad earlier in the year that work wouldn't interfere with my tournament tennis. Having turned 13 in January, I would be competing with the 13 and 14 year-olds this summer. The talent around the Salt Lake valley was deep in that age division, but I felt that if I could play and practice often, I could be competitive in that age group.

So, what to do? I was suddenly torn between making money and giving up tennis to spending time with my cousins in a place that I'd never heard mentioned before in family circles.

By now, it was late afternoon on Saturday and I had yet to get up enough courage to ask my mom and dad if I could spend the Summer with my cousins in Fallon.

"How's dad going to feel about my wanting to take the rest of Summer off," I wondered, "and why should I give up making money and playing tennis just so I could go to some dusty little town in Nevada with my cousins?"

I knew my mom wouldn't be too anxious to let me go either, but in my own mind I began to rationalize that summers are supposed to be brief periods of fun for young people who have temporarily thrown aside the boring regimen of school.

The more I thought about it, the more enticing Bob's invitation appealed to me. Making money, even playing tennis, suddenly became secondary issues and I was caught up in a momentary wave of adventurous dreaming.

"If I couldn't hang out with my boyhood pals in my own home town," I reasoned, "why not spend the Summer with my two cousins on their dad's ranch in Fallon?"

Besides, I'd never been on a real vacation before, or even out of the state of Utah for that matter, so the idea of a working vacation on a big ranch in western Nevada seemed exciting to me.

Bob's mom and dad, Jesse and Vera Banfield, had purchased a large ranch and leased another the first of the year. Then Uncle Jesse had moved all of his farm equipment and several of his ranch hands from the South Salt Lake valley to Fallon in early March.

Bob and Jimmy had stayed behind in order to finish school and would be going over to Fallon with their older brother, Dean, to help their mom and dad with the Summer ranching operations. Dean's wife, Tess, would accompany them.

I was having some misgiving about accepting Bob's invitation, so I called him back and asked for more information about the situation in Fallon before approaching mom and dad.

Bob said his dad was in desperate need of help. With some 250 cattle, not including the young calves born in the spring, and some 300 sheep to feed, 38 cows to milk and a 100 acres of alfalfa maturing for a second cutting, plus miles of fence to mend, his dad simply had more than he and his meager crew could say grace over.

The crew consisted of eight workers plus an experienced foreman, Hank Johnson, to help him operate the 1,275 acre South ranch, where most of the work was being performed.

The 1,100 acre North ranch, which Jesse was leasing, had an abundance of water but aside from some good pasture land, it was mostly fallow ground.

Johnson had been with Jesse for 11 years and knew everything there was to know about raising crops, cattle and sheep. But, he was spread thin, help-wise, and needed another three or four experienced ranch hands to effectively manage ranch operations; at least through the Summer and Fall months; the harvest seasons.

How much help we could be remained a big question, but just having their sons, Dean, Bob and Jimmy, at the ranch would give Uncle Jesse and Aunt Vera great comfort. It would also provide Hank Johnson with some extra hands.

According to Bob, Johnson was an old time cowboy and didn't take any guff from anyone. His crew was virtually working from dawn to dusk; five, sometimes six, days a week. Even then, a lot of things weren't getting done around the ranch and Bob said his dad was getting grumpier by the day.

Such long hours not only taxed everyone to their physical limits, but their patience as well. Maybe, Bob said, that was why his dad and Hank had such a hard time keeping a full crew of ranch hands. They simply worked them too hard.

"That's why he needs us over there PDQ."

"PDQ?" I inquired.

"Yeah, pretty damn quick, so let me know if you can go as soon as possible."

Sensing a bit of reluctance on my part to accept his invitation, Bob hastily pointed out that it would be "kind of a working vacation. We'll have some chores to do—like helping to milk the cows, herding sheep and all that kind of stuff—but there'll be plenty of time to ride horses and go fishing."

Somehow, I knew Bob wasn't into the truth at this point of the conversation. "Oh, yeah," I chided him, "I'll bet there'll be a lot more work than play."

Still, I reasoned, it would be fun, since I would be able to spend the Summer with my favorite cousins. But, the work part bothered me since I knew Uncle Jesse's habits from conversations overheard at past family gatherings. He was the closest thing to human perpetual motion everyone had ever seen.

He was always on the go. He even beat the roosters up in the morning and he was the last man standing at night. Somehow, he managed to father 10 children, five boys and five girls, but of all my cousins, I was the closest to Bob and Jimmy Banfield.

When Bob explained the work/play routine on the telephone, I wondered anew if the Summer would be better spent working for my dad rather than laboring for nothing on a ranch in far off Fallon, Nevada. It was going to be a touchy subject to bring up during supper time.

"Getting mom and dad's okay to go might present a problem for me," I told Bob, "but I'll ask them anyway and call you back in a little while."

"Okay," he responded, "but I need to know as soon as possible. We're bailin' out early Monday morning, ya' know."

"You could've called sooner," I groused while wondering why Bob had waited just two days before departing for Fallon to spring the invitation on me.

"Yeah, I should've let you know earlier—sorry about that." I hung up, still having some knawing doubts about leaving my well paying job as a carpenter's helper. It was hard work. I wasn't enjoying it; especially having to get up early every morning, but I looked forward to payday each Friday afternoon.

Chapter 2

The carefree days of earlier years when I could go swimming, ride my bike into the nearby canyons, play tennis or just fool around with my buddies at the Midvale community park were becoming distant memories. Those were the activities I had always looked forward to each Summer. Now, for the second year in a row, my days were filled mostly with work and very little play.

As he had last year, my dad, Roland Collins, had informed me just before school let out in mid-May that he again expected me to work in his construction crew as a carpenter's helper. Until I reminded him, he hadn't even offered to give me a promised raise over the 25 cents per hour he had paid me last year. When I brought that touchy subject up, dad just shrugged his shoulders as if to say "tough luck." Then I reminded him of that promise.

"Okay, I'll give you a 10 cent raise, but that's all I can afford to give you right now. Times are tough, son, just in case you didn't know it."

As an after thought, and perhaps to emphasize the point he'd just made, he added: "Just be thankful that you even have a job."

I guessed he was right on that account. Of course, he also knew I was almost tapped out, money-wise; so, he could be less than generous with the offered hourly rate.

Following dinner, I hesitantly broached the subject of going to Fallon with the Banfields. I fully expected dad to say no; but just the way he responded to my request made my heart skip a beat.

"You planning to spend the rest of the Summer there?"

"Yes," I replied timidly.

Dad pondered the reply for a few moments; then turning to my mom he inquired as to when we were supposed to go on a long-planned, but frequently postponed, family vacation to Lake Tahoe.

We had never vacationed out of the state before, or anywhere else for that matter; except for two or three day outings over the 4th of July holiday or Memorial Day to visit relatives in Northern Utah. Everyone knew those brief get-togethers were more like social gatherings among relatives rather than vacations.

This Summer, though, a special treat was in store for the Collins and the Banfields. We were going to spend a week at Lake Tahoe. My dad's older sister, Judith, and her husband, Stanley Horton, an English professor at the University of Nevada in Reno, owned a beautiful home (with two additional cabins) on the Nevada side, or Eastern shore, of the lake between Emerald Bay and Zephyr Cove.

The Horton's spent their Summers and holidays there and this year, much to everyone's surprise, they had invited the Collins and Banfields to vacation with them in late August. The Hortons were a polished, very reserved, couple who never had children. They didn't seem particularly comfortable around common folks like us; especially kids, so we were surprised when they had extended the invitation to join them at Summer's end.

"We're supposed to meet your sis and Stan at the lake on the 21st of August," mom said to dad. Then, signaling her approval with my request, she added:

"I think we should let Danny go. We can pick him up on our way since Fallon is only about two hours from the lake. Besides, we can stay over for the night and drive up the next morning with Jesse, Vera and their kids."

"Well," dad groused, "we might as well let him go; otherwise, he'll sulk all summer long."

I couldn't believe what I was hearing! No strong objections, as usual; no railing about working and saving money for school. Much to my surprise, Dad didn't fuss at all, but a look of grudging approval betrayed his real thoughts.

Jumping up from the table, I ran to the phone and dialed 267, Bob's three digit phone number.

"Hey, Bob," I shouted excitedly, "mom 'n dad said I could go!"

"That's great, Danny! See ya' Monday morning. We're gonna leave early…about seven, so don't be late."

Getting ready to go to Fallon with cousins, Bob and Jimmy, was turning out to be a big chore. My mom insisted that I have all clean clothes for my Summer at the Banfield ranch which meant a couple of trips downstairs to the wash room for her then standing an hour or two at the ironing board getting each wrinkle out of my shirts and trousers. The little duffle bag I was planning to take with me wouldn't handle everything she had washed and ironed.

"Mom, I can't take everything I own," I complained. There's not enough room in the car for my stuff and everyone else's."

"I know, son, but I'll bring some of your other things along when we come over in a couple of months. I know you can pack three outfits in your bag if you roll them up like the sailors do when they go aboard ship. Just be sure to keep yourself clean. Take a bath every day and brush your teeth every morning and night."

"Does swimming in a pond take the place of a bath, mom? I know we'll be doing that if there's one around."

"Absolutely not! You need soap and water to get yourself clean. Dirty pond water won't wash off the dirt and grime you'll have on you from working and playing around the ranch all the time."

"Ah, mom, give me a break! Water is water as far as I'm concerned."

I loved my mom, but she was always getting on me about keeping clean and what I should be wearing.

As I watched her ironing into the night, I thought back on the difficult times our family had experienced in the recent past. I was too young to remember much about the depression years, the late 20's and early '30's, but the difficulties we had experienced in the aftermath were still fresh in my young mind.

Dad had been doing odd jobs around the Salt Lake valley and by the Fall of 1933, he and mom had another new mouth to feed. My younger brother,

Chris, was born on October 9th, just two weeks after dad had cut off the tip of his index finger on his right hand while planing a piece of wood.

It was a painful experience for him in more ways than one.

He was not only embarrassed by his clumsiness, but it put him out of work for several days; something he could ill afford to do. I remembered how hard he had struggled to make ends meet and provide for our family's basic needs as the country emerged from ravages of the depression.

Then, in the Spring of 1933, he landed a job as a carpenter, building chicken coops up on the Decker farm in Sandy, Utah. I remember Mom telling us how happy she was about that opportunity.

Good jobs were hard to come by in those days even though dad had skills that an ordinary artisan rarely possessed. Not only was he a skilled craftsman and carpenter, but he could design houses as well. Trouble was, no one was building or buying homes at that time. Back then, we paid little heed to the fact that we were poor. I guess we didn't fully realize it at the time as everybody in our neighborhood was in the same situation.

We lived our lives in plain and simple ways—in quiet desperation, really—and while we were not unmindful of our circumstances, we were secure in our belief that a more promising future was just around the corner.

Sometimes, we were in such dire straits that mom had to borrow butter and eggs, even sugar, from our next door neighbors. She was always careful to note those borrowings, though, and she made sure she repaid them later on while reminding us constantly that even though the future looked bleak for us, things were going to get better.

We believed her despite our desperate circumstances.

And our little world did improve. By the mid-1930's the emerging economy presented better opportunities and dad found steady work at the Midvale smelter where they refined mineral products from ore shipped in by rail from the Utah Copper Mine in Bingham.

The mine was in the Oquirrah mountains some 35 miles west of Midvale. The world's largest open-pit copper mine was located there and its ever-widening spill-over could be seen for miles around. By then, dad was making a decent wage and we were living on a small 10-acre farm on State street near 7200 South in Midvale. He had regular hours—8 to 5—and mom knew exactly when to have the evening meal on the table.

At 5:30 p.m. each work day the Collins family, consisting of my mom and dad, Luella and Roland Collins; my older sister, Joline, and my two younger siblings, Sherry and Chris would sit down to eat and chat about what had happened that day.

After supper, we'd do the evening chores; slop the pigs, feed the cows and chickens and clean up the yard. Since we had a coal stove, it was my job every evening to pack in a bucket of coal and an arm full of kindling wood so mom could fire up the stove for cooking meals.

I don't know how dad managed to buy that little farm in 1936. He must have borrowed some money to do it. After moving in, I became more impressed with the barn than I was with our house.

The barn had a large area for storing hay, huge lofts where we could hideout or sleep during the Summer and indoor pens for our animals. The house had two large bedrooms, a bathroom, a comfortable living room and a long, narrow kitchen.

There was a small bedroom upstairs and that is where my younger brother, Chris, and I slept. On cold winter nights, we'd carry up a heated rock or a hot water bottle and put it in the bed to keep us warm for most of the night.

My brief interlude of remembering the past was interrupted when mom finally quit ironing clothes. It was quarter to eleven; well past my bedtime, but she was determined to make sure my clothes were clean and ironed when I left for Fallon on Monday, which, normally, was her day to wash and iron clothes.

As she quietly folded up the ironing board and put it in the closet until another day, I could see the weariness in her eyes and her bearing. The weight of a long day hung heavy on her shoulders; still, she didn't complain. As I scooted off to bed she gave me a motherly hug and again warned me to bathe often and keep my clothes clean while I was at the Banfield ranch.

Chapter 3

Nevada State Prison
Carson City, Nevada
Sunday Morning
June 25, 1939

The grey stone walls of the Nevada state prison loomed ominously in the distance as Bernard (Bernie) McCoy slowed his old '34 Chevy sedan to a virtual stop. As he pulled into the parking lot across from the prison's entrance, a chilling reminder of days past flashed through his mind.

It had been 47 months and 29 days since he had been released from the same prison. His five-year sentence had been reduced to four years for good behavior and being a model prisoner. He was still on probation but that would be up in a year if he stayed out of trouble.

"How ironic," he thought to himself, "I'm coming back as a free man; not as a criminal to be locked up once again."

Now, he was about to pick up his former partner-in-crime, Jacob (Jake) Dalton, who was being released from prison after spending the past nine years behind bars for bank robbery and attempted murder. Both had been sentenced at the same time, but another five years had been tacked onto Dalton's prison term for the attempted murder charge.

It was a crime that had pained Bernie for years and he cursed under his breath when he thought how stupid he and Dalton had been to try robbing a bank; especially in Fallon. In their own hometown of all places! Robbing a store or putting a hit on some unsuspecting soul to steal money in the dead of night was one thing, he reasoned, but robbing a bank and shooting people in broad daylight?

"Not too smart," he told himself.

Dalton had been the trigger man in that bank heist and they both had barely escaped a much longer sentence when the two victims who survived his shooting rampage eventually recovered.

Dalton had been given a more severe sentence than McCoy since he was the trigger man in that failed bank heist. Five arrests and two felony convictions were among the serious items on his rap sheet. That didn't count the many times he had been in juvenile detention for being a troublesome teenager in and around Fallon.

Now 31, Bernie's record was nearly as bad; in and out of juvenile detention since he was 13, three arrests and a felony conviction.

Dalton had informed McCoy by letter that he would be released on Sunday morning, June 25th, at 9:00 a.m. He was more than anxious to be leaving his prison days behind him.

The letter lay on the seat beside McCoy and, as he had many times in recent days, he re-read it again just to make sure that today was the right date and he was on time to pick up his old buddy.

The scraggly hand writing was hard to read since it was written in pencil; especially the cryptic post script which reflected Dalton's anguish about his time in prison:

"Don't be late. I've served enough time in this hell-hole to last me a lifetime."

* * * *

After waiting over an hour, McCoy began wondering if his long-imprisoned buddy was actually going to be freed.

"Surely," he reasoned, "Jake must have known the exact date and time of his release. Otherwise, he wouldn't have written him to be at the prison at 9:00 a.m., his release time."

Bernie felt grateful that he was on the outside rather than on the inside of those ugly stone walls surrounding the prison. It was a brutal place to be incarcerated and he thought back to the times he had spent breaking rocks, being put on bread and water at the whim of prison guards and thrown in the "The Hole" for bad behavior.

That hole was actually a tunnel in a hill behind the main prison building where rock had been quarried since the Nevada State Prison was established as a maximum security facility in 1862.

He remembered his first distressful day in prison and how the guards had taken him and several other new prisoners on an orientation tour of prison facilities to impress on them the futility of trying to escape and what was expected of them while serving their time. He later learned it was standard procedure to show new inmates around the dreary looking premises.

The guards figured a history lesson quickly learned was the best deterrent if anyone was harboring escape ideas. They enjoyed telling the prisoners that if they were going to "get accustomed to the comforts of their new home," they had to become acquainted with prison history. The guards would then reveal how the prison came into existence when the Nevada legislature purchased a run down hostelry, the Warm Springs hotel, and 20 acres of land for $80,000 in 1862.

The inmates were told that the former owner of the hotel, Abraham Curry, became the first warden and he promptly kicked out all the women of the night and set about building new prison facilities that would harbor the most hardened criminals in the state.

After spending a year breaking up rocks, working in the laundry and then making license plates, a prison enterprise for the citizens of Nevada, McCoy had finally earned some soft duty; working in the library where he re-stocked shelves with the volumes of well-worn books that had been read and returned by inmates.

McCoy read a lot while re-stocking the book shelves. Inevitably, he came across prison records and the infamous history of the Nevada State Prison; one of the oldest prisons in the country. In the early years, he learned that Nevada's lieutenant governors also served as wardens of the prison, but when one of them, a fellow named John Denver, refused to yield the prison to the new lieutenant governor, P. C. Hyman, the governor sent in 60 men and artillery to force him out.

The prison had always been Nevada's maximum security facility and while no one had ever escaped, some had died trying. Those who did attempt to escape were severely punished and sent to "The "hole," the infamous, dungeon-like tunnel in a hill behind the prison where the more hostile inmates were sent for solitary confinement.

After a few days or weeks there, the hard core criminals would end up on the rock pile behind the prison yard. Over the years, enough rock had been quarried from that site to build several important structures including the state capitol building in Carson City.

* * * *

As he waited for Dalton to appear, McCoy also remembered his misspent youth and life of crime with his long time buddy. He and Jake had known each other for nearly 18 years. They had begun committing petty crimes in and around Fallon when they were in their early 'teens. When they became suspects in a number of local robberies, they went out of town; to Sparks, Reno and Carson City; returning to Fallon where they divided the cash and stolen goods between themselves.

Being a convicted felon, he thought, wasn't something to be proud of; especially when nearly a third of his life had been spent in juvenile detention or behind prison bars. At 31, McCoy was old beyond his years and somewhat embittered over the way his life had turned out.

His dad, William (Bill) McCoy, had been an out-of-work alcoholic who never cared about anyone but himself. His mother, Elizabeth McCoy, had to work two jobs, as a hotel maid and a cocktail waitress at a local tavern in order to keep the family together.

It was all she could do to put food on the table, buy a few clothes from time to time and pay the monthly rent on their small apartment in downtown

Fallon. Her husband would often beat her if she didn't give him enough money to satisfy his thirst and addictive gambling habit. Bernie was the only child in that unhappy family and he was left alone to fare for himself most of the time.

Undisciplined, lonely and seeking companionship, he began roaming the streets. Before long, he fell in with a group of rowdies, all of whom were a two to three years older than he was at the time. As a new kid amongst the rowdies, he had to earn the respect of his peers which meant robbing some poor soul, with the help of an older member of the gang, and bringing the loot back to a pre-arranged meeting place so it could be shared with his newfound buddies. He accomplished that goal within a month. Jake Dalton was his partner in crime on that occasion.

McCoy was attracted to Dalton, the senior member of the rowdies. Dalton taught McCoy the tricks of their trade. They started working together; robbing drunks and gamblers as the unsuspecting revelers departed the casinos and saloons in and around Sparks, Carson City and Reno.

"Those kind of guys are easy pickin's," Dalton told McCoy. "They're not hard to deal with and they don't offer much resistance." He offered McCoy another piece of advice:

"Put the hit on drunks who have gals on their arms. They're the ones that have won a little money and are goin' to a hotel to celebrate."

Maturing rapidly in physical size and street smarts, McCoy would remember that advice as he robbed unsuspecting "customers;" as they were referred to by members of a loosely-knit band of hell raisers in and around the Fallon area.

Dalton was a rangy, big-for-his size young man who grew up too fast and his fiery temper would sometimes get out of control when he put a hit on someone. He seemed to take great delight in knocking his victims senseless if they resisted.

Recognizing that McCoy was becoming a street kid that could be trusted, Dalton took him under his wing. It actually became a big brother-little brother-type relationship and together they stole and robbed their way through their teenage years.

In Dalton, McCoy finally found someone who would take care for him. They became a vicious twosome as they robbed stores and held up innocent victims while living on the wrong side of the law. School was an afterthought for them and upon being caught, they would spend time in juvenile detention centers or in jail; always promising the authorities they would go straight when they got out.

McCoy was a high school drop out at 16 and Jake had quit going to school after the ninth grade. By the time McCoy was 20, and Dalton 22, they had served over three years of their young lives in juvenile detention or behind bars.

Their wayward paths seemed to run parallel courses whether it was in or out of prison. They always seemed to be traveling down the mean street of life rather than the main street where civility and the rule of law prevailed. But it was the bank heist in Fallon that proved to be their most serious crime and the one that had landed them in prison. Dalton and McCoy weren't content to be small town robbers and panhandlers and, at the time, the Fallon Community Bank seemed to be "easy pickings."

They made the hit, but this time the law caught up with them. Stiff prison sentences were handed out to both of them in the aftermath of that ill-fated venture.

✻ ✻ ✻ ✻

McCoy was suddenly stirred back to reality when he heard voices and the clanging of a gate. He glanced at his watch. It was 10:35 a.m. He had been waiting for over an hour and a half.

Dalton had finally emerged from behind the prison walls and was standing outside a huge iron gate talking to a prison official. Bernie guessed he was the warden.

An armed guard stood nearby as Dalton glanced furtively around while savoring freedom for the first time in years. His street clothes hung loosely on his slender frame and he was sporting a new pair of shoes.

McCoy thought he looked better wearing his new civies than the prison grays he'd seen Dalton wearing whenever he visited him in the past.

When he saw the warden handing Jake an envelope, he knew right away what was in it; Dalton's release papers, ordering him to report within 72 hours to his probation officer in Fallon. For record purposes, the warden told Dalton that a copy of the report would be mailed directly to that officer. There was also a small amount of cash in the envelope—$23—money Dalton had saved while working in the prison laundry. The warden knew that money wouldn't last long given Dalton's lifestyle.

"Make sure you don't spend it all in one place," the warden said sarcastically. As an after-thought, he again reminded Dalton to make sure he reported to his probation officer.

Dalton merely sneered; electing to say nothing. He didn't even shake the warden's hand after emerging from prison. The warden was apparently giving him some last minute advice, but Dalton had some things on his mind other than being told what to do for the rest of his life.

Waiving off the warden, he turned quickly and headed across the street, walking straight toward McCoy who had gotten out of the car to greet him. They shook hands; smiling as they embraced.

"Good to see you again, ol' bud," said McCoy. Dalton ignored the greeting.

"Let's get the hell out of here," Dalton urged as they got in the car.

"Where to?" McCoy inquired.

"Reno, first…let's drive up there 'n take in the bright lights…do a little drinkin' 'n foolin' around; then we can drive over to Fallon tomorrow afternoon.

"I need to check around 'n find out where Cheryl's hangin' out. I haven't seen or heard from her for years. It's not like her to just up and disappear without me knowin' about it."

McCoy was puzzled about Cheryl, too. He'd been out of prison for four years and even though he only came into Fallon once a month to check in with his probation officer, his occasional inquiries regarding the whereabouts of Jake's sister, were either met with shrugs or don't know's.

Across the street, the warden watched the two with a dubious smile on his face.

"Stay out of trouble and get a job or you'll find yourself back in here," he shouted.

His words were like a whisper in the wind as the ex-cons sped away; paying little heed to the warden's solemn warning.

Chapter 4

Prison life was momentarily forgotten as Dalton and McCoy drove up highway 395 toward Reno. The barren landscape offered little to stimulate a discussion. The sun was despairingly hot and a searing wind whipped through the open car windows; nipping and tweaking their faces at will.

It had been a long time, nine years to be exact, since they had spent much time together and it was proving difficult to communicate with each other. For a few miles, they kept their thoughts to themselves, then McCoy finally broke the awkward silence.

"Wanna' another beer, Jake?"

"Sure do, pal."

"I thought you might be thirstin' a bit after the dry spell you've had so I put a couple on ice for you." McCoy thumbed his hand toward the back seat.

"In the bucket on the floor."

Dalton reached back and pulled a slim brown bottle from the bucket. He popped the cap off, savoring the taste as he gurgled down the cool liquid.

"Man, that tastes good after the crap they fed me in prison. The water was terrible and the food was even worse. It got so that I only ate a couple of times a day. Guess that's why I lost some weight in there.

"Speaking of food, it's nearly noontime and I'm gettin' hungry, Bernie. If you see some place along the way, let's stop and eat. I'm buying since you picked me up this morning."

A roadside cafe attracted their attention outside Washoe City. After a quick meal and a couple of beers, they continued on their way. Reno had always advertised itself as the "Biggest Little City in the World" and the ex-cons had spent a lot of time there before going to prison; mugging and robbing unsuspecting victims who happened to get lucky playing blackjack or craps.

Sometimes they would commit two or three robberies a week by simply watching the cashier windows. If their intended victims cashed in a lot of chips, they would follow them after they had left the casino. If the opportunity presented itself, they would put a hit on the unsuspecting victims and then disappear into the night.

They were predators of the worst kind and they plied their trade in Reno, Sparks, Carson City and Fallon whenever they ran low on funds. Dalton was curious what his long time buddy had been doing since being released from prison.

What ya' been up to, Bernie?"

"Tryin' to stay out of trouble mostly. Living in Silver Springs right now. Been doin' a little bar tendin' and workin' odd jobs around the area whenever my money would run low. Nothin' exciting. Otherwise, I've just been existin' from day to day; waitin' for you to get out." He then asked Jake a troublesome question:

"You plannin' to start robbin' again?"

"Hell, Bernie, I don't even want to think about doing anything for awhile, but how else are we going to survive?"

Dalton seemed irritated over McCoy's question. He was a free man now and he was savoring his freedom at the moment. Still, he wanted to make a point.

"Tell me, what are we good at? What skills do we have?" he asked Bernie. "My parole officer's gonna keep a close eye on me, so I've gotta get a job that's legit' and stay out of trouble; at least for a little while. We've got the weekend to have some fun, so let's just lay low 'n see what's happening around town before we decide what to do. We can stay in Reno tonight and drive over to Fallon tomorrow afternoon so we got plenty of time to do some celebratin' before I have to report to my parole officer on Tuesday."

A moment of rare remorse overcame Dalton when he began thinking about his hooligan past and disfunctional family.

"Right after I went in, I used to get a couple of letters a month from mama," he told McCoy, "but then they stopped comin' after a while," he said ruefully.

"I didn't even know she'd died until my sister, Cheryl, came up to see me one day. I believe that was in early '32, soon after mama had passed away. Sis was on the street by then.

"My ol' man got his self killed in a car accident a couple of years before I went into the slammer. Drivin' drunk as usual. Everything started to go down hill after that.

"Then mama suffered a stroke and was forced to give up the farm. By the time she moved into an apartment in Fallon, she had lost all desire to keep on livin'. Probably died of loneliness and a broken heart."

"I never saw my sis again after she visited me in prison that one time. I don't know where she is or what she's doin' now."

Bernie remembered Cheryl.

"Your sis' is a sweet gal. With her good looks, she should've gone to Hollywood instead of hitting the streets. Who knows, maybe she found a sugar daddy in Reno or got herself married and moved out of the state."

"I hope so." Dalton answered. "She deserved a few breaks after what she went through. She had to grow up too fast and I wasn't much help or an example to her."

Cheryl had left home when she was sixteen to make a living on the streets; hawking her ample wares to all takers while Dalton and McCoy were cruising the same streets and nearby towns looking for trouble and innocent victims they could prey upon or rob.

"Mama's two kids didn't turn out too well." Dalton said in self deprecation. "My sis' took to turnin' tricks and I ended up bein' a convicted felon. A couple of real losers, I guess."

They both laughed; knowing if their up-bringing had been better, especially in their teenage years, things might have been far different for both of them as well as for Cheryl.

* * * *

Dalton popped the cap off another beer.

"I know one thing, Bernie, we've got to get our hands on some cash—muy pronto! I stashed a couple hundred bucks at the old place before I went in. I'm sure it'll still there if the well hasn't caved in by now." That statement caught McCoy completely by surprise.

It pained him to even think about that sink hole. It held sordid secrets only he and Dalton knew about. Over time, he'd tried to dismiss them from his mind, but even after years of trying to forget, the screams that echoed up from that dark, murky shaft still haunted him to this very day.

As he drove up the highway toward Reno, he thought about that terrible debacle when, shortly before their ill-fated attempt to rob the Fallon Community Bank, they had dumped a couple of itinerant drunks down the well; beating and robbing them after they had hit a $1,000 jackpot at Harrah's hours earlier. Looking back, McCoy couldn't believe what they'd done to those poor souls.

"I've tried to forget about what we did to those dudes, Jake." Dalton simply laughed at the memory of that frightful night.

"Hell, Bernie, I put it out of my mind a long time ago. We only put 'em inside the well to scare 'em, but they ended up drownin' themselves 'cause they slipped the ropes off their feet while they were tryin' to get out. They should've held on tighter to those iron rungs like I used to do when I explored the well as a kid. I always figured it was their own fault they drowned; not ours."

McCoy didn't want to think about that nightmare again, but he was curious about the money Dalton had hidden in the well. He had often visited the Dalton farm when he and Jake were running wild, but he hadn't paid much attention to the well in the back yard until the night they dumped the drunks inside that cavernous pit.

"You never told me about hidin' money in the well, Jake."

"Yeah, I found a secret hidin' place down there when I was a kid. I was always curious about the well 'cause I could hear runnin' water whenever I poked my head down there. One of my chores was to draw water from it whenever it was needed.

"It was easy at first, 'cause the well had a pump and all I had to do was raise the handle up and down and water would flow into a bucket. Then the pump broke down one day. Pop couldn't afford to fix it or buy another one, so he rigged a big ol' roller drum with a bunch of rope around it; then we could lower and raise the bucket at will inside the well.

"Sometimes, after fillin' up the bucket, I could feel a tugging' at the end of the rope, like somethin' was prevent'n me from raisin' the bucket. When I asked pop about that, he seemed reluctant to discuss the reason why. But, I kept gnaw'n at him. Finally, he set me straight one day. He said a 'gravitational pull' existed down there as a result of a water current flowin' underground. Then he told me the real reason for not tellin' me about what was down in that well; sayin' that 'the Dalton's don't talk to anyone about our water rights. Ever!'"

"Pop was pretty emphatic about it, too. It'd been a family secret for years that we had plenty of water underneath us when other ranchers around us hardly have any. People fight and die for good water rights, 'ya know, so that's why I never told you about how I discovered that secret little hiding place in the well."

The directional sign up ahead indicated the highway 80 intercept was just ahead and that Reno was 12 miles due West. A few minutes later the bright lights of downtown Reno greeted them.

McCoy knew this wasn't going to be a quick visit. Dalton had been in prison far too long, nine years, just to pass in and out of the city in an hour or two. He fully intended to soak up the bright lights of "Glitter Gulch," that infamous strip on South Virginia street where Harrah's, the Golden Nugget and a number of other casinos were constantly aglow in 10 million lights. Then he would do some gambling, drinking and women chasing before the night was over. He managed to do all three of those things within three hours of arriving in Reno.

* * * *

The sun was high in the sky by the time the two ex-cons put their feet on the floor early Monday afternoon. McCoy had moderated his drinking the night before; figuring he had to drive wherever they went. Still, he had drank too much and his head was throbbing. Dalton was in worst shape. He was nursing a king-size hangover and it hurt to even move his head.

A quick breakfast and some black coffee made them both feel better. Soon they were heading East on highway 80. Fallon was nearly two hours away and as they sped down the highway, a wave of nostalgia suddenly swept over Dalton as he thought about returning to his boyhood home for the first time in over nine years.

One thing he clearly remembered was how his mom and pop struggled to keep their farm intact; pay the help and keep food on the table. Dalton and his sister, Cheryl, were clearly victims of the depression.

His dad, Rudolph (Rudy) Dalton, had been granted an early discharge in late 1917 after being badly wounded in France during World War I. He had come home to desolate surroundings and a bleak future. Many homesteaders around Fallon had abandoned their farms and ranches and fled to other cities, or to California, where better opportunities existed. Area ranchers and farmers, at least those who had remained, were barely eking out a living.

Jobs were scarce, too, and there was very little water or financial resources available to plant and raise crops. Even as a young boy, Dalton realized that it took water to make things grow and there was a noticeable lack of it in the Western Nevada desert, but not on the Dalton property.

Somehow, his dad had managed to hold on to a section of land, a 640-acre parcel, that had an abundance of water. The ranch at one time was part of a much larger operation comprising nearly 2,500 acres. As the country struggled and the economy worsened in the 1920's, his dad had to keep selling off parcels of his land while running a cattle operation and harvesting a variety of crops; mainly alfalfa, corn and potatoes.

Dalton had fond memories of his old homestead…of the rows of Summer corn he could romp in as a boy—picking vegetables from a small garden that was in the back yard near a large stand of Cottonwood trees—and a dilapidated, but strange looking, well from which the family drew water for their daily needs. The well, he remembered vividly, was no ordinary hole in the ground. He had seldom thought about it while in prison except to occasionally wonder if the loot he'd stored in there before going to prison was still intact.

He wondered what he would've done with his life if he hadn't discovered that secret little treasure trove in the well. He had always been fearful of the well's murky interior and the discovery of that treasure had brought him a lot of joy at first; then extreme bitterness and a crime-filled life in later years.

Chapter 5

6:45 a.m., Monday
June 26, 1939
Midvale, Utah

Mom made sure I wasn't late for the Banfield's departure to Fallon. We had packed everything the day before so all I had to do was put my clothes on, eat breakfast and have her drive me over to the Banfield's house which was just five miles away.

I'd gotten up at 5:30 a.m. after a near sleepless night of contemplating the days ahead. For some strange reason, a sense of foreboding had overcome me during the night. Here I was, on the verge of departure, and I had already begun to wonder if spending the rest of the summer with my cousins, Bob and Jimmy Banfield, was the right thing to do.

"After all," I told myself, "I was making good money being a carpenter's helper on my dad's construction crew and I would be home every night and sleeping in my own bed. So, why am I giving that up for a working vacation in far off Fallon? By going there, I wouldn't be making any money the rest of the summer, my tennis career was already shot and I wouldn't be able to hang out with my buddies." I'd fussed about all of that before. Now, I suddenly began wondering what to do and we're already out the door and heading toward the Banfield's.

I wouldn't have dared to ask my dad about what I should do. If I had done so over the weekend, I thought, I would be going to work for him this morning rather than going to Fallon. He had reluctantly agreed to let me go in the first place and if I had expressed the slightest doubt about going there, he would have quashed my plans in a heartbeat.

But mom? I knew she would ease my concerns about leaving home for the first time if I just posed the question. I loved her dearly for her thoughtfulness and I trusted her judgement whenever I sought advice.

She was also a wonderfully talented woman; especially in the field of music. In addition to being an impeccable housekeeper (nothing was ever out of place around the house), she possessed an incredible voice and her range of songs defied description. She could belt out lusty tunes, one after another, then slip gently into an operatic aria without batting an eyelash.

She played the piano by ear and wrote numerous songs with her sister, Rosy. None were ever published although everyone who heard them thought they should have been since the melodies and words seemed so pleasant and professionally done. In the depression years, it took money to get songs published and mom and dad didn't have any extra cash at that time. Now, as we neared the Banfield residence, I just had to be reassured.

"Mom, do you think I'm doing the right thing by going to Fallon with Bob and Jimmy"? She waited a few moments before answering.

"Only time will tell, son—but you must always remember that when you make a commitment, or a promise to someone, you are expected to keep it."

"I'm gonna miss you, mom."

"I'm going to miss you, too, son. This is the first time you've been away from home for any length of time. I hope you will be safe and have lots of fun. I'll remember you in my prayers every night." I felt comforted by her words.

As we turned into the Banfield's driveway, Dean and Tess were stuffing things in the back trunk while Bob and Jimmy were holding two large suitcases that somehow had to also be put into the trunk. Among the items already stuffed in the trunk were two pairs of boxing gloves. Dean was a boxer of note—he was the 1938 Intermountain AAU light heavy weight champion—and I guessed he took them along just in case he could find someone to box around with on occasion.

After putting my small duffle bag into the trunk along with an extra pair of shoes and a small radio that I had just purchased, Mom gave me a big hug and kiss good-bye.

Tess said they were ready to go. "It's a long drive and we must leave right away if we're going to be there before dark." "How long's it gonna take?" I inquired to no one in particular.

"About 12 hours," Dean responded as he slung a canvas water bag around the metal ornament on the front hood of his car, a 1937 4door Chevy with a stick shift.

Assurances were given to mom as she departed that I would be well taken care of and that she needn't have to worry about me. Self doubts about my going to Fallon had been dismissed from my mind and for the first time in hours, my sense of foreboding had been washed away by the dawn of a beautiful day and thoughts of spending the Summer with my two cousins on their dad's working ranch in Western Nevada.

As we pulled out of the driveway and headed up State street and onto Highway 80 for the trip West, and unbeknown to us at the time, two other near-simultaneous events were taking place in Western Nevada that would dramatically effect our lives in the days and weeks ahead.

*   *   *   *

It would be a long, hot—and eventful—drive across the Utah/Nevada desert and the water bag Dean had put on the front radiator before leaving home would prove to be a life-saver for us in the hours ahead. Bob, Jimmy and I had flipped a coin to determine who was going to sit in the middle of the back seat to start the trip. Jimmy lost.

Being in the "squeeze" position, he had to endure the first couple of hours sitting in the most uncomfortable seat in the car before, as we agreed, trading places with each other after every stop.

After leaving South Salt Lake shortly after 7:00 a.m., we turned onto Highway 80 and headed due West; passing briefly by small farms bounded by fences and tall poplar or cottonwood trees.

In less than an hour, green farm lands gave way to a barren, desert landscape in Western Utah. It was in stark contrast to the greenery we had been used to seeing in the Salt Lake Valley and along the Wasatch mountain front.

The Oquirrah mountains, a split off of the larger Wasatch range which borders the Eastern rim of the Salt Lake valley, had ended its northerly reach at the southern edge of the Great Salt Lake. From there, the highway turned briefly Southwest in order to skirt the lake which was virtually lapping over the highway.

As we sped Westward, I remembered a little-known, but perilous phenomenon about the lake—its buoyancy! You couldn't sink due to the lake's high salt content. We would visit the Black Rock or Saltair resorts once or twice each Summer and upon entering the water we'd bob around like corks in the shimmering lake.

We were also very careful not to put our heads under water for fear of swallowing its briny contents. Signs were posted all along the beach front warning everyone they should exercise due caution when entering the water and to avoid frolicking around. Only experienced swimmers were permitted to swim or distance themselves from the shore.

We were taught in geography class that a million or so years ago, the Great Salt Lake was part of Lake Bonneville, a vast inland body of water that became trapped when a cataclysmic earthquake caused a great upheaval of the earth; creating the Continental Divide in the Rocky Mountains and sending torrents of water rushing outward to the Pacific ocean.

Soon, another of Nature's greatest wonders appeared; the Bonneville Salt Flats. The whiteness of this eerie landscape was unreal. We were completely surrounded…as far as the eye could see—by miles and miles of pure, unrefined salt. It was as startling as it was spectacular. Off in the distant there were several huge piles of the briny stuff, virtually hiding the buildings and equipment that were in the process of refining salt.

"Isn't this where they set all those world speed records?" Jimmy asked.

"It sure is," Dean answered as he slowed to a stop and pulled off the highway so we could get out and walk on the white, crusty stuff. Suddenly Bob yelled and pointed Northward:

"Look...there's a race car."

We looked to where Bob was pointing just in time to see a silvery, bullet-shaped racer streaking down the Bonneville Raceway.

"Wow! How fast is he going?" Jimmy asked

"Must be going over 200 miles an hour," I guessed.

"Man, I'd love to be sitting in that car right now," Bob marveled. I wonder who the driver is?"

Dean said it was probably Ab Jenkins who was testing his racer before trying to break his own land speed record that he had set the year before.

"I read in the newspaper the other day that he was testing a new engine in his racer that could put him well over the 200 mile an hour mark. It takes a lot of guts to drive an experimental racer that fast," Dean said. We all agreed to that.

It was beginning to get real hot, so Tess retrieved the water bag off the ornament on the hood of the car and, after uncorking it, we each took a drink. Even though it had been pinned to the front of the car, just inches away from a hot radiator, the water was actually cold!

"That's from the wind beating against the wet canvas bag," she said. As we gazed at the vast, white landscape around us, she pointed to a long line of utility poles just off the highway.

"Have you boys ever seen anything like that?" she queried.

We hadn't. The poles were tall and straight, but each pole had a large, balloon-like bulge at the bottom from the salt water that had penetrated (and expanded) the base of each pole.

It made the poles look like they were set in dark, round wicker baskets on top of the salt surface instead of being implanted into the thick layer of salt brine that completely encircled us for miles around. Soon thereafter, we reached Wendover, a dusty, wind-blown, border town in the Western Utah desert. It was a desolate-looking place and as we pulled into the nearest service station, we could see the garish lights of several small hotels and casinos further west on the Nevada side of the border.

It was mid-morning and we were already uncomfortably hot. The temperature gauge on the side of the building confirmed it: 103 degrees—in the shade!

The car's radiator had begun to heat up a few miles before reaching Wendover so Dean decided the radiator needed to be cooled off. He kept the motor running, and after the attendant gassed up the car and checked the oil, Dean sprayed the radiator with a nearby water hose.

"What's he doing that for?" Jimmy inquired.

"He's trying to cool the radiator down," Bob answered impatiently.

Dean then retrieved a towel from the trunk and after neatly folding it into a square, he placed it on top of the radiator cap. He gingerly twisted the cap a turn, then another, to let a little steam out. Waiting a few seconds, he then carefully turned it a couple of more times before fully depressing the cap and gently lifting off the cap.

He quickly stepped back just as a geyser of hot steam bubbled from the radiator like a miniature volcano. Dean kept spraying water on the radiator until it stopped belching steam. He then poured water into the radiator and we were ready to resume our long hot drive across the Nevada desert.

As a precaution, he asked Bob to fill another water bag he had brought along which was then placed along side the other one that had just been refilled by Jimmy. That would prove to be a wise decision!

It was also my turn to be in the squeeze seat.

Chapter 6

The Banfield Ranch
10:30 a.m., Monday
June 26, 1939

As usual, Jesse Banfield was in a hurry and issuing orders on the run to his ranch foreman, Hank Johnson, who had already been in the saddle for over three hours. Johnson had eaten an early breakfast and had spent most of the morning in the South pasture where he checked on the sheep that were going to be moved to the East pasture later in the day. Marauding coyotes were his chief worry at the moment. Jesse had another agenda.

"We need to talk about some things, Hank. Meet me at the front gate right after lunch."

"Okay, boss, I'll be back in a couple of hours—gotta check on the herds and those fencing repairs in the East pasture first. Those damn coyotes somehow managed to get in there last night and kill couple of our young lambs."

Johnson understood exactly what Uncle Jesse meant when he wanted to talk about some things. He knew whenever his boss wanted to meet at the ranch's entry gate that some serious discussions were going to take place. That was where they could talk alone without being interrupted and where Jesse could comfortably lean on the gate and chew on a piece of straw while talking about ranching operations.

It was also quiet time as well as quality time for both of them. The hustle and bustle of ranching operations would be temporarily put aside for a little while. Jesse could think more clearly under such circumstances 'cause he wasn't on the run, while Hank could provide a full and detailed assessment of how things were going around the ranch.

*   *   *   *

It was early afternoon by the time Jesse and Johnson met at the gate. The temperature was boiling upward and would soon top out at 110 degrees. A gentle breeze swirled about them and then began freshening as they stared silently at a familiar landscape before them.

The panoramic sweep of this surreal setting would normally have exhilarated them and brought expressions of satisfaction about how things were going, but on this unmercifully hot day, ranching operations and problems arising from the lack of help were troubling them. So they simply chose to remain silent for awhile; each occupied with his own thoughts.

Before them lay the fruits of their labors. Fields of alfalfa, corn and ripening wheat met their gaze. Fenced pasture lands held Uncle Jesse's cattle herds and flocks of sheep that were being fattened up for the Fall markets.

The second Summer cutting of the huge alfalfa crop was underway near the ranch house, which lay atop a small hill in the middle of Jesse's property.

As far as they could see the serenity of that landscape gave them hope and visions of a bright future for their ranching operations. But, troubling both of them was not what they could see, but what might not get done if they couldn't find some additional hands to assist in the harvest.

Both were searching for a good way to start a discussion about that problem. Things had become a bit tense between them in recent days and the hot, dry weather was making conversations difficult. Finally, Johnson spoke up.

"Looks like another hot one, boss."

Yeah, I reckon so," Jesse replied glumly.

"If it's this hot now," Johnson wondered out loud, "what's it gonna be like in a month or so?"

Jesse didn't answer. By now, he was in an unusually somber mood and clearly frustrated. Things weren't getting done in a timely manner around the ranch and he was searching his mind on how to properly reproach his foreman about those matters without unduly offending him.

Johnson had been with him for seven years and Jesse didn't want to lose him by being overly critical about the way ranch operations were being carried out. Being desperately short of help had caused friction between them and Johnson knew his boss was going to pound on him again to find some extra hands to meet the crush of the summer and fall harvests.

He had already scoured the valley over the past few weeks, but the labor pool had dried up months ago. He was wondering what more he could do. Jesse offered a solution.

"You'd better go in town this week and see if you can round up some more hands. I know it's not a good time to be lookin' around for help, but we're already late in gettin' that second hay crop in—some fences in the East pasture are down and we're losing too many young lambs to the coyotes."

Johnson could see that Jesse was clearly agitated over that problem.

"Hell, it's either the heat or the coyotes," he thought to himself.

"I know we're short-handed, boss. I've got to do a better job of assigning what few men we have while lookin' after everything else around the ranch. No excuses…there just isn't enough time in the day to get everything done with the number of hands we've got."

Jesse nodded reluctantly. He was heartened by his foreman's own self criticism and determination to do better. At least for now, he wouldn't belabor the way Johnson was carrying out his responsibilities as the ranch foreman.

"He's too valuable to me," Jesse reasoned silently, so he wasn't about to be openly critical of his foreman's work performance. He knew that if he pressed too hard, Johnson would quit.

His range hardened foreman didn't take any guff from his ranch hands; even from Jesse when it came right down to it. Johnson was a loyal and faithful worker, but there only so much a man could take and in a time of crisis Uncle Jesse knew it was time to back off.

Faint praise followed.

"Hank, I know you're doing your best, and I appreciate all the hard work you and your men are doing, but if we're going to make it through the Summer, we've got to have more help.

"My boys are coming in tonight from Utah and they'll be of some help, but see if you can round up three or four more hands."

Johnson nodded in agreement, knowing at the moment that his chances of hiring that many men in the middle of the week—and well into the season—would be next to impossible.

"Who's coming over from Utah, boss?"

"Dean and his wife, Tess, as well as Bob and Jimmy. They're also bringing their cousin, Danny Collins. Dean will be a big help, but I don't know how much work we'll get out of the boys. They'll probably fool around more than help us."

*   *   *   *

Another sensitive matter then came up. Nellie, their aging sheep dog, was on her last legs and Johnson reminded Jesse that while Nellie had always been effective in protecting and keeping the sheep rounded up, the time would soon be at hand to ease her pain and the burden of having to work the herd.

"She's the best damned sheep dog I've ever seen," Johnson commented.

"It's uncanny how she's always been able to round up strays and cull out the weak from the strong, but she's having a hard time doing it anymore. That's the main reason we're losing so many of our young lambs to those damn coyotes."

"Nellie's been a good'un alright," Jesse responded with a sigh of remorse.

"I know old age has caught up with her just like it does all of us. Ya' know she's 14 years old now—that's about 84 year's in human life; so she's pretty ancient for a dog."

With all of his troubles and responsibilities, the last thing Jesse needed to think about right then was the plight of his faithful sheep dog. He loved that little creature and it saddened him to contemplate the future without her.

"We're not only short of help around here, but little Nellie can't scoot around like she used to," he lamented.

"Shoot, I hate to even think about it, but I'm afraid we'll have to put her away before too long."

Johnson agreed, but it touched their hardened souls that such a loyal and faithful canine had become so hobbled by age and arthritis that she couldn't perform like she had in the past.

Their interlude at the main gate was broken when Jesse noted that the intense heat of the afternoon sun had begun to beat down on them unmercifully. Surprisingly, they had been at the gate for nearly two hours and the only sound around them had come from a hot wind that was sending withering heat waves rippling across the land. An occasional tumbleweed bounced along only to be snagged on the fence that bordered the road. Jesse was clearly irritated now, but he managed to keep a civil tone to his voice.

"Better get something to eat, Hank—then round up a couple of hands and repair those fences in the East pasture. We gotta do a better job of keepin' those coyotes out of there and Charlie (Hartwell) can't get out of bed fast enough to shoot 'em either. He's been a good sheepherder for years, but he's even slowin' down now." Then, as an afterthought, Johnson got a another reminder from Jesse:

"We're gonna' be in deep trouble if we can't hire some additional help, Hank. There's too much to do and we don't have enough hands to get things done around here."

Johnson nodded silently and said he'd go into Fallon the next day to see if he could find some additional help.

Chapter 7

Enroute to Fallon
Monday, 11:15 a.m.
June 26, 1939

After a drunken Sunday in Reno, Dalton was trying to share the cobwebs from his throbbing head. Even a hearty breakfast of ham and eggs and three cups of black coffee couldn't make his hangover go away.

It had been nearly 10 years since he'd had a drink and his system wasn't used to the amount of alcohol he had consumed during his one day drinking binge in Reno.

Now, they were heading for Fallon and McCoy was growing restive. He was pondering their next move while wondering just how they were going to survive in the days ahead with virtually no money in their pockets. Dalton had busted them both by wild betting at the blackjack and crap tables.

Still, McCoy looked to his old pal for direction as they headed eastward on highway 80. Just past Sparks, he asked Dalton where he wanted to stop first.

"I should swing by the old house and see if my loot is still in the well, but that can wait 'til later. Let's drop by the cemetery so I can pay my respects to mom and pop. We can drive into town after that. Maybe we can find out where my sis is living since you haven't been able to track her down."

McCoy nodded approval. He was also curious why his pal hadn't told him about hiding cash in the dark recesses of that well even though they had dumped a couple of drunks down there years earlier.

"Jake, you've never told me why you hid your money in that well. Must have been a good hiding place to keep it secret from me all these years."

"Let me tell ya' pal, it's no ordinary well! We drew water from it every day when I was growin' up, but it always gave me the creeps whenever I had to do that chore.

"I was about 10 years old when I went into the well for the first time. I was nose'n around in the backyard one day when my mom asked me to draw some water so she could begin cookin' the evenin' meal. I decided to lift part of the heavy hinged cover board off the top of the well so I could look down into it. To my surprise I discovered some steps and steel rungs leading down into the well; so I climbed inside and looked around.

"It was really eery-lookin' and I panicked the first time I went down there, but after a couple of days my curiosity got the best of me and I started to really explore the well with my flashlight."

Dalton then revealed to McCoy how it was constructed, its curious natural features and how he accidentally discovered a hidden treasure deep within its darkened shaft.

The well, he said, was mostly the handiwork of Mother Nature. A previous owner had built a stoop, or platform, atop the well that was about four feet above the ground. Mounted atop the platform was a wooden structure that held a roller drum with strands of rope wrapped around it. A large crank handle on the end of the drum could lower and raise a wooden bucket for retrieving water from the well.

Around the well's exterior and extending out some five or six feet were slabs of ledge rock that had been cemented together. The opening of the well was about seven feet across and it led down into a dark and cavernous shaft where, depending upon the season, running water could be faintly heard some 100 feet below ground.

The part of the well stoop above ground was man-made. Small rocks, embedded in 12 inches of cement and reinforced with an inner lining of bricks formed the wall that supported the stoop while below the ground, and long undisturbed, were jagged, uneven chards of ledge rock that jutted out into the darkness. Holes had been drilled into the well's interior wall and iron rungs had been cemented firmly in place; forming a ladder that extended about eight feet down into the well.

Dalton told McCoy he had often wondered about that strange design feature; why those iron rungs were put there in the first place and why they didn't go further down into the well.

"How in the hell anybody got the nerve to go down there and cement those iron rungs inside that well is beyond me," Dalton said.

One day, after climbing into the well and while holding onto the steel rungs with one hand and shining his flashlight around with the other, Dalton told McCoy he took a serious look at the inside of the well. Mother Nature's handiwork was eerily evident in the illuminated darkness.

Green moss was hanging' from some of the rocks while below him, the well shaft was a pancake makeup of dirt, jumbled rocks and more layers of jutting ledges that lent a strange look to the inside of the well.

Dalton said it looked like a huge earthquake had fractured the earth's subsurface and in the upheaval it had left an uneven, weird-looking, vertical shaft that seemed to expand into several caverns as it extended downward. Dalton said he couldn't see the bottom of the well, but he could hear the faint sound of running water far below him. Then, an object caught his eye. It was lying on a piece of ledge rock deep into the side of the wall so that he had to reach in and retrieve it. Reflecting on that long ago moment he told McCoy:

"I hesitated for a little bit; fearing there might be a snake or a black widow spider in there. Then when I shined my flashlight directly into the crevice, I could see an old cigar box sittin' there so I reached in and tried to slide it out with one hand, but it was too slimy and heavy to hold onto at first."

Dalton said he climbed up a couple of rungs and secured a better hold on one of the steel rungs. Then he reached back down with his free hand, grabbed the cigar box and carefully lifted it upon the well stoop and climbed out.

"That was a clever place to hide something," he said to McCoy. "No one would ever think to look down there."

Rattling sounds in the box told Dalton there was some coins and a heavy object inside. That object turned out to be a fully-loaded Colt .45 pearl-handled revolver that was wrapped in a faded, soft red velvet cover.

When he lifted it out of the box, Dalton said some extra bullets spilled onto the ground, so he quickly scooped them up and put them back in the box.

But it was the money and a faded hand-written note in the box that surprised Dalton the most. As he looked at the stack of crumpled bills that was wrapped in a soiled piece of brown paper, he realized that he had just found a treasure trove. Some shiny silver dollars also cluttered the box.

Laying the bills and silver dollars aside, Dalton noticed another piece of paper that had some scribbling on it which revealed a chronological listing of small amounts of money that had been acquired over a period of time. The last notation read:

"Saved to date: $320. Need $1,485 more to payoff mortgage."

There was no name or signature on the paper, but the faded date caught Dalton's attention. It read: November 13, 1891.

Dalton's dad had purchased the ranch in 1910, just a few months before his only son, Jacob (Jake) Dalton, was born. Jake was only 10 years old when he discovered his little treasure in 1917; so it had lain hidden in the well for 26 years without anyone knowing about it.

If a former owner was trying to payoff the farm debt, Dalton had wondered over the years, why didn't they put the savings in the bank or keep it in the house instead of the dark bowels of an old well? He finally concluded that it must be stolen money. McCoy's curiosity got the best of him.

"Who d'ya' suppose put it there and what did you do with the loot?" he asked Dalton.

"None of that stuff belonged to pop," Dalton replied. I kept the stuff hidden for a long time, but I eventually spent all the money. Kept the pistol, though."

Jake knew his dad was a hard-working rancher who had been a bit of a rowdy himself and who drank too much, but he wasn't the kind of person who would stash a gun and a sum of money inside the darkened recesses of a well.

He also wasn't the type to go around stealing or hitting on people for money either. He'd rather labor in the fields to earn his keep and provide for his family; meager as those provisions were at times. Dalton told McCoy that he didn't know, or even cared, who put the money in the well. That mystery would never be solved.

"As far as I was concerned at the time, it was finder's keepers; loser's weepers."

"How much money was really in the box?" inquired McCoy.

"The same amount that was listed on the note…$320 bucks. I must've counted it a dozen times to make sure it was correct."

The secret little hiding place Dalton uncovered that day would be both a source of contentment as well as misery later in his life. He had vowed never to tell anyone about it; not even his pal, Bernie McCoy. Now, years later, that vow of secrecy had been broken.

As Dalton began his lawless career, he sometimes would store his share of the loot taken from his robbery victims in that same ledge rock compartment in the well, but the money was always frittered away as quickly as it was deviously obtained. And the ivory-handled Colt .45 became his future persuader and means of making a living later in his life.

* * * *

On the outskirts of Fallon, Dalton gave McCoy hazy directions to the cemetery.

"If I remember correctly, it's not too far from my old house in the northeast part of town. If you can find Rio Vista Drive, that'll take us right to the front entrance of the cemetery."

Dalton's directions were correct and within minutes they were at the entrance and wondering which way to turn.

I don't know where mom and pop are buried, but I suppose I can find their head stones in a few minutes," Dalton pondered. McCoy said his mom was buried there, too, but he had no idea where her grave site was either; not having visited there since he was a kid. As they made their way through cemetery, they spotted a caretaker who was preparing a new gravesite.

"Do ya' happen to know where the graves of Rudy and Mary Dalton are located?" Dalton inquired. The caretaker seemed startled at first, then he stopped digging and pulled out a soiled map from his trouser pocket and studied it for a few moments.

"Over yonder," he said, pointing to an area in the Northeast section of the cemetery. "About 30 feet on the other side of those two large monuments."

"How about Elizabeth McCoy," McCoy asked the caretaker who again turned his gaze on the map in his hands.

"Look's like she's buried not far from the Dalton's. Just keep goin' aways past the Daltons; then cross the service road. You'll find her grave site a few feet on the other side of that tall Hanover monument. That's the one that's got a little fence around it."

The caretaker's directions were accurate, but Dalton was shocked to see a third headstone marker next to his mother's. It was his sister's. It simply read:

"Cheryl Ann Dalton—October 9, 1915—August 30, 1934."

His sister had been dead nearly five years! She was only 19 at the time she had passed away. Dalton was stunned. McCoy was shocked, too, as they stared in disbelief at Cheryl's headstone.

No word had reached Dalton that his sister had died while he was in prison. McCoy said he had tried to locate Cheryl after his release from prison four years ago, but no one knew where she was or where she was living.

"I just thought she had moved out of town," so I stopped wondering about her," McCoy informed Dalton.

"I wish I'd known, I had feelin's for her…" He never finished the comment; but he thought it was strange that she had died so young. Dalton was visibly shaken and determined to find out just how his sister could have died so early in life.

"Couldn't be from natural causes…too young for that," he theorized. McCoy agreed with that assumption. Vengeance was on Dalton's mind now.

"Whoever did this to my sis' is gonna pay for it," he vowed. "I'll help you," promised McCoy as they headed into town and some heavy drinking and fooling around at Fallon's most infamous watering hole—the Diamond Bar saloon on South Main street.

Before the night was over, they had uncovered some clues about Cheryl Dalton's disappearance from Fallon, but not about how or where she died.

Chapter 8

On Highway 80
Enroute to Fallon

Tess had thoughtfully provided a travel map so we could track our progress throughout the trip. Since I was in the middle (squeeze) seat, I spread the map across my lap and Bob noted that our next stop would probably be Elko, Nevada, a dusty cattle town about 123 miles West of Wendover, Utah, on highway 80.

An hour after leaving Wendover, we began a gradual climb as we approached the small town of Wells, Nevada, in the foothills of the Humboldt mountain range. Even though we kept the windows partially down, the combination of a hot wind and the temperature over 100 degrees was causing us a lot of discomfort inside the crowded car.

Suddenly, we heard Dean groan:

"Oh! oh! the radiator's heating up again."

We all watched the car's temperature gauge move higher and higher until Dean pulled the car to the side of the road to let it cool off. Bob, Jimmy and I bailed out of the back seat and stood on the side of the road talking to one another and tossing pebbles at a scurrying jackrabbit while Dean lifted the hood of the car to inspect the engine. Tess remained in the car.

Being a heavy equipment operator, Dean was an excellent mechanic and he determined right away that the core of the radiator had somehow become breached and clogged with rust.

"The car's only two years old…the engine shouldn't be heating' up like this," he grumbled.

Tess reminded him that he had already wore out a set of tires and put nearly 60,000 miles on the car in his work around the Intermountain West.

The radiator was hissing and hot misty steam was seeping from it and Dean wanted the car to cool down so he could lift off the cap and again pour water into the radiator from the extra bag that was hanging on the front hood.

Approaching traffic momentarily distracted Dean from his task. Two cars whizzed by us in quick succession; then another and another.

"Too close for comfort," Dean thought.

He decided to pull the car further off the highway so he could examine the radiator more thoroughly. In the distance two large semi-trailer trucks were bearing down on us at a high rate of speed. One of the big-rigs was trying to pass the other one on the two-lane highway. Suddenly, the shrill blast of a horn pierced the air and we were startled to see the truck in the right hand lane coming straight toward us! The truck had inexplicably left the highway and was stirring up a cloud of dust and debris in its wake as it bore down on us.

By now, both truck drivers were frantically honking their horns and Dean's car, with Tess in it, was on the verge of being smashed to pieces. Standing in front of his disabled car, Dean screamed at us to get back out of the way; then frantically motioned to Tess to get out of the car and follow him into the nearby burrow pit.

"Get out—hurray—get out," he yelled as Tess opened her door and began tumbling down the slight slope to where we were standing.

Then, every-thing seemed to go in slow motion for the next few moments. We stopped tossing rocks at the jackrabbit and froze in horror at the scene unfolding before us. Dean was scrambling after Tess and the truck being passed was just seconds away from causing a major disaster. We ducked our heads for a moment; then a giant swooshing sound told us the trucks had roared past; missing our car by a scant foot or two according to Dean. It was a real close call.

In their wake, the trucks sent out violent shock waves that briefly rippled the air and rocked the car back and forth. A swirling cloud of dust and debris engulfed us momentarily; then it became eerily calm as we all breathed a big sigh of relief.

"Wow! That was close," Bob said.

"What the heck was that guy trying to do…run over us?" Jimmy asked.

We all felt grateful and lucky to be alive. At the same time, we wondered why those truck drivers had put us in so much peril.

Dean already had it figured out. From his vantage point at the front of the car, he saw a potential disaster looming behind him. As the one big-rig was trying to pass the other one, the driver of the truck in the right lane inadvertently let his truck slip off the highway.

As it left the highway, the big-rig's trailer had begun to sway back and forth, almost jack-knifing, as the driver fought to get it back on the pavement, but the uneven ridge-line separating the asphalt pavement from the dirt shoulder caused the trailer to sway ominously.

Now aware that he was about to cause a horrible crash if he panicked, the truck driver alertly elected to maintain a steady course by not applying the brakes or turning the wheel ever so slightly. This maneuver allowed him to keep the left half of his big-rig on the pavement and the right half on the dirt shoulder until he could get past us even though it would come dangerously close to our car. It also enabled him to then slow his big-rig down enough so he could gradually get it back on the highway.

We fully expected him to stop and render aid to us, but he must have been in a big hurry as he continued on down the highway. Dean questioned the truck driver's highway manners, but seemed impressed with his split-second strategy in possibly avoiding a disastrous accident.

"I would've done the same thing under those circumstances," he said confidently. "But, I would've stopped to see if everyone was all right. The driver must have seen Tess tumbling out of the car and rolling head over heels into the burrow pit."

*   *   *   *

As the trucks disappeared over a distant ridge, Dean asked Bob to retrieve a medical kit from the back trunk that Tess had thoughtfully brought along for emergency purposes. She had bruised her right forearm and badly skinned her knees scrambling out of the car. She needed attending to and Dean began comforting her after propping her up in the burrow pit.

At that moment, I thought I could be helpful in getting us back on the road. Having watched Dean place a large towel over the radiator cap back in Wendover to prevent burning his hand while slowly letting the steam out, I decided I would do the same thing. I picked up the towel that Dean had dropped on the road a few moments before and, before he could see what I was doing, I placed it over the radiator cap and twisted it.

I must have turned the cap a little too far and too quickly. A hot geyser of steam suddenly shot up out of the radiator, blowing the towel and the cap out of my right hand. The full force of the gushing steam then hit me fully in the face and forehead.

I screamed with pain and I felt that my eyeballs were going to explode as the steam gushed out of the radiator. Fortunately, I managed to close my eyes a split-second before the steam hit me in the face. Momentarily blinded, I groped and stumbled backward, moaning with pain and clutching my badly burned face.

Bob and Jimmy ran to my side and helped me in the car where Tess, forgetting her own injuries for a moment, dampened my face with cold water from one of the bags that had been hanging on the front hood ornament.

My eyebrows and eyelashes had been burned off; skin fell from my forehead, cheek bones and eye lids as she continued to apply cool water to my burned face. This treatment, she said, would prevent the burn from going deeper into my skin. It also prevented my face from becoming badly scarred.

My right hand had absorbed the initial shock of the radiator cap and the towel not only helped to absorb the gush of steam from the radiator, but it surely saved me from being blinded for life.

As it was, that split-second delay, allowed me to duck down so most of the rushing steam had hit me in the middle of my forehead; then it sprayed downward onto my eyelids, nose and cheeks.

The explosive force of the radiator cap hitting my toweled right hand also numbed it so much that I couldn't close it for awhile. The hot steam had seared my face to a beet red color, prompting Bob to comment that I had the complexion of a red strawberry in season. There was so much hurt in me that I couldn't even laugh at that remark!

As we piled back in the car, Dean said that the radiator would have to be replaced so when we arrived in Elko that afternoon, he searched for a replacement while Tess took me to the emergency room in the town hospital. By then, I couldn't open my eyes and she feared they had been severely damaged.

The emergency doctor examined me briefly, saying I was fortunate to have suffered only first degree, rather than second or third degree burns to my face. He told Tess that applying cool water to my burns, as often as possible rather than a salve-like Vaseline substance, would hasten my recovery.

That procedure, he explained, would keep my face moist and enable the deep heat to be drawn from my skin; thus accelerating the healing process. An ointment was given to me with instructions to apply it three times a day. He also suggested that I see an eye doctor before leaving town.

We were lucky. An optometrist was officed across the street from the hospital. When he heard what had happened to me, and after carefully examining my face, he wrote out a prescription for medicated eye-drops and another ointment that would sooth the burned areas of my face.

Fortunately, I didn't incur any serious retinal damage but the doctor cautioned that I must be careful in the days ahead. He also suggested that I avoid the sun for a few days and that I should wear sun glasses whenever I was outside in order to reduce the suns's glare on my sore eyes.

"You're a lucky young boy," the doctor continued. "It could have been far worse—you could have lost your eyesight if you hadn't blinked!"

His sense of humor didn't impress me and not being in a talkative mood, I simply nodded my head and left it at that. I was embarrassed over putting Tess to so much trouble. I also worried that my face might be scarred for life.

*   *   *   *

Our day-long journey from the South Salt Valley to Fallon was also coming to end. We had stopped in Lovelock to eat dinner and gas up the car while Dean replaced a faulty distributor cap.

The worn travel map that lay on our laps told us we were just 55 miles from our destination and one last turn off of highway 80 and onto highway 95 south would take us into Fallon. The Banfield ranch was eight or nine miles southeast of there according to Dean. We all were ready for the journey to end.

Our travels had taken us across Utah's Salt Flats; then the wastelands of the Northern Nevada desert. As we gazed at the barren landscape, we all wondered why, and how, people could live in such an environment, let alone eke out an existence under such harsh living conditions.

For mile after mile, we had followed an asphalt ribbon (highway 80) that weaved interminably through flat, desolate prairie land; interrupted occasionally by dusty little towns, small hills and a few mountain ranges that provided rugged silhouettes in the distance. From Wendover to Elko and westward to Battle Mountain, then to Winnemucca and on down to Lovelock, there was nothing to excite or inspire our imagination.

"Boy, this is ugly territory," Bob commented.

"Is this the way it is all over the state?" Jimmy inquired. "This isn't exactly the scenic route," Dean chuckled. I wondered why people would want to live in the desert."

"Does Fallon look like this." I asked.

"About the same," Tess explained. "Got some trees in town and a few more around the little farm houses in the area, but not enough to want me to relocate there. I'm glad we'll just be visiting for the summer."

Dean told us to check our map and locate Reno, Carson City and Lake Tahoe. We discovered Reno was in the foothills of the Sierra Nevada mountain range as was Carson City, the quaint and small capital of Nevada. We also computed the mileage and found out that Reno was about 81 miles west, or less than a two hour drive from Fallon.

"Reno and Carson City are the gateways to the eastern Sierras—prettiest part of the state," Dean said. In fact, Reno's where your Aunt Judith and Uncle Stanley Harwood live."

I barely knew my aunt and uncle. They would show up occasionally at our family reunions in Utah, but they seemed like such a stuffy couple to me. Uncle Stanley was an English professor at the University of Nevada and Aunt Judith, a registered nurse, was my dad's older sister.

Aunt Judith always looked so prim and proper and was fussy about everything. The Harwoods had surprised everyone by inviting the Collins and Banfields up to their summer home on Lake Tahoe in late August. Everyone wondered what prompted them to do that, but we were all looking forward to it.

"They've got a beautiful place up there," Tess said.

"At Zephyr Cove, near Emerald Bay" Dean chimed in.

"Can you imagine owning five acres in such a heavenly spot," marveled Tess. "It's just a short drive from Fallon—like going from the ugly to the pristine and the lake is just gorgeous. The water is so clear, you can see a hundred feet down."

After our eventful journey across the desert and having to look at bleak surroundings for hours at a time, we all agreed that a change of scenery would be welcomed.

Now, as we turned on to the dirt road leading to the Banfield ranch we all hoped that the next two months would quickly pass by so we could go up to Lake Tahoe.

For the time being, though, my face was hurting as a result of the radiator exploding in my face earlier in the day and I just wanted some relief from the burning sensation I was experiencing at the moment. It was 10:30 p.m. and everyone had gone to bed by the time we arrived at the ranch house.

Chapter 9

At the Banfield Ranch
Early Tuesday morning

The crowing of a rooster broke the silence of the dawn.

It was 4:45 a.m. and it seemed like we had just gotten in bed after our long, near-disastrous trip across the Nevada desert. I was familiar with roosters, having lived on a farm, but to be awakened so early on our first day at the ranch was ridiculous, I thought.

I hadn't heard such loud, raucous screeching since moving to Jefferson street in Midvale a couple of years ago. It was one sound that I could do without the rest of my life; so when Tess mentioned on the way over from Utah that we would be arriving at the ranch house later than expected, I remembered my cousin, Jimmy, saying that at least we would be able to sleep in the first day of our arrival.

Dean had chuckled at that suggestion; implying that wouldn't happen if "Ol' Red was still around."

"Who's Ol' Red?" I had asked inquisitively. Dean and Tess just raised their eyebrows and smiled at each other.

"You'll know soon enough," Tess said while offering a full description of a red rooster that apparently was renowned for his crowing antics at the break of dawn. In every sense of the word, she informed us, Ol' Red was the dominant early bird around the Banfield ranch.

"He's a feisty old rooster that seems to have a built-in time clock inside him. Doesn't even take Sundays off," she added ruefully.

"From the top of his head to his pretty tail feathers, you get the feeling he's a proud, cocky bird…kind of like a watching a walking rainbow," Tess mused.

Then, she added:

"After waking everybody up each morning, Ol' Red struts around like he's the king of the barnyard."

Dean interrupted her comments:

"There's no doubt that Ol' Red rules the roost around there and he really seems to enjoy waking everybody up. Just watch his morning ritual and that'll convince you."

At the dawn of each day, he said, Ol' Red lets loose a few lusty wakeup calls which continue for about three minutes. He then ruffles his feathers and struts around the barnyard to make sure all of his chickens are up and clucking. Thus assured, the cocky rooster then heads for the barn and jumps up on a little red wagon that ranch hands use to tote the large milk cans from the barn to the kitchen so, when cooled, the milk can be used for drinking and cooking.

The remaining cans, Dean pointed out, are left outside the barn for pickup by a local milk processing company which homogenizes the milk before it is sold to local and regional markets.

Sitting atop his favorite milk can in the wagon which, Dean related, "just happens to be painted a variety of colors to match his plumage," Ol' Red clucks nervously as he and the milk cans are towed to Aunt Vera's kitchen by one of the ranch hands.

"The other chickens stay out of his way when this ritual is underway," Tess said. Then came a warning from Dean; chuckling at the thought of what he was about to say:

"Yeah, and if Ol' Red doesn't get your attention with his early morning antics, dad will.

"Dad's the closest thing to perpetual motion you'll ever see—never stops moving from dawn 'til dark.

"Come to think of it," he added reflectively, "I believe dad wakes up Ol' Red 'cause he's always up and about before dawn. It wouldn't surprise me if dad kicks that ol' rooster out of his nesting place each morning just to gets things moving."

*   *   *   *

On this early morning, a little over six hours after arriving at the ranch, and as dawn gently swept away the darkness, Ol' Red emerged in full throat, just like Dean and Tess said he would.

His innate rooster sense apparently told him there were some new arrivals at the ranch so he parked himself directly under our open window and began crowing loudly. Apparently, he wanted us to know he was king of the barnyard and that we had better start paying attention to him each morning.

We got the message. Loud and clear!

As Ol' Red belted out his screechy wake up call, Bob thrust his head outside our window and, waving his arms in a threatening manner, he shouted a warning:

"Get out of here you ol' reprobate or I'll wring your neck!"

Clucking indignantly, Ol' Red fluttered off the porch and nervously jerk-stepped his way across the barnyard; apparently believing that his authority had been challenged by some upstart. His wakeup call wasn't in vain. Bob had been roused out of a deep sleep and he resented Ol' Red's intrusion into our bedroom.

Jimmy and me were thinking the same thing, but we reluctantly got up knowing that around the Banfield ranch, Ol' Red's crowing signaled the start of a new day.

Our feet had barely touched the floor when the door burst open. It was my Uncle Jesse, Bob and Jimmy's father, and he was in a hurry. Directly behind him and barking like crazy was Nellie, their aging sheep dog that had been in the Banfield family for years.

She used to jump up and down and race about when welcoming her pals, Bob and Jimmy, but now as she limped around the room she could only wag her tail furiously and bark a greeting at us.

Hardly taking the time to even welcome his own sons, as well as myself on the first day at his ranch, Jesse simply said he was glad that we arrived safely. Then he issued his first order of the day; saying that his foreman, Hank Johnson, was waiting for us in the barn.

We knew exactly what he was referring to when he said that. Jesse was in and out of the room so fast that he didn't even notice my badly-burned face which was still beet red and feeling that I had dunked it into a vat of hot oil. As he ushered us out a side door of the ranch house, I noticed that the slightest crinkling of my facial muscles produced a lot of pain. The skin on my face was dry as I hadn't had time to dampen it or apply the ointment the doctor had prescribed for me in Elko. Now, that treatment would have to wait for awhile 'til I milked a few cows.

Dean had fore-warned us during the trip to Fallon that his dad, Uncle Jesse, had 38 cows that had to be milked every morning and evening. Since we had stabled a couple of bovines on our little farm on State street, prior to moving into the city a couple of years ago, I knew how to milk a cow, but I now wondered how long it would take to milk, then strip, such a large herd by ourselves.

There's a certain rhythmic process for milking a cow. My dad had taught me the technique when I was only eight years old. Wrapping your palm and fingers around two of the cow's teats, you then gently pull down on them while at the same time a kneading (pulling) process begins; starting with your index fingers, then your middle fingers and on down to your little fingers.

It's a continuous, rhythmic process and once this technique is mastered, a cow can be milked in a matter of minutes.

Stripping involves depleting the cow's total milk supply after it has given up most of its milk. There is always a small amount of milk left in cows' udders and even though it takes only a minute or two to strip a cow, it is normally done every time milking occurs; otherwise the milk remaining in the udder becomes stale and when mixed with a cow's next batch of fresh milk, the overall quality of the milk is then reduced.

*　　　　*　　　　*　　　　*

Bob, Jimmy and I thought at first that it would be our chore to milk all of the cows, but we were pleasantly surprised to find most of the ranch hands in the milking barn. Some were putting hay in the feed troughs outside the barn while others were washing off the cow's udders, in preparation for the milking process, while others were already sitting on their little stools and milking away as fast as they could. They were a noisy group, hollering to one another to get this or that done, as they filled up their milk buckets. One was even singing a well-known western tune; apparently to lyrics of his own making:

"Home, home on the range,
where the sheep and the cattle do play;
where nothing is heard,
only a loud rooster bird;
and the sky's a deep blue every day."

We would soon discover that the voice was coming from a big, broad-shouldered Irishman, Richard (Rich) Henrihan, whose lusty lyrics and clear tenor voice could rattle the rafters in any barn. Even though he was an Irishman through and through, he loved to sing western songs. Rich not only played the guitar, but the banjo and harmonica, too.

As we stood there at the crack of dawn, momentarily caught up in this surreal scene, one of the ranch hands spotted Bob, Jimmy and myself standing inside the barn door.

"Hey, everybody!—the Banfield kids are here," he shouted; leaving us to believe we were something special. Had such a greeting been orchestrated earlier by Hank Johnson or Uncle Jesse? We would never find out, but with that command, six ranch hands jumped up from their milking stools and welcomed us.

Suddenly, I heard a splat and felt something trickling down my chin and onto my neck. Sitting some six or seven feet away, with his mustacheod face grinning wickedly, Rich Henrihan had taken his cow's teat in hand and was spraying us with warm milk. Winnie Poo, the family cat, who was perched on a nearby bale of hay, got a squirt on her whiskers, too.

Rich, we would come to realize, was a prankster with a keen sense of Irish humor and a huge pair of hands that matched his pudgy bulk. He was also a pretty good marksman. He had hit me squarely on my chin with that stream of milk before I could duck away. He next zeroed in on Jimmy's crotch and then as if to display his accuracy, he caught Bob fully in the face.

In a matter of seconds, we had received our official welcome to the Banfield ranch! Our first assignment was to help milk 38 cows…at a little past five o'clock in the morning!

Chapter 10

With six ranch hands involved, besides ourselves, the entire milking process was completed in a little over an hour. My badly burned face felt like it was on fire, but I didn't know how to relieve the pain. Just as we were finishing the milking chore, Uncle Jesse poked his head into the barn door and shouted some instructions.

"After you boys move the cows out, make sure you hang up the milk stools and clean up the stalls."

A few minutes later, Aunt Vera sounded the breakfast bell. Bob said he and Jimmy would complete the cleanup work and for me to go over to the house and get my face fixed up.

As I left the barn I almost ran into a huge, leggy horse. Astride the magnificent, sorrel-colored animal and looking like a character from an old Western was Jesse's foreman, Hank Johnson. I could see in an instant that he was tough as rawhide. His wiry frame seemed molded into the saddle and his weathered facial features revealed tell-tale crow's feet wrinkles at the corner of his eyes; evident clues that he had spent long days in the sun.

Those wrinkles softened his otherwise flinty gaze, but not his ruff demeanor. The way he held his horse's reins really impressed me. An experienced cowhand has a special way of holding them. As Hank sat straight in the saddle, he controlled his nervous mount with only slight movements of his wrists and the reins.

His right hand was extended out from his chest and the reins were held tightly in his fingers. The wrist was arched in such a way that a mere nudge on the reins, right, left or backward, would signal the direction Hank wished his horse to go.

I was standing in the barn yard, barely six feet from his jittery horse's flared nostrils as Hank kept reigning in his fidgety mount and patting its neck at the same time.

After dismounting, he looped the horse's reins around a nearby railing. He'd come in for breakfast after being in the field for nearly an hour.

"Wow!" I thought to myself, "he's a real cowboy."

Hank spotted me eyeing him so he thrust out his hand.

"You came over here with the Banfield's?" he gruffly inquired as his hand clasped mine in a vice-like grip.

"Yes, sir!" I grimaced. I almost went to my knees from his crunching handshake and my fingers felt like mangled pretzels after he released his grip.

"You here to work or just play around?" he inquired.

"Both, I hope."

"You'd better do more work than playing around here," he retorted. Then, fixing his flinty eyes on me he asked:

"What happened to your face?"

"The car's radiator exploded on the way over from Utah." "What the hell were you doin' with your face that close to the radiator?"

He apparently wasn't interested in my answer. He just shook his head and ambled into the ranch house for breakfast.

To an impressionable 13-year-old, Hank looked for all the world like he had ridden straight out of a Western movie and onto Uncle Jesse's ranch.

*   *   *   *

Bob and Jimmy had made a swift cleanup of our milking stalls and within minutes, they we were dashing across the barn yard and into the back door of the ranch house.

They hadn't seen their mom since early spring, when she and Jesse had sold their farm house in the South Salt Lake valley to begin ranching operations in Fallon. Bob and Jimmy had stayed with Dean and Tess until school had let out in mid-May. Aunt Vera gave her sons a warm hug; telling them how glad she was to see them and giving each a big kiss on the cheek.

The genuine affection was mutual and I could tell they had missed their mom the past few months. Then, turning to greet me, she gasped as she took a closer look at my face. It was still puffy and beet red. Shreds of skin were still hanging from my forehead and cheeks where my burns were the most severe.

Upon arising earlier in the morning to help Aunt Vera prepare breakfast for the ranch hands, Tess had told her about our trip across the Nevada desert; how many times we had to stop because of car trouble and nearly getting killed by a huge big-rig truck and how I managed to severely burn myself.

"Oh, Danny, what in the world happened to you?" she asked. "The radiator exploded in my face—guess I didn't lift the cap off the right way," I replied.

"I didn't realize your burns were so severe," Aunt Vera said. "I've got to take care of you right now."

Then, putting her arm around me and forgetting breakfast preparations for a moment, she led me to a bathroom down the hall, while leveling a charge over her shoulder at Uncle Jesse.

"Don't think for a minute you're going to take Danny into the fields this morning! He's suffering and he's going to stay right here with me."

I knew I looked a mess, but I didn't know how bad it was until Aunt Vera let me look in a mirror. I was even startled at my appearance.

She was quite upset with Uncle Jesse for making me milk cows before she could attend to my burns. She also let me know that I wasn't going to be allowed out of the house for the next two or three days. It was futile to protest.

Jesse didn't resist either. He just shook his head, smiled that ever-present Banfield smile, and set about eating a hearty breakfast that had been prepared for the ranch hands.

✶   ✶   ✶   ✶

The pleasant smell of breakfast wafted through the ranch house and into the bathroom as Aunt Vera began gently dabbing my face with a clean, wet wash cloth.

"How long's it going to take?" I inquired impatiently. "I'm hungry."

"Never you mind," she said firmly. "This is more important right now. When we're finished, I'll make sure you get something to eat." Then, stepping to the door of the bathroom, she called down the hall towards the kitchen:

"Tess, would you please bring me the whites of six eggs. I don't need the yolks, just the whites—and bring me my stirring spatula while you are at it."

I was getting more curious by the minute while wondering what the white stuff from eggs and a spatula had to do with fixing my face.

While filling the bowl up with water, Aunt Vera said Tess had told her of the ointment the doctor in Elko had prescribed for me. I reached in my pocket and brought out a little silver tube that contained a jelly-like substance. The directions on the tube simply said: For burns, apply as needed.

After examining the contents, Aunt Vera shook her head and said that type of ointment was too moist and that it would prolong healing.

"Don't use it for the time being, she said, "I have a better treatment that will speed your recovery."

"Treatment—treatment?" I murmured. Her words sounded more like something for a cold than a remedy for my healing my face.

By now, I just wanted some relief from the burning sensation I was still feeling on my face. I became a cooperative patient and Aunt Vera's comforting manner provided calm assurance that she knew what she was doing.

"First," she explained, "we've got to make sure you're face is perfectly clean before we put anything else on it. I'm going to gently dampen your face with cold water several times so you must remain perfectly still. Then, while it's still moist, I'll apply the treatment.

What kind of treatment?" I inquired again.

Aunt Vera thought for a moment, then said she didn't have a special name for it, but that she had always referred to it as a mud pack.

"My mother—your grandma, Harriett Collins—learned how to treat burns from an old Indian—a Navajo or a Ouray—when we were living in Vernal near the Fort Duchesne (Dushane) Indian reservation in Northeastern Utah."

"Mother said Indian children were always getting burned in camp and teepee fires in those days; coming in contact with hot rocks or burning wood all the time. Since they were constantly around fire, their medicine men had to concoct a treatment that would be both a fast and effective healer for burns."

Although the treatment varied from tribe to tribe, Aunt Vera explained that cool mud packs were highly effective in treating serious burns. The tribes, she said, revered Mother Earth and believed it possessed magical healing powers.

"Indians not only drew strength from the Earth, but felt whatever was taken from it could cure all ills," she said.

*   *   *   *

When Tess brought the egg whites, Aunt Vera poured the contents into the large porcelain bowl that was atop the bathroom counter. She then reached down inside the counter and extracted a large deerskin bag containing several bottles. A smaller, heavier bag held some finely grained red dirt that Aunt Vera said came from the canyonlands of Eastern Utah.

Three scoops of dirt from the bag went into the bowl along with the egg whites. After pouring about half of the contents from one of the brown bottles on top of the dirt and adding a bit of water, she began rapidly stirring the contents with the spatula that Tess had brought from the kitchen.

"Yuk, I said, "that looks like a red mud pie to me. You're going to put that stuff on my face?"

Aunt Vera just smiled and nodded affirmatively. I couldn't contain my curiosity.

"What's in that brown bottle?" I asked

"It's an old Indian remedy." she replied. "Extracted from boiled Mesquite bushes."

Smells like rained-on sage brush to me," I complained.

"My mother said eggs served to soften and cool the mud and draw the heat from burns. I've been mixing them into my mud packs ever since I can remember."

I could tell Aunt Vera wasn't anxious to answer any more queries about egg whites and the contents of that Indian medicine bag. She had other tasks to do in the kitchen; especially since the mixing of the mud had stopped.

"Now, you must stop talking while I'm applying this mud pack to your face."

With that she led me across the hall to the cot where I had slept the night before; telling me to lie perfectly still so she could spread that ugly looking stuff on my forehead and face. With my head propped on a pillow, Aunt Vera began gently applying the mud to the burned areas; even on my eyelids.

"You've got to keep your eyes closed," she said.

As she began applying the mud pack, I immediately began to feel a soothing feeling on my skin and had the sensation that heat from my burns was being drawn from my face and forehead.

It was then that I remembered how my own mother used to apply some weird-looking green substance, mixed with egg whites, to her face. I had come home from school one day and mother had greeted me at the door. I was so startled to see her looking like some green creature from outer space that I almost dropped my books.

"Mom—what's that stuff you've got on your face!"

"I'm giving myself a facial. It freshens the skin and improves my complexion," she replied without hint of a smile. Mother didn't need to improve her complexion; she was an attractive woman anyway; but, I reasoned, women sometimes do strange things to preserve their beauty. So I just shook my head in wonderment over how she looked; noting that her mouth barely moved as she was talking to me; apparently so the green stuff on her face wouldn't crack. I didn't press her for a further explanation; fearing she might want to put some of it on me with my pimples and all.

*   *   *   *

My memories of the past was suddenly interrupted when Aunt Vera said she was going to put a damp wash cloth over the top of the mud pack so that it would be in a moist state when she took it off.

"It won't irritate your face if I keep it moist," she explained, "so just lie still for a little while and I'll be back to freshen up the wash cloth in a few minutes."

After several dampenings and even though it was only on my face for an hour, I was surprised at how heavy the mud pack had become. I was anxious to have it removed so I could get up and about. Sensing my anxiety, Aunt Vera carefully, but surely, began removing the thin layer of mud from my face.

A feeling of relief swept over me as she removed the final piece of mud. My face felt cool and refreshed as she gently cleansed the skin on my forehead, cheeks and eyelids while telling me the treatment would be repeated again in the afternoon.

"We'll repeat the process twice a day for the next two days. The swelling and burning feeling should be gone by then and your face will be as good as new." She then delivered more bad news.

I'm not going to allow you out of the house and in the sun for a couple of days, so don't plan on joining the boys in the field and doing chores; especially milking, before the end of the week." I couldn't believe what I was hearing.

"You mean I have to have those mud packs put on my face again?" I complained.

"Yes, you do, young man!"

"Aunt Vera, I can't stay in the house for two or three days in a row," I pleaded. I've got to earn my vacation by helping out around here."

"Danny, you can help me around here. Don't worry about getting outside too soon with the condition your face is in."

I was wary of what the term helping out meant. It didn't take long to find out. Since I couldn't spend time in the fields with Bob and Jimmy, or even be allowed to milk the cows, what would I be doing in the house? All day long?

Aunt Vera already had it figured out. She put me to work in the kitchen—peeling potatoes and washing dishes between mud packs!

I never realized how many potatoes could be eaten each day by ranch hands. We had fried potatoes for breakfast, boiled potatoes for the noon meal and mashed potatoes for dinner. Every day!

To get ready for each meal, I peeled Russet potatoes for an hour in the evening, so they could be served at breakfast the next morning, and for two hours in the afternoon in preparation for the evening meal.

I didn't need to peel potatoes for the noon meal as we used the New Red variety. I simply washed and scrubbed the skins real hard then Aunt Vera put them in two huge pots where they were boiled on top of a coal burning stove.

Seldom did the potato menu change and out of that experience came a determination never to be a cook when I grew up. My ambition was to become a champion tennis player, but that career choice had been put on hold for a Summer. Instead of serving tennis balls to my junior competitors, I found myself serving potatoes to hungry ranch hands.

Chapter 11

A pounding on the door stirred Dalton out of a deep sleep. He looked around the semi-darkened room trying to figure out where he was and what he had been doing to feel so lousy.

A fierce, headache gave him his first clue. Then he realized the drinking binge he and McCoy had been on for the past couple of days was the cause of his plight.

His mouth was dry. He smelled awful and his hands trembled as he lit a cigarette. Inhaling the smoke deeply into his lungs, then exhaling, he tried to clear his mind so he could figure out where he was at the moment.

For years he had been awakened by a guard clanging his night stick on the bars of his prison cell. Now, disoriented and suffering from a king-size hangover, he sat on the edge of his bed and surveyed his surroundings. It was Tuesday afternoon and he finally realized he was in a guest room at the back of the Diamond Bar saloon.

The small, sparsely furnished room offered little in creature comforts and the lone window high above the bed was clouded with dust and didn't afford much light. But there were no prison bars preventing his escape. What a relief, he thought. He shook his head, trying to remove the cobwebs from his addled brain.

"How in the hell did I end up here?" he asked himself.

Suddenly, it all came back to him. He had been out of prison for two days. He was a free man! No clanging of prison doors or guards to silently curse. His room was one of several at the back of the Diamond Bar saloon that the owner and a long-time friend, Johnny Hayden, provided for his best customers and the women of the night who hung out at his saloon.

The loud knocking continued. Even that sound made his head throb. It was McCoy, inquiring about how he felt.

"Ya' feelin' alright, Jake?"

Staggering to the door, Dalton urged McCoy not to talk too long or loud lest the sound hurt his ear drums.

"Damn, Bernie, I think we've been overdoing it the last couple of days."

"You've got that right," McCoy replied. "We're already broke and we'd better start taken it easy for awhile so we can at least begin to think straight."

Dalton just kept shaking his head and wondering about it all. After spending the past nine years in prison, returning to normalcy and adjusting to being a free man was difficult for him.

He was used to the slower and more restricted pace that prison life forced upon him. Now his head ached and a jumble of thoughts pierced his mind like flash points in a raging storm—his release from prison on Sunday—the wild night in Reno—the visit to the graveyard to pay his respects to his mom and dad only to discover his sister, Cheryl's, headstone next to those of his parents. Things were happening to fast for him.

Two days of binge drinking had taken its toll; not only on his physical well being but his mind as well and he wondered how he was going to be able to handle living outside those prison walls.

Now, he was free to move about, go where he wanted to go and do things he wanted to do without fear of being disciplined or put into solitary confinement for petty things dreamed up by his prison guards.

He really hadn't realized until now how precious his freedom meant to him. Still, his mean-spirited persona hadn't changed. Vengeance was on his mind. Learning that his sister, Cheryl, had died why he was in prison really troubled him.

"How could she have died so young?" he kept asking himself. The more he thought of it, the more his suspicions mounted.

"Could her business on the street have put her in the grave," he asked McCoy?

"I dunno, Jake, but there's gotta be a reason. She was too young to just pass away from natural causes. Somebody must have did her in. She was a good gal, so why would anyone want to harm her?"

"Hell, I wish I knew, Bernie, but I"m gonna' find out if it's the last thing I ever do."

"It puzzles me, too, Jake. When I first inquired around about her whereabouts after I got out, all I heard from people on the street was that she just up and disappeared a year or so after we both went to the pen."

"No one around here told me she'd passed away. When I couldn't find out anything, I just forgot about it."

Despite her zest for living on the wild side, Dalton and McCoy both knew that Cheryl had enough street smarts to take care of herself. At least in most situations, anyway. In their own minds, they kept asking themselves:

"How could she have just disappeared without anyone knowing about it."

The more they talked about it, the more they felt that someone had ended her life when she least expected it. By now, Dalton's head had cleared up and he was steamed.

"I'll tell you something, pal, there's gonna' be hell to pay if some miserable son-of-a-bitch killed her. If that's the case and I ever catch up with him, he'll die a slow death, believe me."

They both agreed that if Cheryl was murdered, it was done in a quiet way so that no one in Fallon knew about it.

* * * *

By mid-afternoon Dalton looked and felt like a new man. After shaving, showering and putting on clean clothes and eating a stout breakfast with McCoy, they drove over to the police station where Dalton had to check in and start his mandated one year probationary period.

He found himself matching stares with Jeb Harrington, deputy sheriff of Washoe Country and McCoy's probation officer.

"So, you're the infamous Jake Dalton—McCoy's partner in crime, eh?" Harrington said in a derisive tone.

"Bernie said you might be checkin' in soon. Where's your papers?"

Jake handed them to Harrington who dutifully stamped and annotated them while indicating he had just received his copy in the morning mail.

"Your reputation's preceded you, fella," he told Dalton, "and I'm here to tell ya' to stay out of trouble if you're gonna' live in this town. Otherwise, you'll find yourself behind bars again."

Then, in a further display of arrogance, Harrington reminded Dalton that the terms of his probation required prompt monthly checkins. If he failed to do so, Harrington told Dalton he'd come lookin' for him in a hurry.

"It won't be a pretty scene if I have to do that," the sheriff warned.

Dalton gave his new parole officer a contemptuous look and strolled out of the police station as if he didn't have a care in the world. McCoy was waiting for him.

"Get signed in?"

"Yeah, that little pip-squeak thinks he's God—tellin me I'd better stay out of trouble or he's gonna come after me. He even changed my monthly checkin date to coincide with yours. The guy's trouble; I can feel it in my bones and see it in his eyes. There's nothing he'd like better'n to see me behind bars again."

The two ex-cons were determined to stay out of trouble; at least for awhile. They were both parolees now and didn't relish the thought of being back in prison; especially McCoy as he had tasted freedom longer than Dalton who was just getting used to being a free man. He was also anxious to find a steady job.

"Let's do a little scoutin' around this evenin' and see what the job prospects are and maybe we can also find out about Cheryl as well," McCoy suggested.

"Otherwise," he cautioned Dalton, "we're gonna have to start robbin' again."

Dalton agreed. They mulled over what to do first. Both felt that Cheryl's disappearance and subsequent death merited a serious investigation. They could ask the town barber, Sal Menowitz, if he knew how Sheryl died; or they could quiz the employees at Hansen's mercantile store or even Rusty Trudeau,

Johnny Hayden's right hand man and head bartender at the Diamond Bar saloon.

McCoy felt they would have to do some quiet probing around town if they were to learn the true facts of Cheryl's death.

"Hell, Jake, somebody around here's gotta' know what Cheryl was doin' before she died. I'm for findin' out about it right away." Dalton nodded a silent approval. A hearty meal of steak and eggs and several cups of coffee, made his king-size hangover gradually go away. He could now think more rationally.

Several times during the past evening, he vaguely recalled asking a couple of old timers and the bartenders at the Diamond Bar if they knew any details or the circumstances surrounding his sister's death. A conspiracy of silence greeted them.

No one offered up any clues, but McCoy said he remembered noticing something in the eyes of one of the bartenders the night before; a telltale look of guilt that betrayed him when they began questioning him about Cheryl's death.

"Did you see how the guy blinked when you asked him about your sis?" he asked Dalton. "That cagey bastard knows something he's not telling us." Dalton agreed.

"You're damned right I noticed. I'm gonna find out his name and then I'll wring the truth out of him one way or another."

*   *   *   *

Dalton had mentioned to McCoy a couple of days earlier that before going to prison he had stashed some money in the well behind his parent's old ranch house, but in the first hours of enjoying freedom, he hadn't been interested in trying to retrieve the loot he'd hidden years ago; only how much alcohol he could consume and how fast he could find a woman to share his pleasure. Now, in a more sober mood and being virtually broke, his thoughts turned once again to the well and its secret contents.

He told McCoy that he didn't think anyone had been living in the house since the bank repossessed the property in the late '20's and they should inspect the premises as soon as possible.

"If no one's livin' there, I can retrieve the cash I stashed in the well and we can hang out there for a few days before decidin' what to do. The place is too far out in the boondocks for anyone to bother us."

As they drove down the dirt road leading to the old ranch house, no sign of activity could be detected. It was evident the place hadn't been lived in for years. Weeds were sprouting up around the foundation, the windows were broken and the front door was hanging on one hinge.

McCoy offered a simple assessment of how his pal's old house appeared to him.

"Looks in pretty bad shape to me."

Dalton nodded in silent agreement while thinking to himself:

"If the outside looks this bad," it must be a real mess inside."

It wasn't a pretty sight that greeted his eyes as he stepped inside the front door. Chards of broken glass from shattered windows lay everywhere. Debris and empty beer bottles littered the floor. Most of the wallpaper had been peeled, or torn off, and two old mattresses lay side by side in the middle of the room. Ashes were scattered about and a half burned log lay in a once attractive fireplace that had featured a hand carved wooden mantle.

Dalton remembered that mantle. It was where the family's big clock had sat and where, as youngsters, he and Cheryl had hung their bright red stockings at Christmas time.

The kitchen was an unsightly mess, too. An old table with three of its legs missing was upside down in the center of the room and a soiled table cloth lay crumpled next to it. The ironlegged kitchen stove was hunched like a battered relic against the far wall; its oven door half off its hinges and a piece of disconnected stove pipe hung loosely from a hole in the soot-blackened ceiling.

Not a single wooden cabinet was left hanging on the walls. Apparently they had been busted up for kindling wood years ago. Jake didn't venture into the two back bedrooms where his mom and dad and Cheryl once slept and he only gave a brief look at the stairs leading up to the small loft area where his bed was once located. He didn't want to tarry inside and further recall the sad memories of his youth so he quickly stepped outside and glanced around the back yard as Bernie trailed behind him.

It was like going back in time; only now it wasn't a pretty picture to behold. The out buildings; especially the barn and the nearby tool and equipment shed were sagging from the ravages of the weather and years of neglect.

Weeds were everywhere.

The Cottonwood and poplar trees that formed a scenic backdrop to the backyard were also showing signs of stress. Crumbling bark and broken tree branches were scattered around the yard, but it was another structure that caught Jake's attention and triggered a flood of youthful, but painful memories. Directly in front of him, nearly 100 feet away, was the well that had caused him so much misery and anguish in the past. He remembered that exact distance as he had stepped off those 32 yards many times when lugging heavy pails of water into the kitchen.

The well's above ground structure of rock and brick were still intact as was the stoop that had once held a roller drum and heavy rope attached to a bucket for extracting water from the depths of the well. The drum for holding the strands of rope had long since disappeared, but the extra long piece of rope that was used to lower the oaken bucket down into the well lay strewn about the yard in uneven coils.

The flat ledge rock base surrounding the well was still in remarkable condition, even though several pieces had become loosened and broken off over the years. The bench surrounding the well, where everyone sat for family picnics, had been partially torn away.

After surveying his surroundings, Dalton wondered if the loot he'd hidden in the well's darkened shaft nearly 10 years ago was still there. As he reached the well and discovered the heavy board cover still intact, a fleeting thought crossed his mind.

"Surely," he thought to himself, "no one would ever think of going down there; especially if the house was vacant."

Casting the cover boards aside, he peered into the darkened interior of the well. The steel rung handles and steps were still in place—just as he remembered them.

McCoy watched in fascination as Jake unhesitatingly climbed atop the well stoop and descended into the well's interior; thinking that it must have taken a lot of guts when Dalton was a young boy to go exploring into that darkened pit.

Seven rungs down, Dalton lit a match and as it flickered in the darkened shaft, he flared it around to see if he could find his secret little hiding place. Just to the right of the fifth rung a piece of ledge rock extended slightly out from well's interior wall revealing a small cavern.

The match was beginning to burn his fingers so Jake discarded it and lit another one so he could peer into the opening more carefully. Then he slowly slid his hand into the hole until something stopped his reach. He flinched momentarily, then realized it was the old cigar box he'd stashed his money in years ago. The shout up to McCoy echoed and re-echoed off the jagged walls of the well.

"Hey, Bernie, I found my little box—hope my money's still in there."

Dalton climbed up out of the well holding a battered, old cigar box. Lifting the flap, he began counting the cash inside it. The tens and twenties, with mildewed edges, were counted twice and both times the amount turned out to be $190; the exact amount he remembered stashing in the well years before.

"Looks like we can get by without robbin' anybody for awhile, Bernie. Can't find a better place to hide money than in an old abandoned well can ya?"

McCoy shook his head in amazement and smiled; knowing their latest cache wouldn't last long at the rate they were spending money.

Dalton put the cover boards back in place on top of the well and told Bernie the next thing they had to do was to go back into town and make further inquiries about his sister's mysterious death.

"I guarantee ya, pal, we're gonna make somebody do a little talkin' before this night's over."

Chapter 12

Hank Johnson's demanding schedule was nearly consuming him. He had promised his boss, Jesse Banfield, that he would go into town as soon as possible and look for help, but there were other priorities he first had to take care of around the ranch.

He had spent all day Monday with several of his ranch hands repairing fences in the South and East pastures while directing other workers in gathering and stacking the hay that had lain for several days in the fields West of the ranch house.

It was now late in the afternoon on Tuesday and he had made the short nine-mile drive into Fallon and filled his pickup truck with Aunt Vera's much needed supplies at Hansen's mercantile store.

Now, he was like a hunter stalking prey. Only this time, he was seeking humans—additional ranch hands—not animals. He checked the usual places where out-of-work cowboys and ranch hands usually hung out—in front of the Hansen's on South main street. He knew serious job seekers always gathered there. Farmers and ranchers always stopped at Hansen's to pick up their weekly supplies before quenching their thirst at one of the local watering holes.

This chore was always done when everyone was still sober. Serious drinking would start shortly after that at the local bistros. But on this day, not a solitary soul was hanging around Hansen's looking for work. Hank was getting discouraged.

Two doors down from Hansen's was Sal's barber shop. Sal Bonatari knew everybody's business in town and he clipped and talked constantly. If anyone was seeking work, Sal would know.

Sometimes, Hank remembered, Sal would burst into song at the drop of a hat. His booming, but brief, Italian arias would be a bit scratchy at times but he could sing a little bit. He always seemed to be in a jolly mood. How he ended up as the town barber in Fallon, Nevada, was a mystery to everyone.

"With my cultured voice," Sal would tell Hank or anyone else listening to his constant banter, "I should be with Metropolitan;" a clear reference to the storied Metropolitan Opera in New York.

His customers knew he was joking, but their standard rebuke to his claim to fame always brought him back to reality.

"A voice like that needs insurance, Sal," some critic would always chime in, which was an obvious reference to the old insurance company of the same name.

Sal would then act miffed, change the subject, and go on clipping and talking at the same time while telling his customers they didn't appreciate great talent.

Further down South main street, was another source for finding potential workers; the infamous Diamond Bar saloon. Hank knew that the Diamond Bar was the gathering place for all sorts of characters.

"If I can't find some help elsewhere in town," Hank thought, "the Diamond Bar might produce something."

Sal suggested he check with Rusty Trudeau, the flamboyant manager and bartender at the Diamond Bar. "That ol' feller knows where all the bodies are. If he can't help you find some hands, nobody can."

Hank was wary of even setting foot inside the Diamond Bar. The saloon's owner, Johnny Hayden, had recently refurbished that glitzy, but notorious saloon. The place was like a magnet; attracting a diverse clientele—city slickers, transients and shady characters—as well as hard working ranch hands who loved to carouse around and chase after the women of the night who were always lounging around the saloon.

Hank knew all about the Diamond Bar. He didn't like the place, but that was where all the action was and he always seemed to end up there whenever he came into town. It would be his last stop before heading back to the ranch. If his efforts failed this time he would be in a real quandary about what to do about finding some extra hands.

*   *   *   *

Rusty Trudeau was at his usual station behind the huge, angular bar that was the centerpiece of attraction at the Diamond Bar. It was made of solid oak and the carvings and bullet holes in the top of the bar spoke volumes about the type of activity that had taken place in the past.

Trudeau presided over his domain like a judge in a disorderly courtroom. Nothing escaped his wary eyes and he made sure his customers were well taken care of—in more ways than one!

Service was his credo and he treated (and greeted) everyone as if they were long time friends whether they were casual acquaintances or first time visitors.

Everyone was Rusty's friend, but there were few customers in the Diamond Bar this night. Like the other hangouts in Fallon, weekdays were slow. The action never really heated up until Friday afternoon when the ranch hands got paid. Spying Hank as he ambled into the saloon, Rusty greeted him in his usual light-hearted manner. They shook hands and exchanged pleasantries. Rusty slid a cool one into Hank's knarly hands while wondering why he was in town.

"Howdy, old friend, what brings you in here so early in the week? Not just to hoist a few beers, is it?"

"I'm afraid not, Rusty. Had to pick up some supplies and see about hirin' some additional hands. Nobody was hangin' around Hansen's and Sal said you might know if anyone was lookin' for work.

"You that desparate—comin' into town in the middle of the week?"

"Sure am. We're gettin' behind on our work and I need to do some hirin' as soon as possible."

"It's slim pickin's right now, Hank. Your distant neighbors, Sam Swenson and Henry Bisbee, came in here last weekend looking for help. They checked the usual places—Hansen's and Sal's; even here—but they didn't have much luck as far as I know."

Rusty then startled Hank when he revealed that a couple of strangers had been hanging around his saloon the past couple of nights.

"Where are they now?" Hank inquired.

Rusty nodded toward the end of the bar.

"Down there…see those two guys huddling by themselves?"

"Yeah, I do," Hank said. "What d'ya know about 'em?"

"Nothing. I've been off for a couple of days and when I came in for the evening shift, one of my bartenders, Sid Franklin, said the two had been in last night and were drunk as skunks by ten o'clock.

"Sid said they were laughin' and hollerin' and raisin' a ruckus. When he asked them to quiet down, they told him to get lost—that they were friends of Johnny Hayden's and they could do what they wanted in his place.

"They were actin' pretty belligerent, so Sid put a couple of girls on 'em in order to quiet 'em down. Before long, they disappeared with the girls into the back room. They came in a couple of hours ago and have been pretty quiet so far—probably recovering from a hangover after last night.

"Hayden's out of town this week, but I've gotta find out if they actually are his friends or just hangers-on. Johnny usually alerts me to special visitors coming to town, but he didn't tell me about those two characters. If they're friends of his, I'll havta' take good care of them. If not…" Rusty left his comments unsaid, but Hank clearly understood his implied thoughts: The rowdies could stay if they behaved themselves, but friends or not, if they got loud and disorderly as they had the night before, he would throw them out and tell them not to come back.

Rusty abhorred disorderly conduct and said he had reputations to uphold—his and the Diamond Bar's—and he wasn't about to let a couple of new arrivals spoil it all with their crude and lewd behavior. Even if they were friends of Johnny Hayden.

He worked the bar for a few minutes longer; then he told Hank that he would find out more about the strangers.

"If they're good guys, we've made some new friends and you might've got yourself a couple of additional hands."

*　　　*　　　*　　　*

A few minutes later, Rusty came back with a concerned look on his face. He'd gathered conflicting information on the strangers and didn't know just what to believe about them.

"I was told they were originally from around here and had returned home a couple of days ago after doing construction work around the state for the past 10 years. Then I see a couple of my old friends, Gordie Alsop and Rich Pastore, motioning for me to come over to their table.

"I thought they wanted another round of drinks, but Gordie whispered to me that those two characters were ex-cons and had done time at the state prison in Carson City."

Hank shook his head in disgust at that disappointing news and ordered another beer while trying to figure out what to do next.

"If they've done prison time and are now out," he began rationalizing to himself, "they've paid their dues to society. If so, why not put 'em on the payroll."

Hank knew his options were limited now. He could either go back to the ranch and inform his boss, Jesse Banfield, that he had again failed in his quest to find some additional help, or he could sidle down the bar and engage the two strangers in a conversation to see if he could glean some information from them about their past as well as their experience in ranch operations.

If he could satisfy himself on those matters, he thought, he would hire them. Moments later, his good judgement impaired from drinking too many beers, he introduced himself to the strangers.

"Hi fellas...Rusty tells me you're new in town. Just passin' through or lookin' for work?" Warily eyeing Hank, the strangers momentarily ignored the tall, lanky cowboy who stood beside them.

"Who the hell are you?" Dalton asked in a belligerent tone. "Hank Johnson, foreman at the Banfield ranch Southeast of here."

The strangers reluctantly introduced themselves.

"I'm Jake Dalton—this here's Bernie McCoy."

With handshakes exchanged, Hank ordered a round of drinks as they moved to a nearby table..

"You fellas new around these parts?" Hank inquired. "We both grew up around here—been away for awhile," Dalton responded. "Why ya' askin'?"

Neither he nor McCoy were anxious to reveal details about their sordid past, but Hank was insistent.

"I need a couple of extra hands for the rest of the summer. Know anything about ranching operations?"

"I was raised on a farm," Dalton offered, "and Bernie here—he knows just enough to be dangerous." They all laughed at that statement.

"Where'ya in from?" Hank inquired.

"Been up in Winnemucca 'n Elko, doin' construction work," Dalton answered.

Dalton was lying and becoming irritated. He wasn't used to being grilled; especially by a stranger, but the opportunity for work overcame his anger.

"We may be pullin' out and headin' for Vegas in a day or two if we can't find some work around here. What're payin?" Dalton inquired.

"Board'n room 'n seventy-five bucks a month," Hank answered quickly.

Dalton and McCoy looked at each other and shook their heads. The ex-cons were not too anxious to become employed at that paltry sum. Dalton spoke up.

"Not interested," he replied.

Those extra beers and the warm atmosphere within the Diamond Bar saloon had begun to blur Hank's normally good judgement about hirings.

He didn't want to return to the ranch and tell his boss he'd failed in his mission to hire extra hands. He even deferred asking more questions about Dalton and McCoy's background lest he find out something really troublesome.

"These are desperate times," he told himself. It was getting late and he had to make a quick decision.

"Alright, make it a ninety a month," Hank offered. "Take it or leave it. That's the best I can offer you." Hank stood up and prepared to leave.

Dalton looked at McCoy "How about it, pal?"

"Sounds okay to me. When do we start?" McCoy asked. Hank was ready with a quick answer.

"Thursday morning. You can move your stuff in tomorrow if you want to."

They shook hands and Hank gave the ex-cons directions to the ranch. A sense of relief swept over Hank. Even though he had failed to question Dalton and McCoy about their shady pasts and prison records, he thought he had at least hired two experienced workers.

He knew Uncle Jesse would be happy about that, too, but he decided not to reveal their criminal records to his boss for the time being. His normal good judgement now impaired due to excessive drinking, Hank rationalized his latest hirings.

"They've served their time," he reasoned, "so why bring up the past?"

Chapter 13

Peeling potatoes and doing dishes wasn't exactly the way I had envisioned starting off my stay at the Banfield ranch. Aunt Vera had performed a miracle and my face was healing rapidly as a result of her special three-times-a-day mud packs. Still, I was anxious to get outside even though the burns on my face were not completely healed.

Kitchen work wasn't for me. My hands were sore from peeling spuds with a dull paring knife and I had so many cuts on my fingers they looked like I'd jammed them into a corn shredder.

"Enough of this," I thought, "where's the fun part of this vacation?"

At least Bob and Jimmy had been able to get out and about the ranch and enjoy themselves a little bit and being a farm boy at heart, I was eager to join them.

I had always liked being outdoors; so while peeling potatoes, I kept my spirits up by remembering Bob's promise that we would have some fun this summer; like riding horses or fishing in the Truckee river. Of course, I knew from the start that it wouldn't be all play and no work for us. We were expected to help in milking the cows and do small chores around the ranch house for Bob and Jimmy's mom and dad, my Aunt Vera and Uncle Jesse.

We were also to assist the ranch workers in mending fences, herding the sheep and cattle and hauling the newly-cut alfalfa from the outer fields. But, for some unknown reason, having fun on the Banfield ranch was proving as elusive as handling quick silver.

The ranch hands seemed to get along alright and the big Irishman, Rich Henrihan, kept everyone loose with his jokes and booming tenor voice; especially when he had a cow's teats in his hands. He was at his accurate best when the early morning chores started and he really enjoyed spraying us with warm milk as we entered or exited the barn.

I took a liking to Henrihan even though he had drenched me with squirts of milk when we had come into the barn the morning after our arrival at the ranch.

Now, three days later he plunked himself down beside me at the breakfast table and began asking Bob, Jimmy and myself all sorts of questions about ourselves when the ranch foreman, Hank Johnson, interrupted our discussion by introducing two new hires to everyone.

"Meet Jake Dalton and Bernie McCoy. They'll be working with us for the rest of the summer."

That introduction was short and simple, but Hank didn't seem overly enthusiastic about doing it.

Uncle Jesse welcomed them and they acknowledged the greeting and thanked Vera and Tess for fixing breakfast for them. Normally, there was a lot of chatter going around the breakfast table, but for some reason everyone ate in subdued silence after that introduction. There was a definite chill in the air and a strange feeling came over me. It felt like a wave of evil had just entered the house.

I was sitting next to Jimmy when he whispered to me. "Those guys look pretty mean, don't they?"

I nodded my head in agreement. Bob's only comment was to hope that the new hires would "pitch in and work hard" like the rest of his dad's ranch hands.

After the crew had gone into the fields, Jimmy again whispered to me. "Those two guys are walking trouble—I hope we don't have to work with them." I didn't like their looks either.

"That older one—Jake Dalton—he's got the meanest-looking face I've ever seen," I responded. "Looks like he could stare a hole right through you if he wanted to."

Jimmy agreed as we helped Vera and Tess clean up the kitchen. A sack full of potatoes sat nearby; awaiting our morning ritual. During the mid-day break for lunch, Jesse said he would be going out in the afternoon to check on his sheep and cattle in the eastern pastures. He invited Bob and Jimmy to go with him.

"How about going, too?" I inquired while looking toward my Aunt Vera for approval.

Jesse knew I couldn't go unless Vera said so. Surprisingly, she nodded her consent, but warned me to stay out of the sun and for Jesse to watch his driving.

"You be careful, Jesse—and Danny, you keep your hat on. Your face hasn't healed completely so don't stay out in the sun too long." Then, for good measure she added:

"Before you go, be sure to put the ointment on your face that the doctor in Elko gave you."

I heard and obeyed every word Aunt Vera said, but if Jesse was listening, he paid no heed. Like always, her words went in one ear and out the other. His mind was elsewhere and he was anxious to inspect a rather large herd of sheep and a some new lambs that were feeding in the South pasture in preparation for their impending move to the North ranch, which we learned, was some nine miles away.

Jesse was leasing that 1,100 acre spread from another rancher as he said it had some good pasture land on it.

"Good place to fatten up the herd before we sell 'em this Fall," he said.

Since he was short of ranch hands, he had informed us that we, Bob, Jimmy and myself, were going to be the shepherds in moving the sheep up to the North ranch in mid-August. We were happy to be given that assignment, but upon hearing of it, Aunt Vera again objected.

"The boys are too young to handle that responsibility, Jesse. That's a chore for Hank's crew; not the boys. Besides, that's a full day's journey and they shouldn't be out in the sun that long; especially Danny. His face is just now beginning to heal good."

"Aw, mom," Bob interjected. "Danny's face will be okay by then. We can handle that job and have some fun doing it."

"Sure we can," Jimmy added supportively.

I added my two cents worth as well. "I'll be okay by then, Aunt Vera."

She just smiled and shook her head. A momentary flash of anger appeared on Jesse's face.

"Vera, for heaven's sake, the boys'll be alright. You can fix 'em some sandwiches and canteens of water and we'll keep an eye on 'em during the day. They'll need to be re-supplied with food and water along the way, as will the sheep. Hank and I will be working on those details in the next few days so don't fret about it."

Vera got the last word in.

"That's still too hard a job for the boys," she protested. "Listen, Vera, if the boys get too tired, we'll pick them up and a couple of the ranch hands can finish the drive."

* * * *

With the lunch break over, we piled into the back of Jesse's battered old pickup truck and sat among the bales of hay that had been put there by one of the ranch hands as drop-off feed for the cattle in a nearby pasture.

By the time Jesse had gunned his pickup out of the barnyard and onto the heavily rutted road leading to the Southeast pasture, we knew he was going to completely ignore Aunt Vera's warning about driving carefully. He seemed to have only two speeds when behind the wheel: Fast and faster. Pedal to the metal seemed to be his credo.

It was a wild and scary ride even for Bob and Jimmy, who were used to riding with their dad at breakneck speeds, but it was a frightening experience for me. After dropping off the bales of hay in the east pasture, we spotted three sick lambs lying in the alfalfa field adjacent to the Southeast pasture.

The lambs had apparently gorged themselves on the tender alfalfa shoots after wandering through a hole in the fence. They were clearly in distress and were also suffering from heat prostration when we found them.

Adding to their misery, as well ours, was a blazing sun that was beating unmercifully down on us. Jesse said it was 105 degrees when we left the ranch house, but the searing wind that raked across landscape scorched our faces and made it feel much hotter than it really was at the time.

The lambs' swollen stomachs told a sad story. They had become bloated from eating too much alfalfa. Their survival was doubtful.

"I'll probably have to stick 'em," Jesse said ruefully as he surveyed his precious cargo and the damaged fence at the same time. I winced when he said that as I was familiar with such a procedure. Years earlier, my dad had given me a baby lamb for my sixth birthday. I loved that little creature; fed it with milk in a baby bottle every day and it followed me wherever I went around our 10-acre farm in Midvale. One hot summer day, my buddies and I had decided to go swimming in the nearby Jordan river; so I ditched my pet lamb for awhile. It was a sad and fatal mistake.

Upon returning home, I found him lying on his side in the neighbor's alfalfa field. He had eaten too much of the newlymowed hay and had become bloated. He was still alive when my dad came from work late in the afternoon. He immediately knew what had to be done even though it was a radical procedure.

Quickly taking out his pocket knife, he punched a hole in the under side of my little lamb's stomach in order to let the air and digestive juices out of the puncture. It was a procedure that worked sometimes, but not all of the time, depending upon how much hay a lamb had eaten and how soon the procedure was applied after it had become bloated.

This time it didn't work and my lamb died shortly thereafter. I mourned for my furry little munchkin until my dad's brother, Uncle Ralph, came by one day with another baby lamb in his arms.

"You'd better take care of this one," he said in an admonishing tone, "or you'll never get another one from me!"

I thought about that period in my young life as I looked with sadness on the similar plight of the three little lambs we were cradling in our arms in the back of Jesse's truck.

*　　　*　　　*　　　*

As we raced back to the barn to get the sick lambs out of the sun, it was all we could do to keep from flying out of the truck bed. Jesse was speeding down the dusty, rut-filled road leading to the ranch house like he was in a road race.

Each rut and pothole we hit seemed to be bigger than the last one and that ever-present rooster tail of dust spewed out behind us as we sped toward the barn with our precious cargo. We couldn't see those pot holes from our vantage point from the back of the truck, but we could really feel them.

It was also painful on our butts and our arms ached from trying to keep from flying out of the truck while holding on to our suffering lambs.

Problem was, Jesse seemed totally unmindful of our plight.

"Why is he driving so fast," I kept thinking to myself? "He must know where all of those potholes are by now; especially near the ranch house."

Suddenly, the truck started to swerve; first right, then left as Jesse tried to avoid the gaping ruts in the road. Too late!

He hit a big one and everything seemed to go in slow motion after that.

As he slammed on the brakes, putting the truck into a slithering, sideway skid, a huge dust cloud began billowing up behind us as we careened back and forth across the road. We clawed at the side panels to keep from falling out, but the truck tipped upward; then slowly rolled over as it slid into a barbed wire fence that paralleled the road.

We all went flying through the air along with our precious cargo as the swirling dust settled upon us. For a few seconds, it was eerily quiet; then I heard a weak bleating sound.

Regaining my senses, I found myself entangled in a barbed wire fence and the baby lamb I had been holding onto was lying underneath me. The little creature had apparently helped cushion the impact as we flew out of the truck and crashed into the fence. It raised its head for a moment and let out a couple of bleats, then it lay still; barely breathing.

Jimmy was sent tumbling through the air in a free fall and came to rest on his backside in the alfalfa field bordering the road. In attempting to protect himself and the lamb he was holding after being ejected from the back of the truck, he not only jammed his left shoulder, but he had broken his left forearm when he hit the ground in an awkward position.

The lamb he was trying to save suffered a worst fate. With gasping bleats, it tried to stand up; only to fall on its side. Moments later it was dead.

Somehow, Bob had been hurled over the fence and was still holding onto the lamb he had been cradling in his lap. He had miraculously escaped with a wrenched knee along with a few bumps and bruises, but the lamb he was holding had died instantly upon impact with the ground.

*　　　　*　　　　*　　　　*

When I realized that we were going to roll over, I had somehow managed to grab the truck's tailgate for a brief moment before being hurled into the fence post. I heard something crack, then a numbing pain surged through my right shoulder. I thought it was broken, but it was the fence post that had snapped when I had banged into it.

While the post had somewhat cushioned my fall, the barbed wire attached to it had raked across my tender face and head; causing a ragged gash to once again scar my already tender face. The prickly barbs had opened up a cut on my right cheek bone and eyebrow before tearing opening a long gash on the side of my head just above the ear. I was fortunate not to have lost the sight in my right eye.

By now, I was bleeding profusely from those cuts. I was also gasping for breath from having the wind knocked out of me. I had also become entangled in several strands of barbed wire and part of the broken post was laying across my chest.

Being the least hurt, and seeing my predicament, Bob hurried over and pulled the wires and broken post off me. He looked afraid and startled at the same time.

"Geez, Danny, you're bleeding pretty bad. I think you're gonna need some stitches in a couple of places."

"I'm hurting more than I'm bleeding," I gasped. "My chest aches and my ribs feel like they're broken."

After regaining my senses, I realized that I had suffered no broken bones as I was able to flex my arm and shoulder muscles without too much pain. That was a good sign, but the blood was streaming down the side of my face and onto my shirt. Suddenly, a voice pierced the silence.

"You boys alright?" Jesse shouted anxiously as he kicked open the door and struggled out of the driver's side of his truck. We weren't alright.

Dazed and shaken up, we were hurting all over. Jimmy's broken arm looked ugly; my chest hurt and I was having difficulty stemming the flow of blood from the gashes on the right side of my head and face.

Jesse was shocked and bewildered over what he had done. He kept telling us how sorry he was as he walked back and forth in quiet desperation while wondering how he was going to get his truck back on its wheels so he could rush us to the doctor in Fallon.

Shaking his head, he sighed ruefully over the misfortune he had brought on to everyone.

"I gotta get you boys to a doctor real quick."

Sobbing quietly and in severe pain, Jimmy turned to his dad. In anguish, he thrust out his arm.

"Look, dad, my arm's broken. Geez, it's really hurting—I think my lamb's dead, too."

"Gosh, son, I'm sorry—I should have been more careful." I could tell Jesse was truly distressed. He couldn't stand to look at his son's broken arm. It was grotesquely mis-shapen and becoming more painful by the minute, so he turned away momentarily; shaking his head and wondering how he was going to get his truck upright so he could rush us to the doctor.

Chapter 14

In a nearby pasture, Hank Johnson and two other workers, Tim Olsen and Tony Minnoti, were mending fences while tending to a herd of cattle when they noticed Jesse speeding along a nearby road that led to the ranch house. They knew their boss was always in a hurry, but this time they didn't know why he was driving so fast until they saw us being thrown out of the truck while holding onto our young lambs.

Dean also witnessed the accident. He and another ranch hand, Clint Murdock, had just finished stacking hay near the barn and were returning to the field to pick up another load when they saw Jesse's truck speeding down the road toward them; leaving in its wake a swirling cloud of dust.

When the truck began to swerve violently, then tip over and sending bodies and lambs flying everywhere, they knew immediately that help would be needed. Whipping the hay wagon around, Dean yelled some instructions to Murdock before heading back to the ranch house.

"Get over there as fast as you can and give 'em some help. I'm gonna get the car—I'll be there in a few minutes."

Dashing into the ranch house, he shouted at Aunt Vera and Tess who were busily preparing the evening meal.

"We've got an an accident up the road—Mom, Tess, you'd better come with me."

"Oh, goodness! What has Jesse done now," Vera wondered out loud as she and Tess gathered up a medical kit, some towels and a jug of water before jumping in the car with Dean.

From his vantage point in the nearby field, Hank Johnson had also noticed Jesse's truck swerving from side to side. When he saw bodies hurtling through the air, he sprang into action.

"C'mon, boys," he shouted, "we'd better hurry over there; Jesse and the boys could be hurt bad." As they raced toward us, Hank muttered under his breath: "Jesse's gotta stop driving like a maniac or he's gonna kill somebody someday."

As it turned out, he did! Two of the lambs, just 90 days old, had died shortly after impact; either from being thrown violently out of truck and crushed or from being bloated. I knew the lamb I had been holding wouldn't last long either as it wasn't moving or responding to my attempts to revive it.

Upon seeing our plight, Hank acted fast. He wasn't about to be critical of his boss, but he knew what had to be done in a time of crisis; the biggest of which was an urgent need to get us to a doctor for emergency treatment.

"We've gotta get this truck back on its wheels, boss, so the boys can be taken to the doctor. They're gonna need some fixin' up and the sooner we get them there the better off they'll be."

As I sat on the side of the road, I could feel myself growing weaker by the minute from losing so much blood. Johnson could see I was in distress and on the verge of fainting. He whipped the bandana from around his neck and tied it around my head in an effort to stop the bleeding from the gash on the side of my head. Then, he borrowed another bandana from Clint Murdock and told me to hold it against my cheek and eyebrow to stem the flow of blood from those gashes.

"Those'll do until we can get you to the doctor," he said.

Turning to Jesse, who was leaning on the front of his truck and still woozy from the tip-over, he gently offered a suggestion.

"Boss, stand back for a minute and we'll get on the right side of the truck 'n rock it back and forth—that'll tip it back on its wheels."

It worked and in seconds, Olsen, Minotti, Murdock and Hank had the truck back on the road that led to the ranch house. A short distance away, Jesse could see a car coming toward him. It was Dean, Vera and Tess hurrying to help us.

As the car skidded to a sudden stop, he knew in an instant he was in deep trouble.

Scrambling out of the car with a canteen of water and towels in her hands, Vera was concerned and angry at the same time.

"Good heaven's, Jesse, what have you done now?"

Without even stopping to hear his reply, she hurried over to where Bob, Jimmy and I were sitting to assess our condition. Tess followed with a small medical kit that Aunt Vera always kept handy since accidents were always happening around the ranch. Dean helped his dad into the truck and said he would drive him back to the ranch house.

* * * *

Observing that we were going to quickly need medical help, Vera knew this wasn't the proper time to vent her growing anger at her husband for what he had done. That would come later.

Getting us to the doctor was her main concern right now. Still, as she helped us into the car, she saw the plight of our precious cargo of lambs and sadly shook her head. Not realizing that two of them were already dead and the one I had been holding was dying, she instructed Jesse to look out for them.

"You get those lambs back to the barn and out of this heat just as fast as you can."

"Vera, don't worry about the lambs," Jesse responded. "They're goners—just get the boys to the doctor."

As she helped us into the car, Aunt Vera asked Tess if she wouldn't mind going back to the ranch house and finishing dinner preparations for everyone while she was away.

"I'll be back as soon as I can," she said. Then pointing her finger at Jesse, she couldn't resist admonishing him one last time.

"Don't you ever pull that stunt again! You could have killed the boys and then how would you have felt?"

Jesse hung his head, but didn't answer. With that Vera sped off toward Fallon with Bob and myself in the back seat and Jimmy sitting up front holding his broken arm and telling her to hurry.

"My arm's realling hurting, Mom. Can you go a little faster?" "I'm hurrying as fast I can, son, but I'm not going to be a reckless driver like your father," she replied.

"I'm so mad at him for what he's done to you boys I could just give him a good kick in the pants." That brought a little levity to a painful situation and prompting Bob to respond.

"I can just see you doing that, mom. You couldn't catch up with him to do that. He moves around too fast."

* * * *

Two hours later, we were all patched up. It had taken the doctor and two nurses over an hour to set Jimmy's arm and put it in a plaster cast. Bob suffered only minor cuts and bruises and a sprained knee, but my injuries were a bit more severe.

Twelve stitches were required to close up the gashes on my cheek and eye brow and it took 17 more to sew up the cut on the side of my head. With my face still tender from the burns I'd suffered when the radiator exploded in my face, I was a real mess.

The doctor determined that the pain on my right side was caused from a bruised chest and ribs so he wound me up like a mummy, from the top of my chest down to my waist. He said I couldn't do any strenuous activities for awhile; especially riding horses.

On the way back to the ranch, Aunt Vera began querying us about the accident. Bob provided the details. The more he told her, the faster she drove until Bob and Jimmy pleaded with her to slow down.

Bob said that after we had picked up the sick lambs, his dad had wanted to get them out of the heat and back to the barn as fast as he could.

"That's why he was driving so fast, mom."

"Don't make any excuses for him, son," Vera replied. His hurryin' was bound to get him in trouble eventually. Now it has."

No matter the circumstances, she said Jesse shouldn't have been driving so recklessly; especially when we were sitting in the back of the truck with nothing to hold onto.

Aunt Vera had always been so calm, cool and collected around everyone. But now, her voice betrayed her emotions and she was visibly upset with Jesse for what he had done to us.

"He could have killed all of you, including himself. It just makes me furious the more I think about it," she fumed.

It was apparent that Jesse wasn't going to get off easy this time. Later that evening, behind closed doors, we could hear Aunt Vera berating him over his reckless driving around the ranch. Not a word of protest or excuse could be heard from Jesse in response.

It was a frightfully sad—and painful—way to start the first week of my so-called Summer working vacation at the Banfield ranch. I had been gone from home just four days and had two serious accidents and one near miss by a huge truck that almost ran over us outside of Elko.

My face was a mess from burns, cuts and stitches. Jimmy had suffered a broken arm and Bob was limping noticeably from the wrenched knee he had sustained when we were thrown out of Jesse's truck. I wondered what could possibly happen to us next.

Chapter 15

> "Early to bed, early to rise,
>
> get out of bed and watch the sunrise."

Jesse wasn't a poet, but for some reason he delighted in yelling out that little ditty, or something similar, when he would wake us each morning. On this day, Friday, the final work day of the week, his wakeup call to rise and shine would fall on deaf ears.

> "C'mon boys, Ol' Red's a crowin' and we gotta' get goin'…"

"Oh, dad, stop it for pete's sake," Bob protested. Jesse paid no heed.

> "No time for sleepin' in 'n foolin' around,
>
> so wake up and hit the ground."

With that, Jesse hurried out the door and headed for the barn. Bob and Jimmy just rolled their eyes and threw pillows at the door over their dad's attempt at poetic reveille as I made a sleepy-eyed exit to the bathroom.

We were not only sleepy, but stiff and sore from being thrown out of Jesse's truck the day before. We were also in no mood to listen to his catchy rhymes, but that didn't matter to him. Evidently, he was a poet and didn't know it.

When Jesse burst into our room and rousted us out of bed with his corny wakeup limericks, I wondered how anyone could be so full of pep and energy at 5:00 o'clock in the morning.

Magically, especially for him, everything seemed to come alive at that ungodly hour around the Banfield ranch. Lights flicked on in the ranch house and the barn as the dawn began to peek at us from the Eastern sky.

Ol' Red, the raucous rooster, had already broken the silence of the dawn with his lusty crowing and was again strutting around the barnyard like he was the cock of the walk. I noticed that even Nellie gave the rooster a wide berth whenever she was in the barnyard.

I had already begun to hate Ol' Red and was harboring some devilish thoughts about what I would like to do to him.

"If I could just get my hands on that wily old rooster," I told Bob and Jimmy, "I'd wring his neck for creating such a ruckus in the barnyard each morning. They both laughed; knowing I had two chances of ever catching him: slim and none!

"He's too cagey to get caught," Bob said. "Others have tried and failed so everyone just puts up with him although none of us would feel badly if he just disappeared someday."

I had also begun yearning for the good old days when I was a carpenter's helper on my dad's construction crew. At least I wouldn't have to put up with a rooster crowing in my ear each morning and hearing Jesse's lyrical wakeup calls.

Jesse had already issued his first orders of the day to his ranch foreman, Hank Johnson. The new hires, Jake Dalton and Bernie McCoy, were assigned by Johnson to start bringing in the newly-mowed hay from the West pasture and stacking it in the field next to the barn. Being new workers, they kept to themselves; mostly nodding when receiving instructions.

For some reason, their presence gave me the creeps and their sullen looks and furtive glances made the other ranch hands a bit nervous. We all suspected that Johnson had even begun to have mis-givings about the hasty hiring of those two guys.

"They just don't seem to fit in with the rest of the crew," I told Bob and Jimmy. They both agreed with that assumption.

Vera and Tess had prepared a big breakfast for everyone and after helping to clean up the kitchen, I found myself peeling potatoes once again. Only this time, I had company.

With his arm in a sling, Jimmy couldn't be very helpful with the early morning chores, like milking the cows or slopping the pigs. Neither could I with my cuts, bruises and stitches, so, Vera had us doing menial tasks in the kitchen and peeling potatoes. We both wondered if we would ever see daylight again.

Friday was always payday at the Banfield ranch and Hank Johnson wanted to make sure his men put in a good days work before taking the weekend off. Pay checks were handed out promptly each Friday at 5:00 p.m. and not one minute earlier. Everyone got a full paycheck except Dalton and McCoy. Since they had only worked two days, their checks were small, but at least they were employed and the Banfield ranch provided a temporary safe haven for them.

Dalton already knew what he was going to do over the weekend: find out what really happened to his sister Cheryl. A good place to start, he told McCoy, was going to be the Diamond Bar saloon.

It was there that he hoped to unravel the mystery behind her untimely death. He felt that fishy-eyed bartender they had met the first night they were in town knew something about his sis's death and he was determined to wring it out of him one way or another.

*   *   *   *

The tinkling of a bell could be faintly heard in the distance. Two ranch hands were forcing a large herd of sheep through a counter gate and into a field about a half-mile south of the ranch house where they would be pastured for a few days.

The flock not only had to be counted, but carefully inspected for heat prostration and other ailments that may have occurred since the last count in the Spring.

During breakfast, Bob said the inspection and selection of the bell sheep would be carried out in the early afternoon after the count was finished. The fittest and strongest one in the herd, he said, would be fitted with a bell that would enable Nellie and the ranch hands to keep track of the herd. It also signified leadership qualities as only the strongest and most dominant sheep would be fitted with the bell.

"We arrived just in time to watch this process," Bob said. "As soon as they finish the count, we'll go watch Nellie do her thing. Dean'll drive us out there if we want to go." Me and Jimmy couldn't get out of the kitchen fast enough.

The work of selecting the bell sheep, Bob pointed out, would be done not by the ranch hands, but by Nellie, their aging sheep dog. I was instantly curious; not only to escape the ranch house, but to actually view the selection process that Bob spoke about.

The procedure of counting sheep on the Banfield ranch took place three times a year he said; in the Spring, Summer and Fall and at each counting a new Bell Sheep was selected.

"This little ritual needs to be seen to be believed," Jimmy told me as we finished peeling a large batch of potatoes.

"Dad's taught Nellie everything about herding sheep—all the commands and stuff—but how she's learned to pick out that Bell Sheep has been a mystery to all of us for years.

"I'll tell you one thing—if she isn't the smartest dog in the world," I'd like to find the one who is."

One of the ranch hands came in from the field to announce that the counting process was about to be finished, so we all hopped into Dean's car and sped out to the south pasture where the sheep were gathered.

This was grand theater for Nellie and she instinctively knew she was going to be the star of the show. Her stage was the entire south pasture and even though her flock was scattered about she knew what had to be done.

The show was about to begin and she was nervously flitting about as best she could on hobbled legs. Arthritis had afflicted her in recent years, a condition that had slowed her down considerably; but she was still up to the task.

The wagging of her tail revealed that much. Charley Hartwell, the sheepherder who had responsibility for the entire herd, handed Jesse a wrinkled piece of paper with a breakdown of the sheep count.

"We counted 327 this time around, Jesse. That includes 79 lambs and 248 ewes. Those little sweethearts will fetch a good price this Fall."

Charley used that affectionate term to describe the young ewes in his charge. A lifelong bachelor, he was always being kidded about his nomadic lifestyle and abstinence from a social life.

His home was actually a covered wagon; only it had rubber tires so it could be moved quickly by horse or truck. Inside, it had a bed, a small kerosene stove for heating and cooking and a fold out bench on the side of the wagon where he could make minor repairs.

A tell-tale stove pipe atop the wagon always revealed Charley's whereabouts on the ranch. If there was smoke coming out of the pipe, Charley was "in." If there was no smoke, he was "out" with the herd or doing other chores around the ranch.

Charley had been Jesse's sheepherder for years and even though he was 63 years old, he was as spry as a spring chicken. He also had a mischievous sense of humor. His constant reference to the young ewes being his sweethearts always brought a few smiles to the faces of the ranch hands. He never learned to drive a car, but he liked to tell the story about how he once tried to obtain a driver's license.

When taking the road test, he was told by the lady official to perform the usual maneuvers, like parallel parking and turning left and right while making the appropriate hand signals for each maneuver.

Finally, when they were ready to return to the station, she asked Charley: "Can you make a U-turn?"

"No," Charley quickly replied, "but I can sure make her eyes wobble!"

The startled young lady flunked him on the spot and Charley never again applied for a driver's license. No one ever believed Charley's story, but the flash of merriment in his eyes when he told it countless times revealed a keen sense of humor for a person who had spent many lonely years herding sheep in virtual solitude.

"Shoot," he would say, "I was just kiddin' that young lady. She shouldn't have been so riled up—Anybody should know the difference between a Ewe and a U-Turn!"

Chapter 16

By now, the Banfield's and most of their ranch hands had gathered to witness Nellie do her thing. Jesse gave a shrill whistle and the show was on.

"Let's go, Nellie," he shouted…round 'em up."

With that command, Nellie took off running as best she could. Everyone there knew that Nellie's days of herding sheep were numbered. Still, she darted here and there and raced excitedly about as she began circling the herd.

Some strays bleated in defiance and scampered off; only to be sharply nipped in the butt or legs and forced to turn back toward the herd. Nellie could still make some fast moves when she had too. Within a few minutes, she had the entire herd rounded up and tightly bunched together like a cluster of grapes hanging on a vine.

That chore done, and with her tongue hanging out and tail wagging wildly, she returned to Jesse for further orders. But first, she fully expected to receive a few words of praise and a curtain call. It was important to her that this praise be done before she performed further work.

"Good girl, Nellie," Jesse said as he gently patted her on the head.

"Now, find me the best ones," he commanded.

She again fully understood her mission. Racing back into the herd, you could hear her sharp bark as she nudged and nipped while separating several sheep from the herd. Her selection process was a mystery to everyone but herself. In milling about the herd, Nellie managed to select six sheep she felt would be the best candidates to carry the bell.

She then herded the selected sheep toward us. That done, and with one of the ranch hands clanging the bell, she was asked:

"Who's this belong to?"

With that command, she began circling the small group of sheep; silently smelling and sniffing about. Suddenly, she nudged herself into that tightly bunched group, and with a sharp bark, apparently only understood by herself and the sheep, she sent them bleating and fleeing back to the main herd—all except one. Nellie kept that one from running away by circling around it and barking in a frenzy as if to say:

"Here's the one; here's the one!"

It was uncanny how Nellie could cull the strongest and fittest sheep from the herd and then present her lone choice for the Bell Sheep to Jesse.

It was also a special Rite of Passage for Nellie, a ritual she performed around the Banfield ranch each spring, summer and fall. Sometimes the entire crew would gather just to witness Nellie select the Bell Sheep.

Nellie also felt it was her duty to choose the person who would fit the bell on the sheep. She would dutifully retrieve the bell from whomever had it at the time and with the leather collar clenched between her jaws she would run about for a few seconds; shaking the bell vigorously so it would tingle loudly. She would then present it to a selected member of the Banfield family or one of the ranch hands.

According to Bob, it would usually be Jesse, who had raised her from a pup and had taught her all of the commands for herding sheep. But, not so surprisingly on this occasion she limped over to Bob and nudged the metal bell and leather collar into his hands.

"She wants you to put it on the one she's just selected," said Jimmy.

Bob tenderly fastened the collar around the newly selected Bell Sheep; then Jimmy whacked it on the butt. With a startled bleat and the bell tingling, the sheep trotted off toward her minions she would be leading for the next several weeks.

*   *   *   *

None of us realized then that this would be the last time Nellie would ever select the Bell Sheep on the Banfield ranch. Jesse revered Nellie and she could often be seen sitting beside him with her head stuck out of the window, sniffing the air, as he sped around the ranch in his pickup truck. There was no doubt she knew that she was something special.

She also had good genes and Jesse knew dog genes. I came to know that first hand. When I first noticed Nellie limping around the ranch after our arrival, I remembered a time when Jesse talked about dog species during a family get together at our little farm on State street in Midvale.

I was nine years old at the time. Bob, Jimmy and myself, as well as a couple of other cousins, were romping with our dogs, Pal and Nellie, when Jesse began comparing the two species. We learned that day Jesse was as knowledgeable about dog breeds as he was about sheep and cattle.

A sharp, short whistle and a verbal command had brought Nellie to her master's side. My dog, Pal, had followed and was licking Jesse's outstretched hand when he simply said: "stay." Nellie responded instantly; settling back on her haunches waiting for a further command. Pal paid no heed. I'd never trained Pal to do anything since he was a mature dog when I found him.

"Look-a-here," Uncle Jesse said as he held my dog's head in his hands. "He's a back alley street dog—a mixed breed. Gotta a lot of mongrel in 'im. I can tell by the shape of his head and the size of his paws that he's not a purebred—no way, shape or form." I was disheartened at my Uncle Jesse's remarks.

I didn't know Pal's pedigree or where he came from. He just showed up on our doorstep one day and I immediately claimed him as my own. He was solid black in color except for white paws and a tipped white tail. Another distinguishing white mark ran between his eyes and encircled his neck. As far as I was concerned, he was an All-American Dog; not a back alley mongrel that Jesse had labeled him.

While Jesse was explaining my dog's genes to everybody, Nellie had been waiting patiently. She kept nudging, then nipping his hand; waiting for another command. He ignored her for a moment and then dismissed her as he continued his discussion of explaining Nellie's heritage.

Nellie, he said, was a "Sheltie," a Shetland Sheepdog whose species had originated in the Scottish Highlands. As far as he knew, Uncle Jesse said, Shelties and Collies came from the same ancestral species. One species evolved into a larger breed, the Collies, another one into a smaller species, the Shelties. The common ancestor, he said, was the Border Collie which came from Scotland and was specially bred to herd sheep in the Shetlands, a chain of islands off the Northern coast of Scotland. The harsh weather conditions there, along with the rocky terrain and scarcity of food, created small, but sturdy animals over time, Jesse explained.

He pointed out that other animal species, like the Shetland pony and Shetland sheep and cattle, also came off the Scottish Highlands, but the Shelties became the best known because of a selective breeding program that produced a fiercely loyal, courageous and obedient animal.

We were all amazed at Jesse's knowledge of such things. I couldn't resist asking him a question:

"How'd you come to know so much about dogs?" I asked inquisitively.

"Talkin' to old sheep herders and reading books," Uncle Jesse responded.

"I'll tell you something else about Shelties," he offered. "They're the most loyal and obedient dogs you'll ever come across. Good breeding's done that and over time they became known for their herding ability."

When and how that canine species came to the United States is unknown, but Jesse liked to recall the first time he ever saw "lil' Nel," as he affectionately called her. He had carried her off a sheep ranch in Eastern Utah in his battered, old cowboy hat some 14 years ago. She was only six weeks old at the time and had come from a litter of six puppies. Jesse liked to brag that he had the "pick of the litter" because an old sheepherder friend, Mac McGrady, owed him a favor.

"As soon as I saw that little critter, I knew she was the one I wanted," he reminisced. "She was the liveliest one of the bunch; crawling all over her mother and nudging the other puppies out of the way all the time. "Even then," he laughed, "she was bossing everyone around."

Through the years, Nellie dutifully accompanied Jesse in his itinerant wanderings throughout the West while always remembering the commands she had been taught and always quite willing to display her uncanny skills in tending sheep.

This Summer, though, Nellie was having trouble moving as sprightly as she used to in the past; especially rounding up stray sheep. That required a lot of energy and relentless running and Nellie simply couldn't do it as efficiently as she used to.

The Banfields had taken good care of her, but she had been slowed by ever-progressive arthritis in recent years. Now, she could barely get around just when the most was expected of her abilities. Her days of herding sheep, culling the ailing ones from the rest of the herd and selecting the Bell Sheep were finally nearing the end.

Now, in addition to worrying about their ranching operations, Jesse and Hank had to wonder about how they would be able to move the herd to the North ranch if Nellie couldn't make the trip. Resting her weary legs would help, he thought.

Five sheep and two young lambs were separated from the main herd right after the Bell Sheep had been selected. Four of them, including the lambs, would become our bill o' fare at the dinner table in the days ahead. The remaining three, the weak and the ill ones, were put out of their misery and buried in the outer pasture by the ranch hands so the coyotes couldn't get them.

The culling process was important this time of the year. The herd had to be fit and ready to be moved to the North ranch in a few weeks where they would remain until the Fall selloff; so only the healthiest sheep would be permitted to make that grueling trip. The move would require a full day's march and several ranch workers. Despite Aunt Vera's mis-givings, Bob, Jimmy and I were still hoping that we would be the shepherds on the drive to the North ranch.

We never lacked for daily servings of lamb chops or beef. Vera amazed us all by her dextrous culinary skills and her recipes and servings she used in the preparation of her daily meals, including soups, salads and vegetables, was remarkable in content and variety.

Still, it had been less than a week since I my arrival at the ranch and I had already begun to feel like I would throw up if I had to see one more lamb chop on my plate.

Sadly, Nellie's hard work of selecting the bell sheep was all for naught. That same night, Charley Hartwell was awakened by a commotion in the south pasture. Taking his ever-present shotgun in hand, he discovered the bell sheep and three young lambs lying amongst the rest of the herd. They been virtually torn apart by a roving band of coyotes who, apparently sensing Nellie's absence and vulnerability, attacked the herd in the dead of night.

Jesse had relieved Nellie of most of her sheep-tending duties a couple of months ago, opting to keep her in the ranch house at night; otherwise, she, too, would have been killed by the coyotes.

When he learned of the attack, it was a near-breaking point for Jesse. I had never heard him swear or raise his voice even though adversity seemed to follow him like a dark cloud, but he was clearly upset now.

"Damn it to hell! Why is everything happening all at once?" he asked no one in particular.

Based on what had happened to me since leaving home five days ago, I wondered the same thing and hoped the weekend would give all of us a welcome respite from the rigors of ranch life.

Chapter 17

Friday evenings in Fallon were always loud and raucous. It was no place for the faint hearted. By early evening, it would turn into a rip-roaring Western town. The rowdies, cowboys and plain working stiffs who drifted in from surrounding farms, ranches and nearby homes were ready for a good time after long hours under the Sun. They were going to celebrate and woe be unto those who tried to stop them.

Jake Dalton and Bernie McCoy fit right in with that crowd.

There was something for everyone; especially if you drank, caroused around or sought women of the night. The fortunes of the town rose and fell sharply based on the pay periods.

Depending on who you worked for around the valley, payday was either monthly, semi-monthly or on the Friday of each week. Uncle Jesse preferred to pay his workers weekly and he promptly did so at 5.00 p.m. each Friday.

That's when the Eagle screamed, as payday came to be known around the ranch.

He used to pay his workers at 3:00 p.m. as a lot of other ranchers did, but according to Dean, he had found out a long time ago that if he paid them in mid-afternoon, little work was accomplished after the noon meal. His ranch hands used to go through the motions of working on Friday afternoons while watching the clock.

They would loiter about the barn or in the fields right after lunch as they knew payday was only a couple of hours away. That didn't set too well with Jesse. He expected a full day's work for a full day's pay from his ranch hands, so he started paying everyone at the end of the day.

Most of them lived from pay check to pay check anyway and he knew they would blow most of it; either on booze or women who frequented the area bars and saloons. He merely delayed the inevitable by paying later in the day.

While there were several watering holes in Fallon where everyone could quench their thirst, the most popular place being the Diamond Bar, which was located on South Main street.

Dalton and McCoy headed there after picking up their meager first week's pay check from Hank. They were on a mission to find out what happened to Jake's sister, Cheyrl, and they expected to find some answers at the Diamond Bar; either amongst the regular patrons or from the bartender that had given them some evasive answers earlier in the week about his sister's death.

They first wanted to talk to Rusty Trudeau, Johnny Hayden's head bartender. Trudeau was plying his trade behind the magnificent bar that had always been the center piece of discussion among the patrons who frequented that notorious place.

Visitors went out of their way just to see if the rumors and stories about the saloon's infamous bar were true. They never left disappointed; especially if they talked to Trudeau.

Born "somewhere in the deep South," Trudeau fancied himself as a True Southern Gentleman. His mother was of French Creole descent from the bayou country near New Orleans and his father was a pure Irishman.

Rusty liked to brag that he had a "little bit of Irish, a little bit of color and a whole lot of French blood" coursing through his veins.

At 6' 3" tall, he cut an imposing figure and he was as much a conversation piece as the bar itself. His flowing, curled-at-the-end mustache and silvery grey hair presented a stark contrast to his white shirt, bow tie, red vest and black trousers. Trudeau was a combination bartender and bouncer and when Johnny Hayden wasn't around, the manager of the Diamond Bar.

No one was foolish enough to mess with him except an occasional drunk who didn't know any better or who would chide him too much about his flowing mustache.

If it got too personal, Trudeau would come around the end of the bar, pick the rowdy up by the seat of his pants and scruff of the neck and deposit him on the boardwalk outside the saloon.

"If you can't say any kind words or conduct yourself properly around here," he would tell the drunk, "don't come back to the Diamond Bar" which was littered with actual diamonds that were embedded in the bar top and coated with a clear shellac so bar patrons could gaze at the sparklers while drinking.

According to workers at the Banfield ranch, Trudeau liked to recount stories of drunken cowboys trying to dig out the diamonds only to have their hands impaled on a knife that suddenly appeared in Rusty's hand.

To protect himself, he also carried a small single shot derringer in the pocket of his vest. Another one was strapped to the inside of his left leg just above the ankle.

He never had to use them, but he would regale his patrons with tales of shootings and fights of yesteryears that had been passed down, and surely embellished upon, when the bar was located in Virginia City, a once-notorious mining town 65 miles Southwest of Fallon.

"When you belly up to this bar," Trudeau would tell his patrons, "you're touching a bit of history."

* * * *

On this night, Dalton asked Trudeau the name of the fellow who, at the moment, was serving customers at the far end of the bar.

"That's Marco Forlani. Johnny brought him up from 'Vegas when he bought this place five years ago. You wanna' talk to him?"

"Yeah. I think he might know something about how my sister died. Just wanna ask him a few questions."

"You'd better talk to him soon—his shift is about to end. I'll send him over."

Several minutes later, Forlani came over to Hank and Bernie's table with two beers; compliments of Trudeau. He appeared a bit nervous and was sweating profusely. Trudeau had apparently told him that two friends of Johnny Hayden wanted to talk to him. Forlani offered a timid greeting:

"Hi fellas..Rusty said you wanted to see me?"

"Yeah," Dalton answered. "We inquired the other evening when we were in here if you knew my sister, Cheryl, before she died. You seemed reluctant to say anything then. D'ya wanna' tell us anymore now—like how, when or where she died?"

"I don't know anything about her," stammered Forlani as he fidgeted nervously with the drink tray in his hands. "I never knew her. I'm not from around here 'ya know—came up from 'Vegas with Johnny Hayden when he bought this place a few years ago."

For some reason, Dalton felt Forlani wasn't telling all that he knew about his sister's death. Maybe it was the bartender's body language, his nervous glances, or his fishy eyes. Whatever it was, Dalton wasn't totally satisfied with the answers he got from the little Italian bartender.

"Okay, Marco, we'll talk to you later." With that, Jake dismissed him with a wave of his hand. Then he told Bernie:

"That little bastard is lyin' through his teeth. He knows something about Cheryl that he's not tellin' us. I'm gonna wait outside for him when he finishes workin' tonight."

Bernie issued a word of caution:

"Hold on, Jake, don't do something stupid right now. Let's due a little more sleuthin' before we take matters into our own hands. Marco isn't going' anywhere soon and if we have too, we'll beat the truth out of him later on."

Sensing trouble, Forlani finished his shift and departed out the back door and disappeared into the night as Jake and Bernie drank themselves into another stupor.

★   ★   ★   ★

Saturdays were half-work days for Jesse and the few unmarried workers who chose to remain at the ranch rather than to spend the weekend in Fallon, Carson City or Reno. They could catch up on a few things around the ranch and assess what had to be done in the coming week.

Jesse also wanted to start sprucing up the area around the ranch house as he and Aunt Vera were going to host the monthly gathering of area ranchers and their kinfolk the first Saturday in August.

This highly popular social event was only held during the summer months, and Jesse wanted to make sure that everything would be "lookin' good" when it came time to host the social get together.

It was like a family reunion. Ranch owners, their wives and workers would gather for a huge early-afternoon barbecue followed by foot-stompin' music featuring guitars, banjos, harmonicas and violins. A real hoe-down! The kids would play games, the men would play horseshoes and the women would gather in groups to chat about ranch life and what their kids were doing.

When it cooled down in the late afternoon, some of the younger ranch hands liked to display their prowess with boxing gloves. Nothing serious and side bets were common; just one ranch hand against a neighbor. All in good fun. The 13-ounce gloves were like powder puffs and no one could get seriously hurt, but the sting was there nonetheless; especially if you caught a blow squarely on the chin.

Hoot Gibson, who owned a large spread several miles up the road from the Banfield ranch, was going to host the July event this coming Saturday. Jesse and Vera were planning to attend so they could get some ideas on how to plan their summer get-together in early August. It was something they were looking forward to according to Vera.

"We want to be good hosts and have a good time," she told everyone at breakfast.

"That means everyone has to pitch in and do their part in making our social really special."

As the morning wore on, Jesse was surprised to see a car coming down the road toward the ranch house. A few moments later Jeb Harrington, the Washoe county deputy sheriff, stepped out of his car and extended a hand of greeting.

"Hi, Jesse, how's things goin'?"

"Been pretty hectic the past few days," Jesse replied.

"I understand you and the boys had an accident a couple of days ago. Hope no one got hurt."

The sheriff was probing for something, but Jesse wasn't anxious to tell him anything about the accident—or anything else for that matter. He knew the sheriff was the nosy type and wondered silently what had really brought him out to the ranch. Surely not the news about the accident, he thought.

"What brings you out to these parts, Jeb?"

The sheriff didn't waste any time in getting right to the point.

"Jesse, there's something you need to know about the fellas you hired a few days ago. I don't know if Hank Johnson's told you much about 'em, but that Jake Dalton and Bernie McCoy are ex-cons with records a mile long."

Jesse was stunned to hear that news; then he became furious that his reliable foreman had not told him about hiring two convicted felons. Still, he didn't let his anger show.

"We've been goin' fast and furious this week, Jeb, and I haven't had much time to talk to Hank about anything, but I'm going too now that you've told me about 'em. What'd they go to prison for?"

"Bank robbery, attempted murder, among other things. They're career criminals, Jesse, and you and Hank need to keep an eye on them. You're still fairly new here, so you wouldn't be familiar with their past, but before they went to prison, they had been stealin' and thievin' for years around here.

"They're still suspects in the disappearance of two fellers from Sparks who came into town lookin' for work a few years ago. Those fellers got lucky one night and hit a thousand dollar jackpot at the Silver Dollar saloon.

"Later in the evening, they were seen with Dalton and McCoy at the Diamond Bar and that's the last anyone ever seen or heard of 'em. Dalton and McCoy always claimed they left the two fellers at the Diamond Bar to do some bar-hoppin' around town, but regular patrons at those bars couldn't verify their alibi.

"Since no bodies were ever found we couldn't formally charge 'em. It's been an open case in our files for over 10 years. We've long suspected those two ex-cons were somehow involved but the evidence we had was hearsay and we knew it wouldn't holdup in court so we didn't prosecute them.

"I know you're surprised about all this, Jesse, but I thought you should know. Ol' timers in town are talkin' about your new hires; so just be careful. They're still on probation; so if they give you any grief or trouble, let me know right away. I won't hesitate to lock 'em up again."

Jesse's temper was at a boiling point now, but he managed cordial response.

"Thanks, Jeb, I appreciate your lettin' me know. We'll be watchful and I'll be sure to talk to Hank about our conversation. They shook hands and the sheriff departed.

*   *   *   *

For a long moment, Jesse thought about what he had just heard. Desperate as they were for help, he couldn't believe his trusted foreman, Hank Johnson, would hire two ex-cons without talking to him. He wanted some answers and he sought out Hank who was in the barn and didn't see or hear the exchange between his boss and the county sheriff.

"For hell's sake, Hank, why didn't you tell me more about those fellas you hired a couple of days ago? It really upsets me that you'd put somebody on without checkin' on them, or delvin' a little into their backgrounds. "Shoot, we have enough troubles around here without putting up with the likes of those two jailbirds."

Hank winced at Jesse's biting comments. In his desperate search for help, he knew he'd used poor judgement and he had sensed it from the start.

"I'm sorry, boss, I should've told you. I guess I was so desperate to hire some hands my good judgement failed me. I can either let 'em go now or keep 'em on for awhile. If we keep 'em, I'll make sure 'n keep an eye on 'em."

Jesse still had deep misgivings about having two bad guys on the payroll even though they had paid their debt to society.

"I dunno, Hank, you made the hire; so I guess you're gonna' have to make the best of a bad situation. Desperate as we are for help, it worries me, I can tell you for sure; especially since they'll be working' around the boys."

With that said, Jesse stomped out of the barn leaving his troubled foreman shaking his head and fervently wishing he'd never made that hire; then not telling his boss about it.

At the dinner table that evening, Dalton and McCoy were noticeably absent having left early for Fallon where they had gone to make further inquiries about Cheryl Dalton's death. Jesse informed the few workers who had stayed over for weekend duties that a couple of ex-cons were in their midst and that they had better be cautious in their dealings with them.

"Hank hired 'em and I'm holdin' him responsible for keepin' 'em in tow. If they start causin' trouble, they're outta' here as far as I'm concerned!"

Jesse and Vera looked genuinely worried. Their anxious glances around the table revealed their true concern for their sons, Bob and Jimmy, as well as myself.

Chapter 18

For a farm boy, nothing invigorates the soul more than the smell of newly mowed alfalfa. A slight Westerly breeze was pushing the scent toward us as we prepared to go into the field after a hectic first week on the Banfield ranch.

It was early Monday morning. During breakfast Uncle Jesse informed Bob, Jimmy and myself that gathering and stacking hay would occupy our time for the next two days. We were even going to be allowed to drive the hay wagons while we were out in the field.

Hank Johnson told us we would be the wagon-masters, a glorified term he made up to make us feel important. Actually, we were mere peons performing menial labor that no one else really wanted to do.

Our assigned task was to ride atop the flat top wagons and guide them alongside the rows of hay while workers, using longpronged pitch forks, tossed the hay onto the wagons. We were to then stomp it into a compact pile before driving the wagons from about a half mile West of the ranch house to two large haystacks near the barn where the hay would be off-loaded by a couple of ranch hands and used as fodder for the farm animals.

"This is going to be better than peeling potatoes and washing dishes—at least I'm outside now," I told Bob and Jimmy.

Since arriving a week ago, I had wished more than once that I was back home working for my dad. I had finally gotten out of the house after a week of confinement that allowed my face and bumps and bruises to heal following two harrowing accidents. The steaming radiator that had exploded in my face on the way over from Utah and the frightful rollover when Uncle Jesse's pickup truck went spinning out of control were now just lingering memories.

For some reason, Uncle Jesse's foreman, Hank Johnson, assigned me to work with the new hires, Jake Dalton and Bernie McCoy. I had seen little of them since they had come to work several days ago. Just being around them made me nervous.

They were a sinister, unfriendly pair and they just didn't fit in with the rest of the crew at the Banfield ranch. Even the horses were extremely fidgety around them, but as they hitched up the team to my wagon, I noticed how they kept their cool when the horses initially rejected the bits that were inserted into their mouths. Instead of immediately forcing the bits back in, Dalton and McCoy gentled the horses; holding the bridles in one hand while patting them with their other free hand.

Horses normally reject the bit that is being slipped into their mouths the first time it is attempted, but will reluctantly accept it the second or third time if it is done in a gentle way.

"These guys have been around horses," I thought. I knew from experience that horses won't allow bridles to be slipped over their heads and bits into their mouths if they don't instinctively trust the person who is trying to bridle them.

As Dalton and McCoy hitched the team to our wagon and slung the long reins from the bridles up and onto a tall, ladder-type structure at the front of the wagon, they engaged themselves in horse talk. Even though they hadn't worked with animals for a long time, it was apparent they knew what they were doing.

"Calm down, now," Dalton kept repeating while holding onto the bridle and re-assuring our nervous team that everything was going to be okay.

Then spotting me, he said: "C'mon, kid, get on the wagon 'n grab those reins; we're ready to go." With that order, I hopped up on the wagon and unfurled the reins from the ladder as Hank Johnson gave us a word of advice.

"You fellas have the most sensitive team in the stable; so be careful how you handle 'em," he pointed out. "Don't make any sudden moves or loud noises around 'em or they'll bolt on you."

That was a discomforting thing to hear since I was going to be the wagon master and the one that would be driving the team out in the field. Dalton and McCoy acknowledged Hank's advice by merely nodding their heads.

As we moved through the field, the horses seemed agitated by my constant "giddup and ho" commands. They always wanted to keep going even though I kept reining them to a temporary halt so that Dalton and McCoy could pitch the freshly mown hay onto the wagon.

*   *   *   *

We were well into our second day of hauling and stacking hay. While they kept grumbling about the hot weather, the two ex-cons were actually behaving like model ranch hands. This surprised me given what we were learning about their sordid pasts. They had been treating me pretty well, too, and I began to think they weren't such bad guys afterall. My thinking was short-lived.

As they pitched the last few piles of hay onto the wagon shortly before quitting time, I noticed them whispering in front of the horses; then laughing to themselves as they separated.

They had just hatched something that I hadn't expected; even from those two hardened characters. The warning from Hank Johnson to avoid startling the horses was about to be ignored.

A sharp whistle suddenly split the air and my already-nervous team bolted and began galloping at full speed across the field; over ruts and bumps and across a ditch, which threw off most of the hay as the wagon dipped into it. Then, they found a dirt road and took off in a frantic gallop back to the barn.

I tried to rein them in while bouncing about on the wagon bed, only to be tossed out on my rear end a short distance from the barn. The stampeding horses went right through the gate in the barnyard and hit the open barn door in full stride; wedging themselves in the door so tightly that it took about half an hour for Uncle Jesse and a couple of other workers to free them.

In the meantime, I had gotten up and staggered into the barnyard unhurt but a bit shaken and bruised from the experience, only to receive a good tongue-lashing from Uncle Jesse.

"You tryin' to get yourself killed, Danny? That's a good team you let get away from you. What caused them to stampede anyway?

No amount of explaining on my part would he let me put the blame where it really belonged—on the shoulders of the two renegade ex-cons who seemed bemused by their antics. Dalton seemed to be the real culprit of the two. He was also the meanest as far as I was concerned.

McCoy just seemed to tag along and do whatever Jake commanded him to do. I told Bob and Jimmy my side of the story and predicted that the two ex-cons would likely pull off other pranks in the future.

"You just watch, they'll try something else before long. I don't think they like us; especially me, for some reason or another."

I silently vowed to get even with them for the embarrassment they had caused me. Even though Jesse blamed me for letting my team of horses get spooked, Bob and Jimmy, as well as some of the ranch hands, supported my contention that it wasn't my fault. They knew Dalton and McCoy were the real culprits.

Two nights later, after the work day had been completed and everyone had gone to bed, I happened to look out across the barnyard and saw a light coming from a corner room of the bunk house. Until then, I hadn't paid much attention to where the ranch hands slept, but on this dark, moonless night I was curious to see why that light was on. There wasn't a soul stirring in the house. Bob and Jimmy were sound asleep, so I slipped out the back door and crept across the yard.

As I drew near the bunk house, I could see Dalton's silhouette framed in the dimly lit room. He was sitting on a chair with his arm dangling outside the window and talking to his sidekick, McCoy, who was lounging across the room on his bed. The window was open all the way and was propped up by a wooden stick.

As I looked at the open window, a tantalizing thought came into my mind: If I could somehow manage to tie a piece of string around the bottom of that stick, a gentle little tug could send that window crashing down on Dalton's arm. Maybe, it would even break it.

I told myself I'd save that bit of pay back for another time. For now, I just wanted to overhear what they were saying.

As Dalton puffed away on a cigarette, he kept flicking the ashes down to the ground while talking to McCoy in a low voice. I stayed in the shadows so they couldn't see me.

When I reached the bunk house and peered around the corner of the building, I discovered I was so close to the open window Dalton was sitting by that I could almost reach out and touch his arm. After drawing back momentarily, I slowly poked my head around the corner again so I could hear what they were discussing.

"Maybe," I thought, "I could find out who these sinister characters really are who had come into our lives so unexpectedly."

Dalton was talking about a bartender named Marco Forlani; a saloon called the Diamond Bar and a fellow named Johnny Hayden who was apparently the owner of that glitzy gathering place in downtown Fallon.

I couldn't make much sense out of what I was hearing at first; then I was startled to hear Dalton make a reference about a sister named Cheryl who had died a few years before. Based on the conversation, she apparently was a victim of foul play. Both Dalton and McCoy seemed positive about that.

…"Ya, know, Bernie, I've been tryin' to put two and two together the past few days—kind of been sortin' through the bits and pieces we've been able to find out about my sis's death.

"I can't put my finger on it right now, but I have a feelin' someone must have did her in while she was doin' her thing on the street."

"It sure as hell wasn't from natural causes, I can tell you that." McCoy retorted.

"D'ya think it was one of her customers that took her down, or was it someone she had known for awhile?" he inquired. Dalton was puzzled, too, and he kept vowing revenge.

"I don't know the answers to those questions yet, but if I find out that somebody killed her on purpose, the bastard's gonna' do some sufferin' before he dies, believe me."

McCoy knew exactly what Dalton had in mind if they found out that Jake's sister had, indeed, died at the hands of some killer.

"Ya' gonna stick him in the well—like we did the others?" Jake pondered Bernie's question for a few moments; inhaling deeply and blowing the smoke from the corner of his mouth and out through the window into the darkness.

"That's not a bad idea, pal. If we did, it'd be hard to pin the crime on us 'cause they couldn't find the body if we dropped the guy down there.

I couldn't believe what I was hearing from those two ex-cons; especially about Dalton's intent to kill the person who may have murdered his sister. And the well? Where was it and what did they mean about putting someone in it?

I watched McCoy stand up and walk over to the window. For a moment I thought he had heard something in the darkness so I pulled my head back around the corner of the building; fearful that I'd be caught spying on them. Surely, I thought, he couldn't have seen or heard me.

It was too dark outside to be discovered. Besides, I was barely breathing; even shaking from what I was hearing from those two bad guys. I peeked around the corner again just in time to see McCoy toss his cigarette out the window; virtually at my feet.

After peering into the darkness for a moment he went back and sat down on his bed. In hushed tones, he offered a thoughtful theory on what might have happened to Cheryl.

"Here's my take on Cheryl's death if you're interested, Jake."

"Yeah, what is it?"

"We've been nosin' around town the past few nights talking to a few people who knew her when she was on the street. Nobody's been too anxious to tell us anything, have they? Without giving Dalton an opportunity to reply, McCoy continued:

"My gut feeling is that manager at the Diamond Bar, Rusty Trudeau, knows a helluva lot more than he's tellin' us. Secondly, he isn't being really forthcoming about anything except to brag on himself and the saloon he's managing for Hayden.

"You saw for yourself that Rusty controls all the gals in his saloon, so we need to find out if Cheryl was hangin' out there at the time she disappeared. Rusty can tell us that." Dalton agreed with that assessment.

"Let's sleep on it for a day or two and see what we can find out," he said.

When the light went out a few minutes later, I snuck back to the house and climbed into bed. I couldn't wait to tell Bob and Jimmy what I had just overheard in the bunk house.

Chapter 19

Jake Dalton and Bernie McCoy seemed to disappear nearly every night after work. They didn't mingle with the other ranch hands and no one knew where they went, except me, and I had only found that out the night before.

Bob and Jimmy were shocked when I told them that after they had gone to sleep I had crept over to the bunk house and listened in on the ex-cons' conversation.

"You can't believe what I found out about those guys last night," I told my cousins. "They talked about a fancy saloon in Fallon called the Diamond Bar and the fellows who run it are kind of strange characters themselves. A lot of hanky panky goes on in that place, I guess."

I had overheard Dalton saying that his younger sister; a girl named Cheryl, once hung out there and he thinks she was killed for some reason.

"That's why he and McCoy keep going into town," I told Bob and Jimmy. "They're trying to find out if she was murdered and who the culprit was that did it."

"We gotta go see that place if we can ever go into town," Jimmy said excitedly.

"Fat chance of that happening," Bob offered. "They don't let boys in places like that."

I hadn't finished telling them what Dalton and McCoy did to some of their robbery victims so I revealed a real grisly tale to them.

"They kept referring to a well and how they put guys in there after they took their money."

"You mean they drowned them?" Bob asked incredulously. "Yeah—robbed them first and then threw them in the well," I replied. Bob could hardly believe what I was telling him.

"Wow! we knew they were bad guys. Now, we really know," he said; shaking his head in disbelief.

"Shouldn't we tell mom and dad (Aunt Vera and Uncle Jesse) what they've done?" Jimmy suggested.

"In due time little brother. Let's do a little more sleuthing and observing before we go telling everyone else.

"By the way," Bob asked me, "did they say where that well was located?"

"Don't know exactly," I replied. "I didn't find that out except to hear Jake say it was on property his mom and dad once owned. Must be on some ranch around here.

"I also heard Dalton say he'd found a secret little storage area inside the well when he was a kid and that's where he stored his cash whenever they robbed a store or held up someone."

Speculation among the ranch hands was that Dalton and McCoy were merely hangers-on and would be leaving just as soon as they could save a little money. They didn't know, as we now did, that Dalton was obsessed in his quest to find out how his sister, Cheryl, had died. They weren't going anywhere until they did.

*   *   *   *

Every night after work, Dalton and McCoy would go into Fallon and made inquires about her death and who could have possibly been involved in her untimely demise. Every time they visited the Diamond Bar saloon, they queried Rusty Trudeau about her activities while she worked there, but he could shed no light on when she was killed or who did her in. They also kept a wary eye on Marco Forlani; the shifty-eyed Italian bartender.

While they were still celebrating Jake's release from prison, their drinking and carousing around town merely disguised their real intent and purpose.

They were determined to find out how his sister, Cheryl, had died and woe to the perpetrator if they found him.

"Surely," Dalton kept thinking to himself, "someone around Fallon knows what had happened to her," but apparently all he ever got from the people he and McCoy questioned were shrugs and vacant stares.

The more Dalton thought about it, the more convinced he became that Forlani, whom he and Bernie had questioned several nights earlier, knew more about Cheryl's disappearance than he was revealing. When Forlani's swing shift had ended on Friday, payday night, he had departed out the back door; fearing that Dalton and McCoy would confront him if he walked out the front entrance.

Now familiar with Forlani's working hours, and anticipating his departure through the rear entrance, Dalton and McCoy lay in wait behind the saloon.

The darkness hid their shadowy figures. When Forlani came out the door and was preparing to get into his car, Dalton rushed up and caught him by the shoulders; pinning him face down against the hood of his car. Forlani knew in an instant who his assailants were.

He winced as they twisted his arms up behind his back; sending sharp pains shooting into his shoulder blades. Dalton snarled a greeting as McCoy delivered a paralyzing blow to his kidneys.

"Listen, you little bastard, you've been lying to us all along about my sis's death. "You know more than you've been tellin' us; so you'd better come clean or we're gonna put some big time hurt on you."

With that he flicked open his Bowie knife and pressed it against the back of Forlani's neck; pricking his skin just enough to draw blood and causing more pain as he and McCoy kept him pinned against the car.

"Now," Dalton threatened, pressing the knife a little harder, "you either tell us how my sis' died or I'm gonna' slide this knife real gentle-like into your neck and you'll die a slow death.

"Your choice!"

Another little jab brought a howl of protest from Forlani's lips. Terror-stricken and in agony from being roughed up, the little Italian bartender began pleading for his life.

"Honest to God, Jake, please don't hurt me. I don't know how your sister died—if someone killed her or she just died a natural death. Now, just put that knife away; you're hurting me!" Then in a halting voice, Forlani whispered a startling clue:

"Go out to the cemetery—check with the ol' grave digger; he can tell you more than I can."

"Grave digger? You gotta be kiddin' me," Dalton hissed through clinched teeth. "What does he know that you don't?"

"He buried her—and he knows who brought her there. That's all I know."

Dalton pulled the knife away and spun Forlani around so that he faced his assailants. This time, he stuck the tip of the knife at the base of the bartender's throat while threatening him with more bodily harm if that tip about Cheryl's death didn't pan out.

Then, for good measure, Dalton warned Forlani that if he breathed a word to anyone in the Diamond Bar about what had just transpired, he would come after him again.

"The next time, pal, you won't get off so easy," Jake threatened as he waggled the point of the knife in front of Forlani's face.

"Okay, Jake, okay. Whatever you say—I'll keep quiet."

With that, the terrified bartender was released. He got into his car and sped off while Dalton and McCoy went back into the Diamond Bar by way of the front door where they ran into Johnny Hayden for the first time since Jake had gotten out of prison. Hayden had been in Reno and Carson City on business and had been told by Rusty Trudeau that a couple of his old buddies were back in town and had been inquiring about the death of Dalton's sister.

Hayden was delighted to see his old buddies and ordered up a round of drinks on the house; even offering to buy Dalton and McCoy dinner and talk over old times.

The ex-cons weren't hungry after what they had just gone through with Forlani and said they would pass on Hayden's offer for the time being.

"Been partying every night, Johnny, but we can get together a bit later when we have a little more time. Right now, we're trying to find out what happened to my sister. When I got out of the slammer last week, I went out to the cemetery to pay my respects to mom and pop and found Cheryl's headstone next to theirs. That was quite a shock! I didn't even know she'd died." Hayden's face never betrayed an inner emotion and his reply seemed sincere.

"I was sorry to learn of Cheryl's death. She was a great gal and I know it must have been a surprise for you, Jake," Hayden said calmly. Dalton just nodded his head; then he asked Hayden to substantiate his whereabouts at the time of Cheryl's death.

"I was in 'Vegas at the time and didn't hear about it myself until I came back to Fallon a couple of years ago—found out about it from one of my girls," Hayden recalled. Quickly changing the subject, he asked Dalton and McCoy if they were looking for a job or needed a place to stay.

"We got ourselves hired out at the Banfield ranch and we're stayin' there for the time being," McCoy told Hayden. As an after thought, Hayden inquired if they were going to the big ranch party out at the Gibson ranch Saturday afternoon.

"Don't know anything about it—what's it all about?" Dalton inquired.

"Oh, area ranchers get together once a month during the summer and have a big barbecue of sorts. All the ranchers bring food and drinks. They hoot and holler and play music and the women cluck about what they've been doing all month long in the kitchen.

"As far as I'm concerned, the only interesting thing about those get togethers are the boxing matches they hold in the late afternoons.

"When I came back from Vegas a couple of years ago, I wanted to make those matches really big events by bringing in some punks from around the state, but the ranchers didn't want any part of it. They wanted to keep the party small and only let their ranch hands hammer each other for a few bucks.

"I could've built up the purses to where the fighters would've made a thousand bucks or more, but the ranchers, especially their wives, wanted to keep those get togethers more on a social level rather than featuring boxing matches.

"So be it; if that's what they want, it's okay by me." Dalton's interest perked up when Hayden had mentioned boxing for dough.

"You mean they actually fight for money?" he asked Hayden.

"Yeah, but it's only for few bucks," Hayden replied. "They play 'last man standing' and I think the winner usually gets a hundred or so depending upon who is fighting and how many bets are placed on the guys.

"The Banfields have a big Irishman named Henrihan who keeps beating everybody up. I suspect he'll be there tomorrow swinging at everybody who dares challenge him." McCoy nudged Dalton while remembering his pal's prowess with his fists.

"Hey, buddy, that's right down your alley. I wonder why the guys out at the ranch didn't tell us about such goings on?"

"I guess we haven't been there long enough," Dalton replied. But we can damn sure drive out there tomorrow and see what's going on. Might pick up some easy money, eh?."

The Gibson's were relatively new land owners so the ex-cons didn't know them.

"Remember the O'Sullivan ranch?" Hayden asked Dalton and McCoy? "That's the Gibson spread now."

They both remembered the big ranch that was once owned by an immigrant family from Ireland.

"Like a lot of other folks around here," Hayden recalled, "the O'Sullivan's had to keep selling off pieces of their land during the depression to survive until all they had left was a section where the ranch house is now located. The Gibson's bought the remaining 640 acres three or four years ago—tore down the old adobe ranch house and built a new southwestern style hacienda.

"As you'll see, they've fixed the place up pretty good. From here, it's on the right hand side of the road just before you get to the Banfield ranch. Look for a big ol' row of poplars that line the entry way…that's where to turn in."

The renegades looked at each other and smiled. Dollar signs were ringing in their ears as they hoisted a beer to that piece of good news.

Chapter 20

We had heard a lot about the Summer Socials held at the ranches in the area. Now, we were in the midst of one.

It was a beautiful Saturday afternoon and Aunt Vera had gotten up early and prepared a large beef roast along with a huge pot of mashed potatoes as her contribution to the get-together at the Hoot Gibson ranch. Naturally, Jimmy and myself got the assignment the night before to peel all of those potatoes.

Gibson and his wife, Maria, had a beautiful spread and the ranch house was surrounded by towering poplar and cottonwood trees that provided lots of shade and relief from the hot Saturday afternoon sun. As gracious hosts, they welcomed us to their impressive surroundings.

As usual, it had fallen to the ranch wives to prepare all the food that was to be consumed and this giant smorgasbord had been placed on tables outside the ranch house. Everyone brought something to the party.

Jimmy called our attention to a small roasted pig that was being placed on one of the tables while others were loaded with all kinds of goodies—watermelons, cantaloupes, cookies and cakes. You could have fed an Army with all of that food.

There was merriment in the air, too, and the excitement of neighbors renewing acquaintances with their counter parts around the valley was evident at the tables that had been placed in the front yard of the low rambling ranch house. The ranchers, their wives, children and hired hands all worked hard during the days and these social get-togethers during the summer months provided a welcome, but temporary break, from the rigors of ranch life.

While the wives were preparing for the food to be served, the men had fashioned two horseshoe pits and were slinging horseshoes back and forth.

A distance away, some of the kids were engaged in a sack race and several girls were jumping the rope while the older boys were running 50-yard foot races in the field behind the barn. We participated in those races for awhile. Bob won the final race and was recognized as the "fastest kid in Fallon."

A couple of the ranch hands were strumming guitars in the shade of an old cottonwood tree; content to pick away while trying to match chords with a banjo player. Obviously, they were rehearsing for a command performance later in the afternoon.

The highlight of the day's activities, as far as the men were concerned, was the boxing matches that took place after everyone had eaten and relaxed for awhile. The boxers couldn't engage themselves until everyone had digested their food, so some lively music followed the hearty meal.

Bob, Jimmy and I were as hungry as three little bears foraging at a campsite. We kept nipping away at some of the food, and getting admonished by Aunt Vera for doing so, when I noticed a young girl suddenly stop skipping the rope and come toward us; only to be diverted to the Gibson table nearby.

I had never paid much attention to girls before, but she caught my eye simply by the way she walked and the way she was dressed. She was rather tall with a graceful saunter and her dark hair was tied smartly behind her head in a pony tail that bobbed about every time she moved her head.

She was clad in shorts and a rather tight-fitting blouse revealed curves I hadn't ever noticed on a girl before. Those curves accentuated a shapely figure and a beautiful face. As she stood at the Gibson family table, she kept glancing in our direction; mostly at Bob, who seemed more her age than mine or Jimmy's.

"Wow," I said to Bob, "who's that?"

"I dunno," Bob chuckled, but she's nice lookin' isn't she?"

A few moments later, the Gibson's came over to our table and introduced themselves and their ranch guests, Tom and Helen Gallagher from Susanville,

California. The Gibson's also introduced their two children; Shawn, a boy about my age, and Natalie, whom I judged to be in her mid-teens.

Aunt Vera and Uncle Jesse introduced Dean, Tess, Bob, Jimmy and myself to everyone. The Gibsons and Gallaghers were friendly and outgoing folks and as we all chatted away about the food that was about to be served, as well as the hot weather and the nice surroundings, I noticed how intently Natalie was eyeing us; particularly Bob who was already well-muscled even though he was only 15. I think he noticed Natalie staring at him, too, as he seemed to blush a bit when he caught her eyeing him.

When Natalie momentarily fixed her gaze on me and smiled, I just melted like butter on hot toast and a rush of excitement engulfed me. The first stirrings of manhood gave me a momentary lift and I felt exhilarated that a girl was actually looking at me since I was a pretty scrawny kid.

Without making further eye contact with Natalie, I shyly kept my head down or just looked around at other people after being introduced, but I still managed to steal a couple of glances of her as she moved about the crowd.

"Holy cow!" I thought to myself, as I watched her walk away a few moments later, "she's got to be the prettiest thing I'd ever seen."

I also wondered how old she could be. With a shape like that I guessed she was 15 or 16 years old. I asked Bob how old he thought she was and before he could answer, Aunt Vera, who happened to overhear my query, replied:

"She's 14, going on 18, so mind your P's and Q's! Her mother told me a little while ago that her daughter was growing up too fast; so you boys had better be on your best behavior and mind your manners around her."

*   *   *   *

With the introductions over and pleasantries exchanged among the visitors, everyone got down to serious eating followed by a couple of hours of wild and raucous, western-style music. Banjo pickers and guitar players strummed to their hearts content.

They were accompanied by two violinists, a harmonica player and an accomplished piano player who just happened to be Aunt Vera.

Her musical talent and repertoire of songs surprised everyone except those who were at our table. Aunt Vera would always perform at our family reunions and sing along with my mother, Luella, in beautiful harmony whenever our families got together. Vera was in fine fettle this day.

After she played several songs on the piano, she belted out a couple of tunes on her harmonica; then, playing the violin, she joined the other musicians in a foot stompin' finale that set the tone for the evening's boxing matches.

By now, and despite the musical beat of some fine, old western tunes and wonderful songs, the menfolk's attention began turning to the area beside the barn where the boxing matches were going to be held.

A late afternoon breeze and the shade from the large Poplar and Cottonwood trees around the Gibson ranch house provided a welcome relief from the sun that was slowly beginning to descend on the western horizon. Wooden chairs, as well as some metal ones, had been setup to form a square ring where the boxers would perform. The men had already begun to gather at ringside.

As the womenfolk cleaned up the remnants of the tasty afternoon meal, area ranchers and their workers began to place bets on who would be the last man standing for the month of July. According to Dean Banfield, who was itching to lace on the loves, the Summer's initial event was held the first week in June at the Clyde Kemper spread which bordered the Banfield ranch to the south.

Uncle Jesse's big Irishman, Rich Henrihan, was the last man standing at that gathering as he punched the lights out of two cowboys who had the nerve to challenge him. Henrihan was the ranch hand who had playfully squirted milk on Bob, Jimmy and myself the morning after we arrived at the Banfield ranch.

In our brief association with Henrihan we had come to admire the enthusiasm he exhibited while working—and singing—around the ranch. We also learned that he was quite handy with his dukes, and he figured he could knock anyone down, if not out, with his huge, ham-size hands. We also wondered how they could fit into a pair of boxing gloves and why anyone would want to challenge him to a boxing match.

"Boy," exclaimed Jimmy, "he must pack a terrific wallop in those mitts. If I had some money, I'd put it on him."

Bob figured his brother, Dean, could out-box Henrihan if given the chance to get into the ring with him. He would be giving away about 50 pounds and three inches in height (the Irishman weighed about 225 pounds and was 6 foot 3 inches tall). But Henrihan was slow afoot while Dean could dance around him all night, if need be, while inflicting punishment with a lethal left jab and a right cross that he could deliver with a thunderous effect on an opponent's jaw.

But when Tess heard us prompting Dean to engage himself in those friendly fisticuffs, she would have none of it.

"Don't you even think about doing any boxing tonight," she pointedly told Dean. "Those matches are for the fellows who work at the ranches. That's their recreational outlet for the month and you don't need to spoil it for them. Besides, you could get yourself hurt; especially if that big Irishman beats you up."

"Ah, c'mon, Tess," protested Dean, "I'm a working stiff, too! Those 13-ounce gloves are like getting hit with a pillow. Nobody's going to get hurt with those gloves."

Tess knew what Dean could do with his dukes. She'd watched him floor too many opponents who were bigger than him in boxing matches around the Intermountain West. She wouldn't budge on the matter this time and Dean slumped dejectedly at the thought of not being able to engage in a sport he dearly loved. Reluctantly, he respected his wife's wishes.

When Hoot Gibson learned of Dean's prowess as a boxer, but wouldn't be boxing, he asked Dean, largely at Bob and Jimmy's urging, if he would be willing to referee the matches. Dean couldn't say yes fast enough. Gibson then invited everyone who wanted to watch the boxers to gather ringside and get ready for the final activity of the day.

"The boxing matches are about to begin, folks; gather round and bet on your favorite fighter," he announced.

The women didn't have an interest in seeing their menfolk knock each other around so they gathered in small groups and chatted away as the men reached for their wallets and began placing small bets among themselves. Gibson held the loot and said he would disburse it at the end of the boxing matches.

The purse was announced at $150 with the winner getting $100 and the runnerup receiving $50. Ranch loyalty played a big part in the betting process. Henrihan was representing the Banfield spread so all the hands, including Uncle Jesse and Hank Johnson, put their money on the big Irishman.

Chapter 21

Only two ranch hands had thrown their hats into the ring. Ringsiders were surprised at that. Normally, three or four hats would be tossed in, but when Henrihan won last month's competition, the word had gotten around that the big Irishman would be hard to beat this afternoon; gloves or no gloves. Henrihan was already sitting on a chair just outside the ring waiting for the preliminary bout to get over. He also wanted to scout his challengers.

He had stripped to the waist, taken off his cowboy boots and had put on a pair of dirty old gym shoes so he wouldn't slip in the dirt. His massive chest was covered with hair and his arms looked like a couple of logs hanging from his shoulders.

"Man, look at that guy," exclaimed Jimmy " who's ever gonna beat him?" The crowd around the ring was thinking the same thing.

When Henrihan stood up to shadow box a little bit, his six-foot plus frame looked like a tree trunk and his huge, ham-like hands barely fit into the boxing gloves that Dean had slipped on his hands to see if they would fit. They did. Barely. Dean then removed the gloves and placed them on the corner tool.

"Nobody can get hurt with those gloves," I thought.

Bob and Jimmy agreed. We could feel the excitement building and the men around the ring were hollering for the first fight to get underway.

Dean stepped into the ring and inspected it to make sure the ropes were taut. He then picked up the challenger's hats.

"Who's these belong to," he inquired while lifting the hats above his head so the owners could be identified. A rangy cowpoke emerged from the cheering crowd to claim one of the hats, which just happened to be white with turned up sides.

"That'd be mine," said the cowpoke who identified himself as "Chauncey Williams—from the Kemper spread." The crowd cheered wildly again.

Everyone apparently knew Williams as a hard worker and a pretty good boxer who had won a couple of the events last summer, but in his first bout this summer, in June, Henrihan had put him down for the full count with a thunderous right hand to the jaw less than a minute into the fight. With powder puff gloves on according to ringsiders!

When the shouting died down, Dean held the other hat aloft; a brand new black one with a silver band around the dome and asked the owner to claim it so he (Dean) could explain the rules of engagement to Henrihan and the two challengers.

A moment later, a lean, mean-looking character sauntered from out of crowd and into the center of the ring. It was none other than Jake Dalton! No cheers this time; only a few gasps from ourselves and the other Banfield ranch hands who were prepared to root for their popular Irishman, Rich Henrihan.

Dalton thought he could rake in some easy money by tossing his hat into the ring, and although he hadn't boxed for several months, he remembered his youthful days when his fists pummeled innocent victims into submission as well as the time he had spent in pen when he took on all comers during the prison's annual boxing tournament.

He was actually the reigning champion of the Nevada state prison when he had gained his release last month. Few ringsiders knew who he was and he relished the role of being the underdog fighter. Bernie McCoy was in his corner to provide moral support for his long time friend. Dalton retrieved his hat from Dean and wanted to know who his opponent would be.

"You're opponent is Chauncey Williams from the Kemper ranch."

Dalton acknowledged his introduction to Williams by nodding and without shaking his hand.

Dean was as surprised as the rest of us to see Dalton enter the ring. He had taken an instant dis-liking to Dalton the minute he had set eyes on him, but he had kept his thoughts to himself and was reserving judgement about him until the ex-con could prove that he was a good guy. Dalton had a cocky sneer on his face as if to say:

"Hey fellas, let's get the preliminary stuff over with so we can get on with the big fight."

Hardly anyone in the crowd knew Dalton and McCoy, except several old timers who had known them when they were teenagers, but they didn't know how handy Dalton was with his fists.

"Hey, Jake, a ringsider shouted, "you're gonna go down early against our man Williams."

Dalton ignored the comment as Dean motioned for the fighters to gather around him at the center of the ring so he could explain the rules.

*   *   *   *

Dean again introduced the boxers and they acknowledged each other with nods as Dean explained the rules of engagement.

"Okay, fellas, when I finish, go back to your corners and slip the gloves on that are lying on your stools.

"No need to lace 'em up," he told the fighters, "I'll do that after I tell you how I'm going to referee these bouts. So, listen up—I'm only going to explain the rules once to you and I expect you to follow them.

"For this preliminary, as well as the title bout, there will be three, three-minute rounds. We don't want you fellas to get overly tired, so there'll be one minute rest periods between rounds and a 15 minute break between the preliminary bout and the final bout.

"If you get knocked down, the other fella must go to a neutral corner. If you don't get up by the count of 10, you lose. No low punches will be tolerated and if you sucker punch your opponent; like hitting below the belt, I'll dock you a point; maybe two, depending upon the severity of the blow. No head butting and no clinches. You're here to box a little; not hold each other. Now shake hands and come out fighting."

Henrihan went back to his chair at ringside. Williams and Dalton retreated to their corners where Dean slipped on their gloves and laced them up.

Seconds later, Uncle Jesse rang the bell and the two fighters met in the middle of the ring; touched gloves, and began sparring while trying to find an opening to deliver the first punch.

It came with a suddenness of a Cobra strike! Barely a half minute into the fight, a looping right hand by Williams caught Dalton flush on the side of the head. Two sharp jabs followed, snapping his head back, and a right hand uppercut sent the ex-con sprawling in the dirt.

Dean waived Williams to a neutral corner and began the count while waiting to have his hand raised in victory by Dean. Williams didn't realize that his opponent was tough as rawhide. Dalton lay still for a moment or two, then he heard Dean counting over him: "four—five—six."

McCoy was pleading: "Get up, Jake, Get up!."

Shaking the cobwebs from his head, Dalton rolled over, got up on his knees and then staggered to his feet as Dean counted "seven, eight, nine…"

He was vulnerable and Williams sensed it, too. Dean wiped the dirt off Dalton's gloves and noticed a glazed look in the excon's eyes as he motioned for the fighters to touch gloves in the center of the ring. Williams moved in for the kill, but Dalton instinctively grabbed him and held on.

"Hold on," Dalton told himself, "just get through this round and you'll be okay."

For a moment Dean thought about stopping the fight, fearing Dalton could get hurt if he allowed it to continue despite the soft gloves they were wearing.

The bell clanged ending round one. No decision for the moment, he determined, as he went over and inspected Dalton who had sprawled on a stool in his corner.

"Have you had enough, Jake," Dean asked, peering into Dalton's dazed eyes once again.

"Hell no—I'm just getting started," the stricken fighter mumbled. Dean was surprised by Dalton's quick answer and he issued a warning to him:

"Alright, but if you go down again, the fight's over."

I was ecstatic about what was happening. I had to have a better seat so I could watch Williams flatten Dalton in the second round. As I edged closer to the ring, I failed to contain my enthusiasm and began yelling and shadow boxing with myself.

"Come on, Williams, dust him off real quick," I shouted above the din of the rowdy crowd.

That was a youthful mistake. Dalton saw me gleefully moving about and shaking my fists at him. His cold glare froze me in my tracks and I quickly melted back into the crowd.

The bell clanged, signaling the one-minute rest period was over. Dean again motioned the fighters to touch gloves in the center of the ring while reminding them that it was "just a friendly boxing match."

Dalton just sneered as he warily danced around Williams. He had noticed that whenever Williams would throw a right hand punch, he would drop his left hand guard down which exposed his chin. Street smart from years of defending himself in and out of the ring, Dalton also anticipated that Williams would again try to throw that looping right hand.

A minute into the second round Dalton saw it coming. Williams's left hand dropped noticeably again and as he prepared to deliver the knockout punch with his right hand, Dalton shuffled forward and launched a stinging right hand that caught Williams flush on the jaw.

Williams staggered backward; a look of bewilderment on his face. Dalton pounced on him like a cat on a mouse. Three left hand jabs and another lethal right hand sent Williams sprawling on his back in the dirt ring. He lay motionless for a moment as Dean began the count; then the cowpoke from the Kemper spread tried to raise himself up; only to collapse again. Dean stopped counting; signaling that the fight was over. The crowd was stunned and couldn't believe that the fight had ended so quickly.

As Dean bent down to assist Williams to his feet, Dalton became enraged that Dean would stop the fight so soon. Rushing from a neutral corner, he tried to push Dean aside so he could get some final licks in against Williams who, obviously, was not in any shape to continue the fight.

Dalton was momentarily out of control and his fiery temper had reached the boiling point. Sensing this, Dean pinned Dalton's arms to his side and shoved him into his corner where McCoy further restrained him.

"Calm down, Jake, the fight's over," McCoy told him.

Dalton was still fighting mad. Sensing he was going to create a ruckus, Dean issued a warning:

"Look, Jake, You've won fair and square; so calm down! You've got a 15 minute rest period before you and Henrihan mix it up. Don't get yourself riled up—you're going to need all your energy to fight the big Irishman."

"Get out of my way, Banfield," Dalton growled belligerently. "I'll fight the way I want to and I don't need you interferin' with me." Then, to emphasize his anger, he growled a warning:

"I'll punch your lights out, too, if you're not careful."

Dean was momentarily taken aback by those unexpected comments so he just smiled and backed away. Then his easy-going manner quickly faded to a scowl. He wanted to make his own point:

"Look, fella, you'll fight by the rules or you won't fight at all. And as for as punchin' my lights out—don't let nothing but fear stop you." Now, it was Dalton's turn to be surprised. Turning to McCoy he growled:

"Who the hell does this guy think he is anyway?"

McCoy was nervously wiping the sweat off Dalton's head and shoulders while at the same time trying to calm him down.

"C'mon, Jake, quit trying to stir up trouble. We've got another fight coming up in a few minutes, so calm yourself down." Then gesturing to Henrihan at ringside, McCoy whispered a warning to his unruly buddy:

"You need to start thinkin' about how you're gonna' handle that big dude sittin' over there—and you gotta' quit irritating the referee."

Neither of them knew that Dalton had just challenged the Intermountain Light Heavyweight Champion to a fight. Dean would have relished the opportunity to get into the ring with Dalton, right then and there, but he didn't want to incur Tess's wrath.

But with that harsh exchange of words between Dalton and Dean, the inevitable was bound to happen. Those two antagonists were going to meet sometime soon; inside or outside the ring—and with or without the gloves on!

Chapter 22

Hearing the restive crowd creating a ruckus at ringside the womenfolk broke up from their little gossip groups and began to filter into the crowd beside their husbands. What's going on they anxiously asked?

A happy Saturday afternoon had suddenly become dampened by harsh words coming from the ring. Except for a few old timers who knew Jake Dalton and Bernie McCoy from earlier years, most of the other folks were wondering how those belligerent cowpokes could have landed in their midst.

Bob, Jimmy and myself were hoping that Dean would accept Jake Dalton's challenge to fight him right then and there. We knew Dean could take him like Joe Louis took Max Schmeling. We also knew that Dean's wife, Tess, would have none of it. Still, Bob couldn't contain himself.

"Hey, Tess," Bob shouted excitedly, "Dean's gonna fight that ex-convict, Jake Dalton."

"Oh, no he's not," Tess said firmly. Then motioning to Dean, she shouted above the noisy crowd:

"Don't you dare think about fighting anybody. We're guests here—and remember, you promised me that…" Dean interrupted her by holding his hand up and shaking his head.

"Don't worry your pretty head. I'm not gonna' fight anybody, let alone Jake Dalton."

"At least not tonight," he was thinking, but his disdain for Dalton and his antics was evident to all who were paying attention to the goings on in the ring.

Some of the ringsiders heard Dalton's rantings and couldn't wait for Henrihan to make mince meat out of the ex-con. The Irishman was sitting calmly on his stool waiting for Dean to slip on and lace up his big 13-ounce gloves so the first round could begin.

That done, the bell clanged and the boxers touched gloves in the center of the ring and they began to feint and jab at each other; always probing to find each other's weaknesses.

The big Irishman towered over Dalton and his huge arms and wide body seemed to engulf the ex-con each time they clinched. Dean warned them both to stop holding and begin fighting. Hardly a blow was struck during the first round.

A voice in the crowd shouted: "Hey, you guys, quit dancin' around and do a little fightin' the next couple of rounds. Those powder puff gloves you got on ain't gonna hurt you."

The ringsiders laughed. The fighters ignored the comments.

Jake told Bernie before the second round started that the big Irishman was slow afoot and that he could out box him and win on points if he could stay out of the reach of Henrihan's tree trunk-sized arms and huge hands.

The ex-con had an uncanny sense of being able to analyze his opponent, but he realized that he'd be lucky to even knock Henrihan down, let alone out. The Irishman appeared to be too big for Dalton or anyone else to handle.

McCoy cautioned Dalton to be careful and if Henrihan began to move in, he should put his left hand jab to good use.

"Just tattoo him like a woodpecker hammering on a tree," he told Dalton, "then step in and smash him with a good right hand to that soft belly of his. He's vulnerable there, I know he is."

*   *   *   *

Dalton heeded McCoy's advice and as they warily eyed each other in the opening minute of the second round, Dalton made his move. Henrihan missed with a right hand and Dalton countered with his left jab…once, twice, three times. The Irishman's head kept snapping back as Jake's lightening strikes found their mark.

Suddenly, Dalton shuffled his left foot forward and made another feint-like jab with his left hand. Henrihan blocked it, but left himself open in the midriff. That's all Jake needed. He swiftly delivered a right hand blow to the Irishman's belly; knocking the wind out of Henrihan. As he reeled back from that blow, Dalton kept jabbing him repeatedly with his left hand while managing to stay out of range of the big man's wild swings.

Dalton was just too swift and light on his feet for the big Irishman. He could dance in and out of danger; inflicting damage to Henrihan's face and bloodying his nose. A deep cut had opened above his right eyebrow from an intentional head butt by Dalton. Dean docked him a point and warned him not to do that again. The cut was bleeding profusely by the time the second round ended.

Henrihan's handler quickly washed the blood off the Irishman's face and applied an ice pack to his swollen left eye. The partisan crowd was going nuts and shouting for Henrihan to take Dalton out, but it wouldn't happen.

Dalton beat the Irishman to a pulp in the third round. Even with those big 13-ounce gloves, his quick punches had severely bruised Henrihan's face and the damaging blows to his body left him doubled over with pain.

Then the out-of-shape Irishman collapsed in the center of the ring before the bell could end the fight. Dalton stood over his stricken opponent for a few moments begging him to get up while at the same time gesturing to the crowd and shouting a new challenge:

"Any of you chicken-livered characters wanna' fight? No one responded.

Everyone was repulsed by his crude behavior and they booed him out of the ring. It took a few minutes to revive Henrihan and Dean worried that he should have stopped the fight sooner in the round. It was a savage encounter; one that had gotten quickly out of control because of Dalton's savagery.

The ex-con apparently wanted to prove that he was the best boxer around. He also wanted to intimidate those who were thinking about throwing their hats into the ring when the next "social gathering" took place at Uncle Jesse's place in August.

The fear factor works on people's minds, he cunningly thought, and what better place to prove that theory than in a boxing ring? Even before a hostile crowd!

With the fight over, Hoot Gibson handed Dalton his take, a hundred bucks, without congratulating him, and he stuffed fifty dollars into Henrihan's pocket while wishing him a speedy recovery.

There were already bad feelings among the Banfield ranch hands about Jake Dalton and Bernie McCoy's employment. They had largely kept their sentiments to themselves; knowing the desperate labor situation and work load the Banfields were facing in the coming weeks.

As the crowd disbursed, Dalton's brutal beating of the popular Irishman wasn't setting well with several of Uncle Jesse's ranch hands. They vented their anger at Hank Johnson about the rogue cowpokes.

"They either leave or we will," they threatened as a group.

In the few short days since being hired by Johnson, Dalton and McCoy had managed to alienate the entire Banfield crew. They also knew about my hay field debacle with the two ex-cons and didn't want to put up with any more nonsense from those two renegades.

The day that had started with so much fun and laughter had ended on a sour note; leaving everyone to wonder if having friendly fisticuffs at a social gathering was a good idea.

Chapter 23

Two days after the boxing debacle at the Gibson's ranch, Uncle Jesse's workers were in no mood for engaging in the light hearted banter that usually went on in the milking barn. A new work week had started, but after the usual wake up call by Ol' Red, the Banfield's cocky rooster, the ranch hands performed their milking chores in subdued silence.

Winnie Poo, the Banfield's calico cat, had taken up her normal position on a bale of hay behind the first cow in the milking rotation so she could get the first squirt of milk from Rich Henrihan, but the big Irishman was not at his usual station.

He was recovering from the brutal beating that Jake Dalton had administered to him on the past Saturday afternoon. When we saw him later in the morning, he was still stiff and sore and his right eye was virtually shut from the repeated left jabs that Dalton had managed to deliver in a flurry of blows during the second and third rounds. It would be another day before Henrihan could sit comfortably on his milking stool and wet Winnie Poo's whiskers with a well aimed squirt of warm milk.

Hank Johnson had told Dalton and McCoy before breakfast to stay out of the barn and to feed the other animals while the milking operation was underway. He didn't want further confrontation between the crew and Dalton; especially Dean who had gained everyone's respect by the way he had handled himself right after the fight had ended.

Dean was a veteran of the ring and realized that fighters have high emotions following a bout; so his calm manner defused a volatile scene. Dalton had been real snarly at the end of the bout and was surprised when Dean didn't back down after Dalton challenged him to fight.

Not to be intimidated, Dean had issued a challenge of his own before they had even exited the ring; telling Dalton:

"Don't let nothing but fear stop you," if he wanted to get it on then and there.

Dalton began to wonder just who was facing him down. He'd only known Dean for a few days and had no idea, nor a clue, that Dean was an accomplished boxer.

A few of the ringsiders had also heard Dean tell Dalton that he wasn't afraid of him. Bob and Jimmy, as well as myself, had done our best to heat up the challenge by disclosing that Dean was the Intermountain Light Heavyweight Champion and that he could whip Dalton's butt if given a chance to do so.

Both Dalton and McCoy were oblivious to Dean's prowess as boxer, but it didn't take long for that fact to filter back to them. Still, Dalton was unimpressed.

"Bernie, I might have to duke it out with that fella' behind the barn one of these days just to see if he's as good as everyone says he is."

McCoy wasn't nearly so cocky.

"Jake, we don't need to stir up any more trouble than we have already. The Banfield crew resents us as it is; so get off your high horse and calm yourself down for awhile."

"You sticking up for those dudes, Bernie?"

"Hell no, Jake, I'm just being realistic. The message Dean Banfield sent you should be a warning. I couldn't see any fear in his eyes and he didn't back down when you challenged him. Appears to me, he'll fight you anywhere, anytime, so just be careful what you're sayin' when you're around him."

Dalton sneered contemptuously at McCoy's suggestions, but he remained silent; knowing there was some merit to that advice.

Uncle Jesse's ranch foreman, Hank Johnson, had attended the Gibson social and when his ranch hands threatened to revolt after Dalton had beat up on Henrihan, and even challenged Dean, he got his crew together and assured them that he was only going to keep them on the payroll through the rest of the Summer.

"After that, they're gone. Right now, we need every hand we can get for the next couple of months so we can get ready for the sheep and cattle shipments coming up. We'll be movin' the sheep out to the North ranch first. That'll be in the middle of August and the first shipment of cattle will be in September right after Labor day."

Hank was too proud to admit that he'd made a mistake in hiring the ex-cons to work on the Banfield ranch, but desperate times meant making desperate decisions. Now, he was suffering the consequences of poor morale among his ranch hands and a growing concern around Fallon that a criminal element had invaded their community.

*   *   *   *

Jeb Harrington, the Washoe County deputy sheriff, was sitting in his office shuffling papers when the telephone rang. It was Hoot Gibson calling to express his concern about the conduct of Jake Dalton following their Saturday afternoon social.

Gibson said he and Mrs. Gibson were happy to have hosted the social and that everyone seemed to be having a good time until Dalton punched out a fellow worker from the Banfield ranch.

"No one told us that this Dalton feller and his sidekick, Bernie McCoy, were ex-cons or we wouldn't have even let them come on our place," Gibson told the sheriff.

"Still, it was a legitimate boxing match, Jeb. No different than the ones we always have at the end of our Saturday afternoon socials, but this one turned a bit ugly at the end."

"What happened, Hoot?"

"Well, this Dalton feller knocked that big ol' Irishman, Rich Henrihan, to his knees and then he just kept comin' after him so the referee stepped in and stopped the fight; fearin' Henrihan might get hurt more'n he was at the time."

"Who was the referee?" Jeb asked Hoot.

"Feller named Dean Banfield. He's Jesse Banfield's son who'd come over from Utah last month to help his dad over the Summer. Brought over a couple of Jesse's younger sons, too; Bob and Jimmy, and their cousin, Danny Collins, to help out around the ranch.

"I'll tell 'ya, Jeb, I was impressed with the way Dean handled the refereein' chore. I didn't know until shortly before the boxing matches started that Dean was a skilled boxer himself.

"How come he wasn't fightin' Hoot?"

"The word goin' around was that he'd promised his wife, Tess, that he wouldn't engage himself so I asked him if we would referee the bout," Gibson replied.

"He's a cool feller, Jeb, and he sure knew how to handle that ex-con when the fight was over."

"Tell me about it, Hoot."

"Well, the first thing he did was to constrain that Dalton feller by holdin' his arms down to his sides when he wanted to keep on fightin'. That kind of upset Dalton and he began to rave 'n rant about wantin' to keep fightin' some more.

"Dean told him Henrihan was finished and that he, Dalton, had won the fight. That's when the fuss started. He told Dean to get out of his way and that he wanted to finish off the Irishman in his own way.

"Dean would have none of that; so Dalton called him out and that's when things started to get real interestin'. About that time, the word was bein' spread around that Dean was no slouch in the ring either. In fact, his younger brothers, Bob and Jimmy, were braggin' on him all afternoon; claimin' he was some kind of a boxing champ over in Utah.

"I thought that was just family enthusiasm, so I asked Jesse Banfield after everything had quieted down and most everyone had gone home if that was true. Jesse just smiled and nodded his head like a proud papa would do under those circumstances. Then he stepped closer to me so no else could hear and said:

"'My boy is a real assassin in the ring. You can bet the farm on him if he ever puts on the gloves with Dalton, but I don't think it'll ever happen 'cause Tess doesn't approve of his boxing people around.'"

Gibson then told Jeb that menfolk around the valley were already beginning to talk about next month's social at the Banfield ranch.

"They're thinking this could be a whale of a boxing match, Jeb. Dalton will be there to defend his right to be King of the Hill, but if Dean's wife won't let him fight, I don't think any of my boys will be anxious to throw their hat in the ring after seeing what Dalton did to Henrihan."

As an afterthought, Gibson said he hadn't seen Jeb at the social so he was calling to inform him about what happened last Saturday evening.

"Thanks for the update, Hoot, I'll go out to see Jesse and tell him we spoke. I'm also gonna' have a talk with Dalton and let him know that his next fight might be inside the prison walls if he is not careful. The guy is bad news and I don't know why Jesse and Hank keeps him and McCoy on their payroll. They must be real desperate, I guess."

* * * *

My cousins and I were full of ourselves after letting everybody know that Dean was the Intermountain Light Heavyweight Champion. Even Uncle Jesse' ranch hands were surprised to learn of Dean's boxing skills. They kept asking questions about how Dean became so good; how long had he been fighting and if he was going to pitch his hat in the ring when Uncle Jesse and Aunt Vera hosted the August social.

Bob and Jimmy filled them in on the first two questions, but whether Dean would fight Dalton was a big question mark. Tess wasn't going to let that happen, but we told the ranch hands at every opportunity that this could be the all-time best fight in Washoe County history if it came about.

We knew Tess was dead set against it, but we had a sneaking suspicion that Dean would be making that decision at the next social. His easy going manner belied an intense competitive spirit and while he deferred to Tess's wishes most of the time, he sometimes drew the line. We also knew it would be Dean's decision to fight Dalton and no else's.

He had been challenged and called out by a rogue ex-con who had no idea about his ability as a boxer. It was in his nature to respond to such a challenge and we were determined to find a way to get them into the ring together despite Tess's objections. The August Social couldn't arrive fast enough as far as we were concerned.

Chapter 24

Aunt Vera was clearly upset about what had happened at the Gibson social over the weekend. She had already given Jesse an earful about the so-called boxing matches that had over shadowed the friendly gathering of ranchers and their families. Now she was chewing on him again for allowing Hank Johnson to hire Dalton and McCoy.

"You weren't that desperate for help were you?"

Jesse pondered the question for a moment before answering.

He had deep mis-givings about that hire, but after he criticized Hank for not initially informing him of their sordid backgrounds, he had relented on his urge to fire them. While they didn't fit in with the rest of the crew, he thought, they were at least doing what they were told to do without complaining.

"Look, Vera, I know those fellers don't have the best of reputations, but we were—and still are—in dire need of help. They're good workers and you know yourself this ranching operation is too big for the number of men we have workin' for us right now, so I've got to keep 'em on for a little while longer; at least until we make the sheep run to the North ranch next month.

"As for supervising 'em, I've told Hank more than once that I'm holding him personally responsible for their behavior. If I hear they're getting out of line, I'll run 'em off myself."

Vera still wasn't satisfied. The fear factor swept over her momentarily and she shuddered to think of what might have happened if things had gotten out of control at the end of the boxing match.

"That Jake Dalton went crazy last Saturday when he beat up on Rich Henrihan. If Dean hadn't kept his cool, we would have had further mayhem." Jesse agreed.

"Yeah, I know. Dean did a good job refereein' and an even better job of controllin' things at the end."

Vera wouldn't let the issue die and she kept pounding on Jesse to make sure he understood her views on the matter.

"Tess was upset that he had even gotten involved as a referee. I'm glad she told the boys they shouldn't have been jumping up and down and stirring up trouble; especially letting everybody know that Dean was a good boxer." Jesse chuckled over our antics at ringside and how we touted Dean's prowess as a boxer.

"They were just being boys, Vera. Shoot, when they heard Dalton challenge Dean, they wanted to make sure everybody knew who he was calling out. Can't blame 'em for that."

Jesse savored that statement. As he prepared to leave, he visualized how his son would handle Jake Dalton in a boxing match. He couldn't resist a final comment and told Vera what he was thinking as a devilish smile spread across his face.

"That would be a good match, don't you think? Maybe we can get them in the ring next month when we host the August social."

Vera shook her head in disgust and shooed him out of the kitchen. That was another worry she didn't want to even think about at the moment. Keeping house and fixing three meals a day, seven days a week, for her family and the other ranch hands was more than enough to keep her constantly on the go from early morning to late at night. Now, she had to start thinking of hosting all the ranchers and their families in the valley as well.

Thank heavens, she thought, how helpful Tess had been since arriving from Utah. She knew her daughter in law would be a big help in the planning of that social and both would do their very best to prevent the boxing matches from being held at the end of he day. They abhorred violence and that's all boxing was—pure unadulterated violence—and they strongly believed it wasn't the way to end a friendly social gathering.

But Vera couldn't worry about that problem any longer. Preparations for the evening meal were well underway. The bill-o-fare would consist of fried lamb chops, mashed potatoes and gravy, boiled carrots, tomatos based in vinegar, hot biscuits, apple pie for desert and plenty of milk to drink.

It would be a meal fit for a king, but I was growing weary of lamb chops and longed for the day when I could return home, sleep in my own bed and go have a milkshake with my buddies at Vincent's drug store.

*   *   *   *

Out in the field, Dean and Hank Johnson, along with Bob, Jimmy and myself, as well as a couple of other ranch hands, were digging post holes and fencing off a new pasture just North of the ranch house.

The sheep would be kept there prior to herding them to the North ranch next month. Uncle Jesse had been telling everyone that we were going to be the shepherds on that drive, but Aunt Vera and Tess weren't keen on the idea; saying that it would be too hot for us to make that day-long trek across the hot desert. Still, we persisted every chance we got even though we knew they were firmly against it.

Off in the distance we could see Uncle Jesse's pickup truck flying down the road toward us; the usual rooster tail of dust shooting up behind the truck in a huge swirl of dust. As he braked to a stop, another car pulled up behind him. It was all black and had large spotlights with Washoe County insignias on the front doors. We knew right away it was a patrol car.

Deputy sheriff, Jeb Harrington, stepped out in full regalia of a law enforcement officer. His uniform was neat and pressed, dark glasses shadowed his eyes and a pearl handled pistol was belted to his side. His spit-polished boots didn't have a speck of dust on them until he exited his car. A picture of Mr. law and order himself, I thought. It even tickled me to see dust get splattered all over his boots.

After grunting a greeting to everyone in his usual brusque manner he extended his hand to Jesse, Hank and Dean and asked if he could visit with them for a few minutes.

"Something serious on your mind?" Jesse asked. "Yeah, Jesse, there is. Where's Dalton and McCoy?" Hank motioned toward the South pasture.

"They're workin' over yonder mendin' fences and movin' some cattle."

Harrington's mannerisms indicated he was really unhappy about something. He asked the men to step away from us, so they moved a short distance away and began talking in hushed voices.

The sheriff then got back in his car and drove toward town. Uncle Jesse also left after asking how the fencing was coming along and saying he was going over to the South pasture.

"What was that all about," Bob asked Dean.

"Oh, don't be so curious—just men talk that's all," Dean replied.

We knew better. The sheriff wouldn't drive all the way out to where we were for a casual visit. That wasn't his style. As the day worn on, we were able to pry bits of information out of Hank about what he, Jesse and Dean had discussed, but Dean wouldn't tell us a thing. Hank said that the sheriff had received some calls about the Saturday night fight at the Gibson social and since the sheriff hadn't been there, he just wanted to hear a first hand account of what went on.

The callers had expressed outrage over Jake Dalton's conduct and had praised Dean for the way he had handled the confrontation with Dalton.

"Is that all he came out here for?" Jimmy inquired of Hank.

"No, as a matter of fact," the foreman answered. "He wanted to meet Dean and hear his side of the story, too. He also wanted to see what kind of a man would stand up to a hardened criminal like Dalton."

Hank said the sheriff left impressed with Dean, his quiet demeanor and his explanation of the incident. He had even complimented Dean on how he had defused a highly volatile situation at the end of the fight between Dalton and Henrihan. Hank said Dean just smiled and shrugged his shoulders over such praise.

"That brother of yours has got a lot of confidence in his self," Hank said afterward to Bob and Jimmy.

"I haven't seen him box since I was in Utah a couple of years ago. Is he still as sharp as ever?"

"Better'n ever," Bob said. Jimmy offered his assessment of his older brother's boxing skills, too.

"His left jab is improved—and his right cross can put you to sleep real quick if you let your guard down."

* * * *

Vera and Tess had fixed a tasty supper for us, and despite the strained atmosphere of having Dalton and McCoy sitting at the end of the table, the ranch hands seemed to enjoy themselves and the food that was served.

Dalton and McCoy ate quickly and left the table without engaging in any conversation, but they were back in the bunkhouse soon after dark.

We thought that was strange, but since it was early in the week, they were probably still tired from their carousing around on the weekend.

Later on, when everybody had gone to bed, I noticed Dalton smoking by the window, so I suggested to Bob and Jimmy that we go over to the corner of the bunk house and listen to their conversation.

Dalton was sitting in his usual place at the open window; his left arm was dangling outside as he flicked cigarette ashes on the ground. McCoy was sitting on his bed and as we peeked around the corner of the bunk house we could hear Dalton talking about confronting some grave digger at the local cemetery. We were puzzled about that conversation and as we picked up bits and pieces of their banter we realized they had been up to no good.

Instead of going into Fallon that evening they had apparently driven out to the local cemetery and confronted the grave digger about who was responsible for burying Jake's sister, Cheryl, over five years ago. By the tone of his voice, Dalton's visit to the cemetery had clearly frustrated and irritated him.

"…It was hard gettin' that ol' feller to tell us anything at first, wasn't it Bernie?"

"Yeah," McCoy replied, "but did you see how quick he came around from denying everything to spillin' his guts when you stuck him with your knife and told him we'd bury him alive if he didn't come clean?" They both laughed at that remark.

We were barely breathing for fear of being discovered, so we scrunched down around the corner behind the bunk house for a few moments.

"He carries a knife!" Jimmy whispered to me.

"Yeah, I whispered back, "it's a big old Bowie knife that Dalton keeps strapped in a sheath on the inside of his right boot."

"How'd you know that?" Jimmy asked

"I saw it when he was sitting on a stool milking cows last week. The handle was sticking out of the top of his boot." Bob shushed us both.

"Be quiet so we can hear what they're saying," he whispered.

McCoy came over to the edge of the window and tossed out what was left of his cigarette butt and promptly lit up another.

"If that grave digger is tellin' the truth, Jake, we may be gettin' closer to findin' out how Cheryl died; whether it was from natural causes or by someone who knew her pretty well."

Dalton agreed, but he was still mystified, even angry, about the mysterious way she had died and her strange night time burial.

"There are a lot of things still puzzlin' me about this whole situation, Bernie. The 'digger said that no funeral or graveside services were held and that he buried her after dark following a hurried long distance call from out of town.

"Now, tell me, Bernie, why 'n hell would anyone want to bury someone in the dead of night unless it was under suspicious circumstances?"

"I don't know, Jake, but did you notice after you asked the 'digger who the caller was and who paid for Cheryl's funeral that he couldn't remember a thing? He was sufferin' a complete memory loss until you told him we'd bury him alive if he didn't cooperate. Then, he spilled his guts."

"Yeah, he sure did," Dalton replied, "That ol' 'digger isn't the guilty party though—he just buried my sis'—but at least he fingered Marco Forlani. That little bastard knows more than he's tellin' us.

"That's why Forlani shuffled us off to the 'digger at the cemetery; figurin' the ol' feller couldn't remember things that happened five years ago and that he was paid off for diggin' a hasty grave and stayin' late to bury Cheryl.

"We're gettin' closer to figurin' this thing out, Bernie. We're going into town this week and have another talk with Forlani. He's either going to tell us the truth this time or we're gonna' dump him in the well."

McCoy winced at that thought, but he was anxious to finally find out who was responsible for Cheryl's death, too, and if it meant tossing her killer down the well, he told Jake, he was all for it.

We were stunned to hear the ex-cons talking so casually about killing someone and wondered who this Marco Forlani was and where he hung out.

Bob ventured the thought that his dad's foreman, Hank Johnson, might know who that fellow might be since he went into town frequently.

We had spied enough on those two ex-cons to keep us awake for awhile and as we slipped back to the ranch house under the cover of darkness we wondered where that mysterious well was that Dalton and McCoy kept talking about.

Chapter 25

The sharp crack of a distant rifle shot echoed through our open window and awakened us out of a sound sleep. A few seconds later another shot rang out.

"Holy cow! Who's shooting at us," Jimmy mumbled; still half a sleep. Even though it was a distance away, the sound startled us out of our beds.

"Hank must have nailed a couple of coyotes," Bob explained.

Then, we remembered that Jesse's foreman had told everyone over supper the night before that he was going to camp out in the South pasture in his pickup truck to see if he could get rid of the coyotes that were harassing and killing the sheep.

As we ran out the door to see what was going on, a dark, starlit sky greeted us. The barnyard was eerily quiet. Even Ol' Red, our raucous rooster, hadn't even had time to deliver his first wakeup call. Jesse was nowhere to be seen, which surprised us. It must really be early, I concluded, if Ol' Red and Jesse weren't up and stirring around.

The first hint of daylight had barely began appearing in the Eastern sky, so I knew it had to be close to five o'clock in the morning. The ranch house and milking barn would soon be bustling with activity and the cock of the walk would, at any minute now, come strutting out of the chicken coop and begin crowing in full throated glory as he jerk-stepped across the barn. Even Dalton and McCoy had come to hate Ol' Red's early morning antics and vowed to quiet the rooster the first chance they got.

Nearly a month had passed since I had arrived at the Banfield ranch for a working vacation. Arising early each morning, seven days a week, was not my idea of how to enjoy the Summer. Cousin Bob had promised that we would be doing some fishing, swimming and horseback riding while working on his dad's ranch outside Fallon.

We'd done none of those things. I had wished a hundred times since arriving that I was back working for my dad. At least, I wouldn't have had to work on weekends. In Midvale, my home town, a nice park with tennis courts was nearby and I could go swimming in the evening or on weekends.

I would also be making good money; thirty-five cents an hour, which translates into $2.80 a day, $14.00 a week, and $56.00 a month. I wondered with each passing day how I could have passed up that bonanza.

Shortly after hearing the rifle shots, Hank drove up with two dead coyotes in the back of his pickup truck. We had just finished our milking chores and as we headed out of the barn to go to the ranch house for breakfast, Rich Henrihan managed to douse his favorite target, Winnie Poo, with a few playful squirts of milk and us, too, while we were trying to hang up our milking stools.

Dalton and McCoy were the first in the milking barn and the last to leave, which seemed to be their habit pattern. Henrihan didn't squirt milk at them as they left the barn each morning and he only nodded to them at the breakfast table. He still hadn't forgotten the beating Dalton had given him a couple of weeks earlier at the Gibson social.

   *   *   *   *

As the ranch hands were finishing breakfast, Hank announced a change in the work schedule. He was dividing his crew into three groups for the day. Dean and three other ranch hands along with Bob and Jimmy were assigned to the North pasture where they would be fencing off the remaining area where the sheep would be kept until the herd could be moved to the North ranch in a couple of weeks. Henrihan and a crew of three would be in the South pasture inspecting cattle, mending fences and counting heifers that were being fattened up for the September sell off, while Dalton, McCoy and two other workers were sent to the alfalfa field West of the ranch house to wagon-in the hay that had been cut the day before.

While all this was going on, Jesse had parked his pickup truck under a lean-to on the side of the barn where he was putting in a new set of spark plugs and replacing a leaky radiator hose. He largely left work assignments to Hank; except on this day he had told his foreman that he didn't want his boys to be working in the same group as the ex-cons.

I was relieved when Hank told me I didn't have to work with Dalton and McCoy either and that I could ride with him in his pickup to string up the carcasses of the dead coyotes, a common practice among ranchers. We were also going to drop off some salt lick and bales of hay in the feeding stalls in the East pasture.

It had been difficult to be around the two ex-cons in recent days; especially after Dalton's confrontation with Dean following the fight at the Gibson social.

Dalton didn't like the fact that we had helped stir up the crowd against him while he was beating up on Henrihan. His comments about our conduct that evening didn't set well with us either.

Whenever we were outside the view of the other ranch hands, Dalton would always try to intimidate us by shadow boxing. He would shuffle around, bobbing and weaving and feinting left jabs toward our chins as if he was going to knock us down.

On a recent day, he told Bob and Jimmy that if he ever got Dean inside or outside the ring he'd "knock his block off." Bob responded by saying that his brother had met far tougher foes than him and had emerged the victor. Then as a reminder, Bob gave Dalton a little jab of his own by saying:

"Just make sure you keep your guard up, Jake, up or he'll flatten you like a pancake."

Jimmy and I howled with laughter over that remark. Dalton snorted in derision. Then McCoy's remark reminded us how cruel and mean spirited those ex-cons could be:

"You little smart asses won't be laughin' when Jake takes your brother down. Jake'll beat him to a pulp if they ever get in the ring together—It'll be worse than the Henrihan fight."

That remark stung us into silence and we just walked away from the two sneering renegades. We had hardly spoken to them since. They knew we held them in contempt and it was hard for us to be on friendly terms with them; whether it was in the field or around the ranch house.

When Hank had invited me to ride with him, I noticed Nellie, Jesse's little sheep dog, eyeing us as if wishing she could ride along. I asked Jesse if she could go with us.

Before he could answer, Nellie had come over and put her two front paws on the running board of Hank's pickup truck, waiting for someone to give her a boost. I lifted her up and gave her a big hug as we climbed into the cab alongside Hank. She promptly climbed onto my lap and stuck her nose out the window so she could feel the wind against her nose and nostrils.

She was in dog heaven! Hank just shook his head and smiled in approval.

As we drove toward the East pasture, I wondered if it would be a good idea to ask Hank a few questions that had popped into my mind after Bob, Jimmy and myself had overheard Dalton and McCoy talking late at night in the bunkhouse. I reminded myself to do it in a way so that he wouldn't think I was being nosy; especially if I inquired about Dalton and McCoy and their sordid pasts. I started off with easy questions.

"How come you invited me to ride along with you, Hank?"

"Your Aunt Vera said you needed to stay out of the sun as much as possible. It's gonna' be well over a hundred degrees today—she said your face needs to heal more; so ridin' around in the truck will shield you from the sun's rays."

"So, it was Aunt Vera's idea instead of yours?"

"Yeah."

"At least you didn't put me with Dalton and McCoy. I hate working with those guys. They give me the creeps and I wish they would go away—for good."

"We need all the help we can muster up around here, Danny. They're stayin' for now."

"How come they go into town almost every night?" I asked Hank.

"What they do after work is none of my business."

Hank's terse answers to my questions indicated he had other things on his mind. By now, we had reached the feeding stalls in the East pasture. He retrieved two large, curved hooks from his pickup and sunk them into the ends of each bale of hay so he could carry them to the feeding stalls.

He clipped the wires off each bale, then he handed me a pitch fork so I could spread the hay all along the stalls while he strung up the hides of the two dead coyotes on a nearby fence. Nellie sniffed the skins a time or two and even growled at them before scampering back to where I was throwing hay around.

* * * *

We would make three more trips to the feeding stalls; each time we would load up Hank's truck with bales of hay from a huge haystack near the barn and distribute them to the feeding stalls in the East and South pastures. Uncle Jesse's cattle and sheep were always well fed. Hank saw to that. On the final trip of the day, I knew it would be my last chance to ask Hank some more questions that were troubling me.

"I hear the guys talking all the time about a saloon called the Diamond Bar. Is it in Fallon?"

"Yeah—on South Main street," he replied. I was getting more bold with my questions.

"The way the guys talk all the time, it must be a pretty wild place with lots of girls."

"It is—and there are."

"Do you ever go there?" I asked Hank

"Sometimes."

"Who's the owner?"

"Fellow named Johnny Hayden."

"Does he really have diamonds embedded in the bar like everyone says he does?" I inquired.

"He sure does—a few people have got themselves shot tryin' to pry them out," Hank replied.

I was impressed. Hank was growing weary of my chatter, but I wasn't through yet.

"Wow!" I exclaimed, "what's to keep people from stealing those diamonds?"

"The bar top has heavy coats of shellac and Rusty Trudeau and Marco Forlani guard 'em like a bear motherin' her cubs. Must be 17 or 18 of them sparklers buried in that bar. Nobody knows for sure, but I've heard people guessin' that bar's worth over $100,000."

With that explanation, Hank cut me off and told me he wasn't answering any more questions. I'd gotten what I wanted to out of him, anyway, and was surprised to hear Hank reveal two now familiar names—Rusty Trudeau and Marco Forlani—that Dalton and McCoy had mentioned when we had eavesdroped on them a couple of nights ago.

Without appearing overly excited, I asked Hank one more important question:

"Who's Trudeau and Forlani?"

"Rusty Trudeau manages the Diamond Bar for Hayden and Marco Forlani is the head bartender there. They're both nice guys."

*   *   *   *

When we had eavesdroped on Dalton and McCoy, we heard them mention that they believed Forlani was somehow involved in the killing of Dalton's sister, Cheryl. Now I knew for sure that he was involved.

I couldn't contain my excitement over hearing Forlani's name. I didn't dare ask Hank if he knew anything about the mysterious well that we heard Dalton and McCoy talking about in the bunkhouse.

"Wait 'til I tell Bob and Jimmy about that," I thought to myself as Hank drove me back to the ranch house at day's end with Nellie sitting on my lap.

When I told them about my conversation with Hank, they were both amazed at what I had found out about Jake Dalton and Bernie McCoy, the Diamond Bar saloon and Marco Forlani, the man who apparently was involved in the murder of Jake Dalton's sister, Cheryl.

We vowed to listen in on Dalton and McCoy again at the first opportunity.

Chapter 26

Following supper, Dalton and McCoy again made a quick departure. No thanks were given to Aunt Vera and Tess for the nice supper they had fixed for them and the other ranch hands nor did they indicate where they were going. We saw them simply nod at each; indicating that it was time to leave. Their furtive movements and lack of eye contact led to speculation among the other hands that they were up to no good.

The ex-cons were on a mission of mayhem. Having visited the caretaker at the cemetery and coercing him into telling them what he knew about Cheryl's death, they had become convinced they were closing in on Cheryl's killer and they weren't going to let him get away with it.

It was nearing payback time. The caretaker had fingered Marco Forlani, the head bartender at the Diamond Bar saloon, as the person who knew more about the details of Cheryl's death than he had originally divulged. Now, they were determined to wring the truth out of him.

As they drove toward Fallon in McCoy's old '34 Chevy, Dalton's mood turned ugly as he thought about the run around Forlani had given them earlier.

"That little bastard was lying through his teeth when he shuffled us off to the ol' man at the cemetery," Dalton complained.

"Forlani figured the digger's memory had become so dim by now that he wouldn't remember what had happened last year let alone five years ago when he buried my sis. I know Forlani's been lyin' to us, so tonight we're finally gonna' get the truth out of him. He'll either 'fess up or he's goin' in the well."

McCoy sensed that his pal was getting overly anxious to confront Forlani and if they weren't careful, their plan would not only be foiled but they could end up back in prison on a battery or kidnap charge.

"Now, look Jake, we've gotta' be careful how we carry this out. So what d'ya have in mind?"

"If Forlani's the guy, I'm gonna bust his chops. If he puts it on someone else, I wanna' know the guy's name so we can go after him.

"One way to get Forlani to squeal and tell us the truth, is to tie him up and dangle him in the well for awhile. That'll refresh his memory real quick.

"If he keeps lyin' to us, then I'll just cut the rope and get rid of him of him for good. Nobody will ever know what happened to him 'cause they'll have no body to prove their case." McCoy had some thoughts of his own.

"Okay, but the first thing we need to do is to find out if Forlani's workin' tonight. Ya' know he usually works the swing shift during the week so when we get into town we can drive behind the saloon and see if his car's there. He owns a '36 LaSalle convertible. If he's workin' the swing shift, we'll nail him when he gets off.

"We've gotta' be careful, too. We don't wanna' be hangin' around Fallon in broad daylight. If we're gonna snatch Forlani and make him sing, it's gotta' be done quiet-like and after dark when there's no one around to see us. Ya' know what I mean?"

Dalton agreed and pointed out that a couple of hours of daylight was still left on the clock.

"We sure don't wanna' be seen drivin' around town before the sun goes down," he told McCoy. "Another thing we need is a good, solid alibi."

The ex-cons knew if Forlani was to suddenly disappear, they would be the prime suspects since they had been seen talking to him in the Diamond Bar several times. McCoy had a solution and a good alibi.

"Tell you what, pards, a friend of mine, Rudy Claskey, is a bartender over at the Silver Dollar saloon in Silver Springs. He'll vouch for our presence there if we need him too. "We can run over there, hit a couple of joints n' hang out at Rudy's place until after dark.

Silver Springs was a few miles West of Fallon and after visiting with Claskey and chasing down several beers and a couple of boilermakers, the ex-cons boldly plotted their move on Forlani as they drove back to Fallon.

They both agreed that the best place to confront him was at the back of the Diamond Bar saloon after he had gotten off work. They lay in wait for him after parking their car where it couldn't be seen.

Forlani's shift ended at 9:00 p.m. and shortly thereafter, he came out the back door and walked toward his car. Just as he reached it, Dalton and McCoy lunged at him from out of the darkening shadows; pinning him over the hood of the car.

Before Forlani could shout, or call attention to his plight, Dalton shoved his head violently downward so he couldn't move as McCoy grabbed his arms and twisted them up behind his back where he tightly bound them with twine. He then tied Forlani's feet together and stood him up upright so he could see who was assaulting him.

The terrified bartender cringed when he saw Dalton leering in his face once again. Shaking with fear, he told the ex-cons that he wasn't the person they were looking for.

"You little bastard, it's payback time," Jake hissed through clinched teeth. "You better come clean this time n' quit givin' us the run around about who killed my sis, or you're dead meat." Forlani was shaking with fear and could barely utter an answer.

"Honest to God, Jake, I swear I've told you everything I know. Please don't hurt me."

Both Dalton and McCoy knew Forlani was lying so they put a gag in his mouth, tossed him in the trunk of McCoy's car and sped away from the Diamond Bar as darkness settled in about them. They hoped no one had seen them come or go.

* * * *

When they arrived at Dalton's old farm house, they dragged Forlani from out of the trunk of the car and into the backyard where they propped him against the broken down bench that partially encircled the well. The glare of the car's headlights cast eerie shadows around the well site and an old nearby shed.

Dalton removed the gag from Forlani's mouth and threatened him with bodily harm:

"You either come clean about who killed my sister, Cheryl, or you're goin' in the well." Forlani pleaded innocent.

"You're talking to the wrong guy, fellas. I'm not the one who killed your sister. I hardly knew her." Dalton and McCoy knew better.

"If you didn't know her, why would the ol' digger out at the cemetery put the rap on you then?" McCoy asked. Forlani tried to explain.

"I don't know, he must have a bad memory, or got me confused with somebody else."

"You're protectin' someone else," growled Dalton. "Let's see how much you can remember after we dump you in the well."

With that, they lifted the struggling bartender atop the stoop, tied two strands of rope around his feet and lowered him down into the darkened pit while securing the ends of the rope to the steel rungs that led down into the well.

Forlani yelled and pleaded for Dalton and McCoy to stop the torture and to lift him out, but the ex-cons seemed to be enjoying his plight and the sadistic nature of their actions.

His cries of "get me out, get me out," kept echoing up from the depths of the well, shattering the silence around them.

McCoy grabbed a flashlight from his car and sent the beam shining down to where the bartender was dangling headfirst in the darkened shaft. As he flashed it into the interior of the well, Dalton slipped his big Bowie knife from the sheaf on the inside of his right boot leg and shouted down to his stricken victim as the flashlight caught a glint of the shining blade:

"You see this, Forlani. I'm gonna' cut you loose in a minute. You've got one last chance to come clean or you're gonna' drown like a rat."

With that Dalton swiped across first strand of rope that was holding the bartender. Now, only one strand of rope was all that was keeping Forlani from plunging into oblivion. Bound hand and foot and hanging precariously by that single strand of rope, Forlani finally realized that Dalton was about to cut him loose. An anguished cry came up from the well.

"Okay, Jake; Okay. I'll tell you what you wanna' know. I'm a dead man either way, so get me outta' here right now."

Dalton looked at McCoy in dim light coming from the car's headlamps and smiled a wicked grin.

"See what a little persuasion will do, pards." McCoy knew Jake had serious intentions of cutting the rope so he didn't comment. He was relieved that it didn't happen and wanted to hear Forlani's confession as quickly as possible so he began lifting and tugging upon the single strand of rope that had suspended Forlani head first in the well. After they hoisted the terror-stricken bartender onto the bench outside the well, Dalton again started probing Forlani with his knife with just enough force to hurt him.

"Alright, Forlani, start singin'. Who really did my sister in? And you'd better be tellin' us the truth this time or we'll dump you in the well without a rope to hold you up." Forlani was suddenly eager to talk.

"Alright, Jake, I'll tell you. The fella who did the dirty work is a guy name Morelli—Gino Morelli."

"Where's he live or work and what's he look like," McCoy growled.

"Over in Reno. He's a blackjack dealer in Harrah's casino. You can't miss him—he's kind of tall and has a black, pencil-thin mustache."

"Why'd he kill my sister?" Dalton asked.

"He was paid to do it. Talk on the street was Cheryl stepped out on her man—broke his trust. He didn't like it so he hired a hit man to take her out."

"Who's the bastard that ordered the hit?" Dalton growled.

Forlani sighed and slumped over, wishing this terrible moment would go away without having to reveal anything more. When he hesitated, Dalton jabbed him with the point of his knife; drawing blood from the wound in his neck and a howl of pain from Forlani.

"It was my boss, Johnny Hayden. He's the one who had her killed. All I did was make the burial arrangements after Gino Morelli snuffed her."

Dalton and McCoy were stunned. They couldn't believe their long time buddy and owner of the Diamond Bar was behind the killing of Dalton's sister.

McCoy shook his head in amazement.

"Holy hell, why would Johnny do a thing like that?" he asked.

Dalton was enraged.

"I don't have a clue, but he's gonna pay for it and so will his henchman in Reno. I feel like goin' back to the Diamond Bar and killin' Johnny right now." McCoy urged patience.

"Calm down, pards, we gotta' take care of business here before we do anything that drastic."

* * * *

His ordeal over, Forlani began to struggle after being bound for so long.

"How about untying me now," he pleaded. "I've told you guys everything I know about your sis's death—I'd like to go home now." McCoy grabbed the Forlani by the shoulder and shoved him back against the well.

"Hold on, pal, you haven't told us all we need to know so we're not gonna untie you 'til you do."

Dalton and McCoy then began probing and prodding Forlani for more details of Cheryl's death. They learned that after Johnny Hayden had gone to Las Vegas, he had enticed Cheryl down there. She became his mistress and he showered her with money, gifts and clothes that she'd only dreamed about before.

After about two years of living in the lap of luxury, she tired of the glitz and glamour of Las Vegas and wanted to return to Fallon. Hayden wouldn't let her and from thereafter, he kept her a virtual prisoner in his home.

As Hayden broadened his business interests, he began spending less time with Cheryl and more time with the show girls he had met on The Strip in Las Vegas, Forlani revealed. Cheryl was an extremely attractive young woman and had made her living on the street before moving in with Hayden, but she no longer wanted to be a kept woman, so she started up an escort service in North Las Vegas. Hayden found out about it and beat her severely; telling her she was "his woman" and no one had better ever lay a hand on her in the future or she would be sorry.

Forlani told Dalton his sister was a "strong minded gal" and wasn't about to bend to Hayden's will. Then the bartender revealed that Hayden had caught Cheryl in bed with another man one night.

"That was it as far as Johnny was concerned," Forlani said. "He had a guy working for him by the name of Gino Morelli. Johnny had brought him down from Reno to be his bodyguard and all around enforcer at a strip club and betting parlor he operated in Las Vegas.

"He ordered Morelli to get rid of Cheryl, so Morelli strangled her and made it look like she had died from natural causes. He had her embalmed at a mortuary in North Las Vegas and then had her body shipped up to Fallon where I arranged to have her buried next to her parents in the Fallon cemetery. I slipped the caretaker there a hundred dollar bill for stayin' late and diggin' the grave and buryin' her late at night."

Now satisfied that Forlani had spilled his guts, Dalton and McCoy untied him and drove him back to the Diamond Bar saloon. On the way, Dalton asked Forlani where he was from and the little bartender said: "Newark, New Jersey."

"If I was in your shoes, I'd get my ass back there as quick as possible if you value your health at all."

Forlani knew his life would be in danger now that he divulged details about the killing of Dalton's sister, but, his choices were extremely limited. He could have taken the hit himself; thereby protecting the real killers—his long time boss, Johnny Hayden, and his henchman, Gino Morelli—and lose his life in doing so, or he could squeal under duress to protect himself. He had wisely chosen to squeal.

The caretaker at the cemetery had also fingered Forlani as an accomplice, so either way, his life had been placed in jeopardy. Going in the well at the hands of two mean-spirited ex-cons was terrifying to contemplate and he knew he would be a dead man walking the minute Hayden found out that he had spilled the beans about Cheryl's death.

*　　　　*　　　　*　　　　*

When they dropped Forlani off behind the Diamond Bar saloon, it would be the last time Dalton and McCoy would ever see the little Italian bartender. It was nearly dawn by the time they got back to the Banfield ranch. Ol' Red had just made his first wakeup call and was strutting around the barnyard in his usual cocky, jerk stepping manner.

As McCoy and Dalton walked toward the bunkhouse from their car, Dalton spied the big rooster directly in front of him, so he took a running step toward the cocky bird. Ol' Red tried to flee, but Dalton's booted toe smashed into the rooster's breast; sending him tumbling and fluttering through the air and crashing hard against the outer wall of the milking barn.

Ol' Red flopped his wings helplessly for a few times after he dropped to the ground. Then he lay still, his breast crushed from Dalton's brutal kick. The Banfield's magnificent, red-feathered rooster had just crowed his last wakeup call.

Dalton and McCoy slunk into the bunk house and began preparing for another day's work as we began stirring in our beds. No one would ever know how Ol' Red died, except those two renegades and they would only smirk when inquiries were made that morning about the rooster's sudden demise.

Chapter 27

When aunt Vera put the word out that she was opposed to having boxing as the finale to her and Uncle Jesse's upcoming Summer social, the womenfolk around the valley were all for it, but the men vetoed the idea.

Boxing at the Summer socials was a tradition and it had been going on long before the Banfields came into the valley. The menfolk weren't about to forego the pleasure and excitement of watching their ranch hands belt each other around simply because the women didn't like such goings-on. Still, Vera wanted everyone to know how she and Tess felt about the inter-mixing of fun with boxing at the Summer get togethers.

"That kind of activity spoils a perfectly good afternoon of socializing," Vera contended.

It was supper time on Monday evening and she was venting her feelings to a less than sympathetic, but captive audience. She realized her and Tess were clearly out-numbered on this issue, but that didn't stop her from chastising the menfolk for inciting violence when the evening should be devoted to music and light hearted chatter.

She had a right to be concerned. The Banfields' were not only going to be hosting the August social in less than two weeks, but the buzz around the valley was that Dean wasn't going to accept Jake Dalton's challenge because of his wife's strong objections.

Dean had been strangely quiet about the Big Fight in deference to Tess. She and Vera were upset with Bob, Jimmy and myself for telling everyone within earshot at the Gibson social that Dean was not only a skilled boxer but he was the Intermountain AAU Light-Heavyweight Champion. Both Tess and Vera had scolded us for spreading the word about Dean's boxing skills and asked us to stop doing that.

Despite that scolding, we found it difficult to control our excitement when talking to the ranch hands about the fight. As far as we were concerned it would be a classic confrontation. Good going against the evil force. Triumph over tragedy in the human perspective.

We believed Dean could whip Dalton's butt if they ever got in the ring together, but everyone around the Banfield ranch doubted that the match would ever take place.

We all knew Tess's position on this matter. Even though the heralded bout had begun to take on a life all of its own, she would squelch all talk of it happening whenever she heard us talking about it. But in his laid back manner, Dean would simply smile, shrug his shoulders and say nothing when he was asked if he felt the fight was going to take place. He didn't want to offend his mother or his wife, so he kept his innermost thoughts to himself. He held faint hope that Tess and Aunt Vera would relent and give their blessing to such a distasteful event.

Being called out by Dalton and not immediately responding to that challenge had been eating away at Dean for days. Without knowing Dean's background as an accomplished boxer, Dalton had made the mistake of belittling Dean after the ex-con had administered a severe beating to Rich Henrihan, Jesse's affable Irishman.

Dean had refereed that bout and he had to restrain Dalton after the fight was over when the Dalton insisted on punishing Henrihan even more than he had during their three round encounter. Dalton had taken exception to Dean's decision to stop the fight, but everyone knew Henrihan was in no condition to continue; except Dalton himself.

Dalton had told Dean to stand aside so that he could finish off Henrihan and if he didn't, he would take Dean out, too. Dean not only called his bluff, but he told Dalton not to let anything but fear stop him. The rebuff stopped the ex-con dead in his tracks. He wasn't used to being challenged like that.

That's when the war of words between Dean and Dalton heated up. Dean had coolly deflected Dalton's tirade to fight him even though he would have dearly loved to take on the ex-con. They had glared at each other in a stare down and ringsiders thought a fight was going to breakout between the two antagonists. It was a tense moment; then Dean had grabbed Dalton, shoved him into his own corner and pinned his arms to his sides with the help of McCoy.

It grated on Dean that he didn't accept Dalton's challenge right then and there, but he didn't want to incur the wrath of Tess who was standing nearby with her hands on her hips and a stern look on her face as if to say: Don't even think about it!

Dean knew it was inevitable that he would eventually clash with Dalton; inside or outside of the ring, but the when and where part of the puzzle was missing at the moment.

* * * *

Knowing there was now bad blood between Dalton and Dean, Jesse's foreman, Hank Johnson, was careful not to put the two of them on the same work crew. The closest they came to being together was at chow time; and even then they sat on the opposite ends of the table.

The other ranch hands weren't so reluctant to discuss what they thought could be the premier boxing match of the Summer. They talked of that possible matchup all the time; in the field, in the milking barn and after work.

They wondered if it would actually happen given Tess's strong objections and Dean's desire to keep peace in the Banfield family, but the fight would be held if Bob, Jimmy and myself had anything to do with it.

We had already been scolded for acting up at the Gibson social and we would really be in trouble with Vera and Tess if they knew how much we were touting the match behind their backs.

Although our audience was limited, our enthusiasm certainly wasn't. Jesse's crew initially thought Bob and Jimmy's exuberance was tinged with sibling pride, but the more they questioned them about Dean's boxing skills and his record, the more they swung over to our side. I would put my two cents worth in every time I got a chance, too, but I had a feeling most of the ranch hands thought I was just trying to stir up trouble. Still, they also began spreading the word in and around Fallon that a classic boxing match was in the works. They talked about it among themselves, with their friends in the valley and even when they were drinking with other ranch hands in the Diamond Bar where they were told by Rusty Trudeau, Johnny Hayden's saloon manager, that some big money would be in the purse if Dean and Dalton were to mix it up at the Banfield social.

Some of the old timers around Fallon remembered how handy Jake Dalton was with his fists and they passed the word that they would be betting on the ex-con if he stepped into the ring with Dean.

On the other hand, Dean was unknown to most everyone except the Banfield's and myself. The betting line was beginning to look like it would be the city slickers against the country folks with a lot more money up for grabs than had been offered in any previous boxing social. Johnny Hayden would see to that.

Early one evening, after Dalton and McCoy had departed for Fallon, some of the ranch hands were lounging outside the bunkhouse; smoking and joking around. Henrihan was picking on his guitar and humming an Irish tune that only he was familiar with at the moment.

Another ranch hand was trying to stay in tune with the Irishman as he blew softly on his harmonica. We were nearby, tossing a beat up old softball around while trying to overhear what the ranch hands were saying. The talk was whether or not Dean could beat Dalton.

Henrihan put aside his guitar momentarily and offered his opinion on the possible outcome of the fight. He had been knocked almost senseless by Dalton at the Gibson social, but he was alert and close enough to see the look on Dean's face when Dalton got belligerent after the fight.

"I saw something in Dean's eyes when Jake called him out that revealed the character of the man," Henrihan informed his coworkers.

"That look told me for sure that Dean's not afraid of Dalton. Funny thing, Dalton seemed to know it, too, and that's what irritated him. He thought he could intimidate Dean by calling him out, but Dean stood his ground and challenged Jake right back."

"You think Dean's that good, eh?" one of the ranch hands asked Henrihan. "We'd put a few bucks on him if we knew he had a chance against Dalton."

"If Dalton fights fair and square, Dean has a good chance of beating him," Henrihan responded. "I've never seen Dean fight before, so I don't know how good he really is in the ring. I heard Hank and the boss braggin' on him the other day, so he must be pretty handy with his dukes.

"Hank told me he'd seen Dean box last year in Salt Lake City and he came away impressed with his boxing style. He said Dean didn't dance around a lot like some fighters do. Figured it's a waste of energy to do that, I guess. Instead, he said, Dean's the type of boxer that just keeps shufflin' forward; bobbin' and weavin,' feintin' 'n jabbin.' Kinda' like Joe Louis does. Then he unloads his right hand that's got dynamite in it."

Upon hearing those opinions of Dean, Jesse just smiled. He knew his older son could even be better if Tess would let him box more. Then he confirmed Hank's opinion of Dean's prowess as a boxer while offering some startling observations of his own; especially his prediction of Dean's highly competitive nature and the outcome of the fight if it was to come about.

"If Tess will give in and let Dean fight, it wouldn't surprise me to see Dalton go down before the third round's over."

"The problem is, Dean get's a bit too serious when he's really boxing to win. He beguiles his opponents into believing he's not an aggressive boxer because he's a shuffler, not a dancer, in the ring.

"Dean will fool around and be gentle with you when nothing's on the line, but when something's at stake, he shows no mercy until the other guy is flat on his back. I think that's the way he'll be if Tess lets him get in the ring with Dalton."

That's all the ranch hands needed to know. They were going to put their money on Dean if he laced on the gloves with Dalton at the upcoming August social.

Chapter 28

Jake Dalton and Bernie McCoy's trips away from the ranch were becoming more frequent now. The other workers dismissed their nightly wanderings as a desire to catch up on their social life at the infamous Diamond Bar saloon and other hangouts around Fallon.

We knew better based on what we had overheard them saying while we were hiding behind the bunkhouse. Their intense, almost nightly, quest to find out who had killed Jake's sister, Cheryl, had paid off and we were the only ones who knew about it at the moment. They were also robbing people so they could sustain their lifestyle of drinking and gambling.

We had also found out some other things about the ex-cons while secretly listening in on their bunkhouse conversations, but we weren't about to disclose what we knew; at least not yet. We had heard them talk about throwing people in a mysterious well and how a grave digger at the local cemetery claimed a bartender in the Diamond Bar saloon called Forlani knew more than he was telling the ex-cons about the death of Jake's sister.

Then when Dalton and McCoy kidnapped Forlani and threatened his life by dangling him head first in a well, he finally came clean and told them a blackjack dealer named Gino Morelli was the hit man who had killed Dalton's sister.

The real bombshell that Forlani dropped on Dalton and McCoy came the night when he told them that the person behind the killing of Dalton's sister was none other than their old buddy, Johnny Hayden. The ex-cons were shocked upon hearing that disclosure. Vengeance was now on their minds, but we didn't know how serious that quest was until later on in the evening.

I hadn't forgotten the dirty trick the two renegades had pulled on me a couple of weeks earlier when they intentionally spooked the horses while I was riding atop a hay wagon. I not only lost a wagon load of hay when the horses ran back to the barn, but Jesse had blamed me for not controlling my team when, in fact, Dalton and McCoy were to blame.

That fiasco not only embarrassed and humiliated me, but I also received a tongue lashing from Jesse. I had told Bob and Jimmy at the time that I would find a way to get even with them. Tonight, I thought, would be a good time to do it.

* * * *

After Dalton and McCoy had left the ranch following the evening chores, I told Bob and Jimmy what I intended to do. We waited until after dark and then we snuck over to the corner of the bunkhouse where their room was located.

With a piece of string in my hand, I tied one end to a stick that was holding up the window and ran the other end around the corner of the bunkhouse where I could give it a quick jerk when Dalton hung his arm out of the window while taking a final smoke or two before retiring. That would put a little hurt on him, I believed, for what he and McCoy had done to me.

We then returned to the ranch house to wait for Dalton and McCoy to return. It was nearly midnight when they arrived at the bunkhouse. All the lights were out and everyone in the ranch house was asleep, except Bob, Jimmy and myself.

We crept quietly across the barn yard to the corner of the bunkhouse where we waited for the light to come on in their room. If they were in a talking mood, we wanted to find out if they had been able to determine who had killed Dalton's sister and what they were going to do about it.

When the dim light in their room came on, we waited breathlessly to see if Dalton could see the tiny strand of string I had attached to the bottom of the stick that was holding the window up. If he could, we knew we would incur his wrath the next day, but in his near drunken stupor, it appeared that he didn't have a clue what was about to happen to him.

He would be hard pressed to see the string anyway since the window sill curved downward and it was pitch black outside. McCoy was sitting on his bed and, as usual, Dalton was dangling his arm and hand out the window so he could shake off the ashes from the cigarette he was holding. We scrunched down and listened to what they were saying.

Sipping on bottles of warm beer, we heard them plotting their next move and gloating over how successful their intimidation tactics had been in finding out who had killed Dalton's sister, Cheryl.

"Things are gonna' be comin' to a head pretty quick now that we've found out who took my sis' out," said Dalton.

We were startled to hear that statement and we started to whisper back and forth until Bob shushed us to be quiet so he could hear what they were saying to each other. Dalton was gloating over their success and how quickly they were able to find out who killed his sister.

"We've done some pretty good detective work, ol' bud, now it's payback time. It just goes to show you what a little bit of persuasion can do to get a feller to spill his guts."

McCoy laughed at Dalton's comments and offered his own assessment of their activities.

"That ol' digger couldn't remember anything until you told him we'd bury him alive if he didn't come clean. Then when he fingered Forlani again, I knew we were gettin' close to findin' out who killed Cheryl." Dalton agreed.

"Yeah, Forlani thought we'd just go away and not bother him anymore, but when we put him in the well and gave him time to think about his future, he started to sing." McCoy had some additional thoughts.

"Getting Forlani to put the blame on that Morelli guy was a big break for us, but the real shocker was findin' out that our ol' buddy, Johnny Hayden, was behind the whole scheme. I can't believe he'd do Cheryl in just because she stepped out on him."

"Man, I can't either. It was a real surprise to find that out," said Dalton in bitter disbelief. "That connivin' son of a bitch is gonna' get his due if it's the last thing I ever do.

"As for that Morelli guy, we'll take him down first, then we'll go after Johnny." We'll probably have to bail out of here after that…jump probation; maybe go to Canada and get us new identities." Dalton indicated he knew an ex-prison mate from Canada who could help them.

"I know a feller who can do that for us. He got out a couple of years ahead of me after serving time for forgery. He's now hangin' out in Vancouver. Does nice work; especially with passports, driver's licenses and social security numbers."

McCoy was surprised to hear that Dalton was even thinking about leaving the country.

"I dunno' about that move—there must be a lot of places we can hide out without goin' to Canada. Dalton was quick to respond.

"Maybe so, but that's a damn good safe haven as far as I'm concerned. McCoy also wondered about Johnny Hayden.

"What're we gonna' do with Johnny?" McCoy asked. Jake didn't have an answer to that question at the moment.

"I dunno. That's a tough problem to figure out right now, but we're gonna' take care of him just as soon as I can figure out a way to do it without gettin' caught. I don't think we should do anything right now."

"Why not?" questioned McCoy. Dalton was becoming irritated.

"Remember, Johnny's stirrin' everybody up in town about the fight I'm supposed to be havin' in a couple of weeks with that Banfield guy—just back off for a while 'cause I could make some pretty good money out of that fight." McCoy realized the need for patience.

"I guess you're right. Johnny's got a lot of confidence in you. He'll throw another thousand bucks into the pot if you end up fightin' Banfield." Dalton relished the thought.

"That tickles the hell out of me; knowin' that bastard's gonna' contribute to my welfare when I'm plannin' to do him in. If the fight comes off, we can pick up some easy travelin' money."

We were shocked and fascinated by the conversation going on between the two ex-cons. We then heard Dalton tell McCoy how confident he was of taking on Dean and what he thought of him if the two met in the ring.

"When we were in the Diamond Bar the other night, Rusty Trudeau asked me if it was a sure thing, 'cause a lot of his customers were gonna bet on me. I told him he could count on it if the fight actually comes off. I don't think it will 'cause the Banfields won't let Dean fight. The guy's a chicken-livered pussy cat and even if he does fight me, I'll have him down and out before the first round ends."

"How 'ya gonna' do that?" McCoy asked.

"I'll give him my ol' bolo punch to the groin. Learned that in the slammer. Then when he's doubled over, I'll snap his head back with a couple of quick upper cuts and smash him to the ground with a hard right hand to the side of his jaw. He'll be out before he hits the ground."

Bob was furious when he heard Dalton's cocky boast and description of his brother.

"Wait 'til I tell Dean what Dalton thinks of him! He'll probably go after that guy before the fight even starts," he whispered to us.

"Those guys are bad news—let's get out of here," Jimmy whispered back.

We didn't think we would find out too much more about what those two renegades were going to do, so I decided it was time to pull the string and give Dalton something to howl about for a few days. A quick jerk on the string released the stick and the window came crashing down on Dalton's forearm. We didn't see him withdraw his arm from the fallen window as we had run back to the darkened ranch house and hid in our bedroom.

Through our open window, we could see Dalton's shadowy figure prowling outside the bunkhouse. He had turned the porch light on and was holding his arm and cursing in pain as he tried to figure out if it was an accident or someone's dirty trick. We laughed and climbed into bed.

As I lay cowering under the covers, I knew that I had finally gotten even with Jake Dalton for what he'd done to me, but my little game of an eye for an eye and a tooth for a tooth had suddenly turned deadly serious.

Chapter 29

It didn't take Dalton very long to figure out it wasn't an accident that the window had fallen on his arm. At the break of dawn he was again outside his window looking for clues.

He soon found what he was looking for. Lying in the dust at the corner of the bunkhouse was the stick that held his window open and attached to it was a knotted piece of string. He pocketed the string and threw the stick aside; cursing out loud as he tried to figure out who had pulled that trick on him.

He knew the other ranch hands wouldn't dare to do such a thing to him. That left Bob, Jimmy and myself as the prime suspects. In my haste to leave the scene, I had dropped the string holding the stick.

I had thought at the time about trying to retrieve it after running back to the ranch house, but I was afraid that Dalton or McCoy would see me, so I had stayed in the safe haven of our bedroom and listened to Dalton curse for awhile after he had come outside to look around.

We had grown accustomed to Ol' Red's shrill wakeup call. His untimely demise a few days ago remained a barnyard mystery, but on this morning, the commotion outside the bunkhouse aroused us.

We hopped out of bed and peeked out the open window. It was Dalton, cursing to no one in particular, as McCoy stood nearby. We could clearly see and hear that Dalton was irritated. Apparently, the falling window had almost broke his left forearm and it was painful every time he moved his wrist or hand too quickly. As soon as he had seen the stick and string lying on the ground he knew who his principal antagonist was and he vented his feelings to McCoy about it.

"The Collins kid was behind that little stunt last night. He's been mad at us ever since we stampeded his team of horses when we were pitchin' hay a while back." McCoy agreed.

"You're probably right, Jake. He and those Banfield boys are gettin' too damn sassy for their own good. If they wanna' play games with us, we can show 'em a trick or two of our own that'll make 'em think twice about foolin' with us again."

Dalton nodded in agreement. Holding the string in front of him, he formed it in the shape of a hangman's noose and as he dangled it in the air, he indicated to McCoy how he intended to give the string back to me.

"I'm gonna' put this around that kid's neck and give it a good jerk. That ought to scare hell out of him."

I was already scared at what I had done. Now, I was terrified after hearing Dalton say that.

* * * *

During breakfast, we didn't dare to glance at Jake or Bernie sitting at the end of the table; fearing we would give ourselves away. They were sullen as usual and didn't even greet the other ranch hands when they sat down to eat.

We desperately wanted to tell everyone what we had overheard the night before, but how and when we would do it worried us; especially since they had threatened us before.

There was a lot at stake here; a demanding work week coming up, the season-ending social this Saturday and the big sheep drive to the North ranch the following Tuesday. We had to think of our own safety as well and time was running short. We also didn't want to spoil Aunt Vera and Uncle Jesse's upcoming social event.

The topic at the table was what was being planned for that day. Strangely, boxing wasn't even mentioned; probably because Vera and Tess were present and the fact that the matches probably wouldn't be held anyway. The ranch hands had been telling us all along that no one wanted to mix it up with Jake

Dalton. They were hoping Dean would toss his hat in the ring, but knowing Tess's feelings, and Vera's, too, they didn't believe it would happen.

Vera told the ranch hands that she and Tess and the other womenfolk around the valley were going to prepare a huge Western style barbecue for the season-ending Summer social.

"You men need to pitch in and help us get the place ready. We'll take care of preparing the food if you will tidy up the outside the rest of the week," she said.

"What are you going to fix, mom," Bob asked.

"I've got four large hams in the smokehouse that we are going to cook. Jesse and Dean are also going to roast a pig and the other wives are going to prepare a delicious potluck…corn on the cob, beans, vegetables and salads and—oh!—I almost forgot; Tess's going to fix two types of potatoes—mashed and scalloped."

As Vera said that, she looked at me and Jimmy like we were her anointed potato peelers and mashers.

"Hear we go again," I thought, upon hearing spuds mentioned. Jimmy just groaned and shook his head.

"Geez, mom, you're not going to make us peel potatoes again are you?"

Sure enough, she assigned Jimmy and me to the potato brigade. That assignment, Aunt Vera said, would start on Friday so there would be enough peeled, cooked and mashed by Saturday noon.

✷ ✷ ✷ ✷

Hank Johnson had already issued his orders for the day and with breakfast over, Uncle Jesse said he had some chores for us to do around the ranch house to get ready for the big event. Beckoning us outside, he gave us instructions that would take us the rest of the week to complete.

"I want you boys to clean up the yard and pull the weeds around the house. Make sure the machinery is out of sight—put it all behind the barn—and paint the front gate. It's been needing it ever since we moved here.

"Later on in the week, you boys can help me and Dean set up the picnic tables and chairs over there."

He nodded and pointed in the direction of a large shaded area in front of the ranch house where some big Cottonwood and Poplar trees stood. Then with a twinkle in his eye and a smile on his face, he pointed to an area just the North of the bunkhouse.

"That's where we'll set up the ring in case we hold the boxing matches, so make sure you clean that area up real good." That statement totally surprised us.

"Does your dad know something we don't know?" I asked Bob and Jimmy. They both shook their heads while wondering the same thing.

We were having anxiety attacks about what we knew and hadn't disclosed and what Uncle Jesse, Dean and Hank didn't know if the boxing matches were held—that Jake Dalton was going to sucker punch Dean at the start of the fight; maybe even maim him so he couldn't continue the fight.

He would then claim the first prize which Uncle Jesse's ranch hands were saying could be at least a couple thousand dollars if Dalton and Dean were to square off in the ring and if Johnny Hayden sweetened the pot as he had been promising his Diamond Bar patrons.

"I know one thing," I told Bob and Jimmy after their dad had departed, "if Tess lets him fight, we gotta' tell Dean so he knows what Dalton's planning to do to him." Jimmy agreed.

"Yeah, he need's to know right away. He's gonna' really be mad when we tell him that Dalton's callin' him a chicken livered pussy cat." Bob told us to calm down and be a little patient.

"C'mon, guys, let's not get so excited. If we tell Dean now, he'll go after Dalton in a hurry and there won't be a boxing match after the social this Saturday. Then Tess will find out and she'll tell mom. Everybody's gonna be in an uproar around here before the party even starts. Let's wait for a day or two and think this thing through before we tell anybody anything."

We reluctantly agreed; then I reminded Bob of Dalton's intention to put a hangman's noose around my neck.

"After I almost busted his arm, he's just waiting to get back at me—mean as he is, there's no telling what he will do if he catches me alone." Bob gave me some reassuring words.

"Don't worry about that, Danny. We'll be working around the ranch house this week. If we stick together, he won't dare to hurt us."

Over the next two days, as we pulled weeds, painted the main gate and tidied up the barnyard, we saw little of the two renegades except when everyone was at the dinner table.

Chapter 30

As Gino Morelli passed out the cards at a blackjack table in Harrah's casino in Reno, he failed to see two sinister characters eying his every move.

Jake Dalton and Bernie McCoy were pretending to be interested spectators at a nearby table, but their eyes were focused on the tall blackjack dealer who shuffled and flipped the cards around the table with the skill and dexterity of a master card shark.

Morelli was good at what he was doing and he fit the exact description that the little Italian bartender, Danny Forlani, had given Dalton and McCoy a few days earlier; that of an impeccably dressed, rather tall, dark haired man with a pencil-thin mustache and a confident manner.

His strikingly handsome face and suave appearance was enhanced by a pony tail that was tightly pulled back behind his head, making him appear that he was more a native American than Italian.

Forlani had fingered Morelli as the hit man who had killed Jake's sister, Cheryl, five years ago and Dalton was determined to make him pay dearly. By now, Dalton was absolutely convinced that Morelli was, in fact, Cheryl's killer and that Johnny Hayden was the one that had ordered the hit. He and McCoy felt the "Well Treatment" could force a confession out of Morelli. Then they would go after Hayden.

After doing some subtle, but thorough, detective work and based on Forlani's description of Morelli, his working hours and where he lived, the ex-cons left the casino in the late evening to stake out Morelli's residence; confident they had identified their man and what course of action they were going to take.

Morelli was completing the swing shift—12 noon to 9:00 p.m—and they wanted to nab him when he returned home from work. He was single and lived in an apartment complex called the Waverly House near the University of Nevada campus.

Jake and Bernie decided to wait him out; reasoning that Harrah's employees typically eat at the hotel buffet line, see a lounge show, or gamble a few bucks at other casinos before coming home.

By the time Morelli pulled into the dimly lit parking lot behind the Waverly House it was nearly midnight. The ex-cons felt confident they could nail him without being seen. As he exited his car, they suddenly emerged out of the shadows of the night and confronted him face to face. Dalton growled a warning.

"Don't do anything stupid or you're a dead man." Morelli found himself staring at the barrel of .38 calibre pistol that was aimed directly at his chest.

McCoy swiftly slipped behind the startled hit man and began prodding him in the ribs with Dalton's big Bowie knife. Believing he was about to become a robbery victim, the quick thinking Morelli momentarily fended off his adversaries by telling them he had some money in his car and if they would just step back he would get it for them. Morelli was no innocent citizen, but a cold-blooded killer, just like his would-be assailants, and he knew all the tricks of his trade.

As he pretended to unlock his car, Morelli purposely dropped his keys to the ground. Feeling he could momentarily distract his adversaries with such a ruse, he bent over and pretended to pick them up. Instead, he reached for a gun that was strapped to his left ankle. Dalton knew instantly what he was attempting to do.

"You'll stay bent over forever if you touch that damn gun," hissed Dalton. "Now, stand up real easy with your hands empty or I'll spill your brains all over this parkin' lot."

Morelli knew he was in deep trouble with those words. While Dalton held a gun on him, McCoy quickly frisked him; retrieving the .38 calibre pistol from a holster on his left ankle and a two shot, pearl handled derringer from inside his vest pocket.

"You're well heeled, pal, an' so are we—so be quiet and keep your mouth shut," McCoy ordered. Morelli stopped resisting.

With that, McCoy quickly bound him hand and foot while Dalton guarded him. Then they tossed him in the back seat of their car and took off for Dalton's old farm house on the Northeast side of Fallon without uttering a word. Morelli finally realized he was in really serious trouble.

"Where ya' takin' me?" Morelli inquired.

"Never you mind," McCoy shouted over his shoulder as he sped down the highway.

"Look fellas, I've got some cash back in my apartment. Let's turn around and I'll give it all to you if you'll let me go.

"You're lyin' Morelli," Jake growled. "You card sharks are like gamblers. You're always busted, so don't give me that crap about havin' some money stashed away in your apartment. You're tryin' to buy time and you ain't got much time left.

"Besides, we're not robbin' you; we're lookin' for some answers and you better damn well give 'em to us or you're dead meat."

"Okay, fellas, what answers are ya' lookin' for? And by the way, who in the hell am I talkin' to, anyway?" Dalton ignored the questions and shot back a query of his own.

"You a friend of Johnny Hayden's?" he inquired of Morelli.

"I know of him, but that's about it."

"He hired you to put a hit on a young lady back in '34. Do you remember what her name was and where she was from?"

"I don't remember that at all. I don't go around takin' people out. I deal cards at Harrah's and nothin' else."

"Quit your lyin' Morelli. We know better," McCoy said, probing for the truth.

Dalton had his pistol pointed right between Morelli's eyes. "We have it on good authority that you put the hit on the girl," he growled at Morelli. "She was my sister. Her name was Cheryl Dalton. Does that refresh your memory?"

"Don't remember that name," Morelli coolly replied.

*   *   *   *

Dalton turned to McCoy and asked how much longer it was to his old ranch house. McCoy looked at his watch and told his sidekick that it would be another 15 or 20 minutes before they arrived at their destination. Dalton knew his question and answer tactics weren't working with Morelli so he took a new tact.

"Maybe we can help you remember, Morelli. We have a well at my old farm house and it's amazing how it refreshes a person's memory when we put them in there. In fact, they have instant recall," Dalton sneered.

McCoy laughed at that description of the well and shouted over his shoulder at Morelli as he drove down the road; telling him he'd better 'fess up and come clean or he was going to a watery grave. Morelli continued to maintain his innocence.

Minutes later they arrived at the farm house. McCoy left the lights of his car on so it would partly illuminate the back yard. Then, they dragged Morelli out of the car and propped him up on the bench that surrounded the well. When Dalton began lifting the boards off the well, Morelli began to panic.

"C'mon, fellas, don't put me in there," he pleaded. Dalton had a quick reply.

"You killed my sister, Cheryl, five years ago and we wanna' know why."

For the first time, Morelli realized that he was talking to Johnny Hayden's old friend—the infamous Jake Dalton who had recently been released from prison. Word had apparently gotten around that Dalton was again a free man, but he never expected to be confronted by his assailant. McCoy also warned Morelli to tell the truth.

"You're goin' in the well if you don't come clean," McCoy said. He then attached a rope to Morelli's legs and hoisted the struggling hit man up on the stoop while tying the other end to the top steel rung inside the well.

Dalton was growing impatient over Morelli's evasive answers. He grabbed him by the front of his shirt and shook him until he was bent backward over the well opening.

"I'm askin' ya' one more time, Morelli, "why did ya' kill my sister."

"I didn't kill your sister—c'mon, fellas, quit playing games and untie me."

"You're goin' down," Dalton growled, and with that, he shoved Morelli head first into the well. The rope snapped taut in Dalton's hands as Morelli bounced off the side of the well.

Morelli screamed in anguish and began pleading for his life. Dalton put the flashlight on him and as he dangled head down in the murky depths of the well he told Morelli to "start singing."

Morelli had no choice.

"Johnny Hayden ordered me to do it," he said. "Your sister was Hayden's girl friend. Soon after you went into prison, he brought her to 'Vegas. She stayed faithful to him for a couple of years, then he caught her in bed with another guy and he flipped."

Morelli's words tumbled from out from the depths of the well like it was an echo chamber. He struggled to free his hands so he could reach up and grab one of the steel rings that led down into the well, but they were bound too tight. He kept talking.

"Johnny told me to whack her and I did it for a couple of grand. I was workin' at the Golden Nugget at the time, but I left town after that and Johnny helped get me a job in Reno. Been there ever since." Dalton cursed at him and said his sister didn't deserve to die so young.

"You're headed down the river of no return," he shouted down at Morelli.

With the slash of his Bowie knife, he swiped across the rope that had suspended Morelli in the well and sent him screaming and twisting into its murky depths. The ex-cons listened for the inevitable splash. The screaming stopped when they heard it. Then it became eerily quiet. Dalton turned to McCoy and smirked.

"One down and one to go, pal—Let's get the hell out of here."

McCoy just shook his head. As they headed for the car he wondered how—and where—they were going to take down their next victim, Johnny Hayden.

Chapter 31

Hank Johnson had given Charley Hartwell and Rich Henrihan the task of moving a flock of sheep into the pasture just East of the ranch house where they would be fed and thoroughly checked daily before being herded to the North Ranch. Only the strongest sheep in the herd would make that hot trek across the desert next week.

We were still pressing Hank and Jesse to let us be the shepherds on that trek, but we didn't seem to be making much headway. We continued with our menial chores around the ranch house while keeping a wary eye out for Dalton and McCoy who were hauling hay from a nearby field.

With 38 milk cows and other farm animals to feed—morning, noon and night—the hay in the barn had to be replenished every three or four days. That chore had fallen to Dalton and McCoy this week.

After they had finished dumping the final load on Thursday, two days before the Saturday social, Bob, Jimmy and myself decided to do a little hay jumping after we had completed our chores.

Just as we entered the barn and had started to climb up a ladder leading to the hay loft from where we would jump into the pile of hay below, Dalton and McCoy slipped in behind us and closed the barn door.

Jake was twirling the piece of string that I left behind the other night when I had sent the window crashing down on his arm. It was formed into a hangman's knot and as he dangled it in front of me, he contorted his face into a wicked sneer.

"You little twerps were listen' in on me and Bernie the other night, weren't ya'? Get an earful, did' ya?" We ignored his questions, but my curiosity got the best of me.

"We heard you talking about dropping people down a well. Did you actually do that?"

"Yeah, and where's it at?" Jimmy inquired.

"None of your damn business," Dalton growled. "You keep pullin' stunts like you did the other night an' you just might end up in there yourselves.

"Another thing, kiddos, you'd better keep your mouths shut about what you heard me and Bernie talkin' about, 'cause if you go blabbin' around, we'll do some bad things to your kinfolk."

That threat really scared us. We now shared secrets with two hardened criminals and were afraid to tell anyone for fear of causing harm to the entire Banfield family if we reported them.

We might even get hanged or thrown in that mysterious well we had heard Dalton and McCoy talk about. The fear of the unknown gripped us like a steel vice. Dalton kept dangling his hangman's noose in front of my face and threatening us with all kinds of bodily harm. We denied hearing anything.

"If you did, your little asses are in trouble, McCoy snarled. Then turning to Bob and Jimmy, he mouthed off again:

"And as for your brother, you can tell him that if he gets the courage to put the gloves on with Jake this coming Saturday, he's gonna' go down in a hurry." Dalton doubted there would even be boxing matches at the social.

"C'mon, Bernie, you know Dean ain't gonna fight me. He's a chicken livered pussy cat who's tied to his wife's apron strings." Bob became livid with anger at hearing that remark again.

"You've called my brother out twice now; claiming he won't fight you. If he does, I can promise you, he'll beat your brains out."

Dalton snorted in disgust.

"Well, smart mouth, if he does decide to get in the ring with me, tell him it'll be a winner take all, no holds barred fight. With that, the two ex-cons disappeared out the door.

As they headed toward the bunkhouse, Dalton told us to "have a good romp in the hay."

We were puzzled by that comment and were now frightened more than ever of those two criminals. Following that exchange of words, and completely unaware of their ominous warning, we decided to take a couple of jumps in the hay before calling it a day. Jimmy was the first up the ladder. I went up next with Bob following close behind me.

As we stood on the loft and looked down at the inviting pile of hay below, Jimmy told Bob that it was time to tell their brother that he'd again been challenged to fight Saturday afternoon. Bob agreed.

"Yeah, it is time, but we can't tell them everything," Bob replied.

"Dean's going to really be mad when he hears what Dalton and McCoy said about him. I just hope Tess let's him fight the guy. He won't know what hit him if Dean connects with that right hand of his."

We then jumped, feet first, into the inviting pile below us; virtually disappearing into the fluffy stuff. As we tried to climb out, Bob suddenly groaned.

"Geez, I've been stuck."

We both looked over at Bob and saw him struggling to get out of the pile of hay we had just jumped into but he was impaled by a pitchfork that had been left upside down in the hay; either accidentally or on purpose. We climbed over to where Bob was laying and discovered that in jumping off the loft and into the hay, his extended right arm had come in contact with the tines of the pitchfork; two of which had penetrated the meaty part of his inner forearm. He couldn't move and he was virtually suspended on the up-ended pitchfork.

Bob was lucky he didn't land on top of it, but that frightful experience was enough to convince us that it was at last time to reveal the secretive past of Jake Dalton and Bernie McCoy to everyone as well as what they were planning to do in the future.

We also discovered another pitchfork embedded in the hay near where I had landed; its tines pointing ominously upward as well. Obviously, it was the sadistic work of Dalton and McCoy. They wanted to hurt us badly; probably to get even as a result of what I had done to Dalton a couple of nights earlier.

*   *   *   *

As farm boys, we knew instantly that pitchforks are never left in haystacks; especially with the tines pointing up. We felt lucky that we weren't severally injured.

Bob had jumped into the pile of hay in such a way that the two outer tines of the pitchfork had only pierced the soft flesh of his inner forearm, causing a superficial wound and some loss of blood.

Actually, it wasn't as bad as it looked or first appeared, but it was painful, so we told Bob to stay as still as possible so we could stabilize his position.

Then, as Jimmy held Bob's outstretched arm steady, I grabbed hold of the pitchfork and gave it a stout downward tug which removed the tines from his arm. We then rushed him over to the ranch house where Vera began examining the wound.

"My goodness, what's happened to you boys now," she asked us.

Bob told his mother that he had accidentally fallen on a pitchfork in the barn. He didn't want to tell her more than that before he told his brother, Dean, what Dalton had said about him and what he was threatening to do to him in the ring.

Vera cleansed the wound, put some salve on it and applied a bandage to protect it from getting infected while telling Bob to be more careful in the future.

Bob thought: "If she only knew what had really happened!"

We had just been frightened out of our skin, but in our youthful zeal to witness the Big Fight, we decided to keep what we knew about Dalton and McCoy a secret for awhile longer; except to warn Dean what to expect from Dalton if the fight was held.

Bob had become upset that Dalton had called his older brother a chicken livered pussy cat. He felt that such a reference alone would be reason enough to justify Dean's stepping into the ring with Dalton. He was right on that account.

Dean was incensed when Bob told him of that remark and that Dalton was going to take him out early in the fight if they were going to duke it following the Saturday afternoon social.

Bob also told his brother that Dalton was going to sucker punch him in the groin early in the first round so it would be easier to put him away. Never one to be overly demonstrative, Dean listened intently; then he simply said:

"So he thinks I'm a pussy cat, eh? Well, we'll see about that."

He then disappeared into the ranch house. We knew there would be a lively discussion this evening in Dean and Tess's bedroom. We also knew what the outcome would be. Despite Tess and Vera's protests, Dean was too proud to not to respond to the challenge after being called out.

He was one determined man now and he was going to be in that ring on Saturday afternoon with Jake Dalton come hell or high water.

* * * *

At breakfast on Friday morning the word had already gotten around that Dean was going to fight Jake the next afternoon. Everyone kept a subdued silence in deference to the women, but we could feel tension in the air.

Dean apparently had told Tess in the close confines of their bedroom the night before that he was going to fight Jake Dalton and that was that. He expressed his feelings in strong and forceful terms. He didn't want to hear another word from her or his mother about the upcoming boxing match. The issue was settled. Finished. He had been called out. There was a matter of pride and personal honor involved he told Tess and only a boxer could know how he felt about it.

Vera, who always seemed to have a wisp of a smile on her face, was in an unusually somber mood, as was Tess, while they were serving breakfast to everyone. But Jesse couldn't contain his glee when Dean told him afterward that he was going to accept Jake's challenge on Saturday following the social and musical entertainment activities.

"Atta' boy—go get him, son," was Jesse's response. We'll put up the ring by this afternoon and then you and the boys can arrange the ringside chairs that everyone's bringin' over to us."

Jesse also revealed that he was going to "put something in the pot;" meaning of course that he would add to the fighter's purse just as Johnny Hayden was going to do. If they did, it would be the richest purse ever offered at those Saturday afternoon socials. The final purse would be announced at ringside, Jesse said.

Hank Johnson was elated, too, as was the other ranch hands who always said they would be solidly in Dean's corner if he ever met Dalton in the ring.

Only the ranch hands knew how close Dean and Dalton came to duking it out in the milking barn that morning. As we were about to begin our milking chores, we saw Dean walk down the line to where Dalton and McCoy were standing with their milking stools in hand.

Dean grabbed Dalton by the front of his shirt and shoved him up against the wall. The move caught Dalton completely by surprise and before he could react, Dean had pinned his arms to his sides. With their faces just inches apart, Dean issued a stern warning:

"Look, buddy, I've had about enough of your lip and big talk around here. You've been telling everybody I'm chicken and that I haven't responded when you called me out.

"Well, I'm here to tell you I'm not a chicken livered pussy cat—I accept your challenge—and since you've declared it to be a no holds barred fight, here's a little of what you're going to get from me tomorrow afternoon."

With that, Dean delivered a paralyzing blow to Dalton's midsection. Dalton doubled over; groaning with pain and gasping for breath. McCoy raised his milking stool as if he were going to hit Dean on the head, but our big Irish friend, Rich Henrihan, and a couple of other ranch hands, sensing trouble, rushed up and prevented a larger altercation.

"Okay, guys, do your fightin' in the ring, not here," Henrihan said as they separated the two adversaries.

After a few anxious moments, the scene in the milking barn returned to normal, but feelings were now running high in anticipation of the Big Fight.

The ranch hands who witnessed the confrontation were impressed with Dean's bravado and Dalton realized for the first time that he would be going up against a formidable foe tomorrow afternoon.

Chapter 32

Saturday morning dawned bright and beautiful. It was going to be a great day for the social get together of valley ranchers and their families even though afternoon temperatures were going to be over a 100 degrees.

Fortunately, the area around the Banfield ranch house would provide lots of shade for everyone. The Cottonwood trees, with a sprinkling of Poplars, stood like giant canopies above the picnic area while over in front of the bunkhouse was the boxing ring that Uncle Jesse and Dean had managed to put up within the last 24 hours. Their handiwork had all the earmarks of experienced ringmasters.

To stabilize the ring, they had sunk four posts in concrete. Then they had wrapped three strands of rope around the posts to form a perfectly square 18-foot ring. Surrounding each side of the ring were several rows of chairs. It wasn't exactly Madison Square Garden, but for Fallon, Nevada, it was state of the art.

Aunt Vera and Tess were even impressed with the way it looked and how quickly Uncle Jesse and Dean had put the ring up, but they weren't looking forward to the rowdyism that would soon be taking place; inside and outside the ring. Instead, they were rushing about and getting everything ready for the big picnic while Uncle Jesse and Dean, with our help, arranged the picnic tables and chairs in a semi-circle around a stage that had been mounted directly in front of a huge, old Cottonwood tree.

Jesse was not the kind of person to openly praise anyone for doing a good job, but he did compliment his sons, Bob and Jimmy, as well as myself, for the work we did in cleaning up the place in recent days. The entire ranch house area looked neat and clean and the front gate had a sparkling new coat of paint on it.

For once, it felt good to be praised, given all the bad stuff that had going on in recent weeks. Even though we would soon be seeing the cool, crystal-clear waters of Lake Tahoe, I longed for home. In my mind, it had been a wild, wasted Summer; plagued by injuries and bad memories. What really hurt was that I hadn't earned a dime!

My Summer working vacation had turned out to be all work and no play so far and the near constant harassment by the two ex-cons kept me scared all he time.

I hadn't come over to the Banfield ranch thinking that everyday would be a holiday and every meal a banquet, but I wasn't prepared to handle the turmoil and the dawn to dark work routine associated with living on a large ranch.

Perhaps today, I thought, I could recapture part of my lost Summer of Fun, and that it would be special for a lot of reasons; namely that everyone was going to see how good a boxer Dean really was and, maybe, just maybe, I might again get a chance to talk to Hoot Gibson's pretty young daughter, Natalie Gibson.

I had managed to keep my thoughts about her to myself ever since we met at the Gibson's social last month, but I knew she had an eye for Bob, not me, 'cause she was a year older than me. I fantasized that perhaps we could at least picnic together at this afternoon's social.

If she wanted to, I would even skip rope with her or play hide and seek in the nearby corn field. It would be easy to get lost in there as the corn stalks had grown to well over six feet tall.

There's a special way to frolic in a corn field. As you race down the furrowed rows, you must hold your hands up in front of you to protect your eyes and face from the sharp edges of the leaves that protrude out from the corn stalks. Then after you've grown tired of getting lost in the maze and swatting leaves and running about, you take a flying leap sideways. The sturdy corn stalks cushions your fall as you crash to the ground. You're exhausted, but exhilarated from that exercise. At Summer's end, kids always knocked down corn stalks back home, but we hadn't had the time or the energy to do it here.

* * * *

The last thing on my mind at the moment was food; probably brought about by our having had to peel a million potatoes (at least it felt like we did) so everyone could select either mashed or the scalloped variety. Jimmy and I thought that having two types of potatoes was too much. A variety of one would have been our choice.

All of the food that had been cooked and baked by area wives presented a virtual foodfest for the guests and it was pouring in by the box load as preparations began for the picnic. As noontime approached, there already was enough of it to feed an army. And more was coming according to Vera.

I especially liked the way Vera and Tess had prepared the hams. After removing excess fat, they next cut a criss-cross pattern on the rounded sides and face of each ham so basting juices would seep deep into the hams. Small cloves were then inserted in several places and a generous splash of honey and brown sugar was added before they were put into the ovens. They were then slow baked and continually basted for several hours before being taken out for cooling.

The smell of those hams was irresistible. Just looking at them made my mouth water. It was the only time in my life that I wanted to be in the kitchen, so I could furtively slice off a couple of small pieces and hurry outside before getting my hands slapped. Both Vera and Tess were wary of my shenanigans and they hovered over their prized creations like troops guarding the gold at Ft. Knox.

The picnic was about to start. Jesse asked for silence and he thanked everybody for coming. He blessed the food and Vera promised some lively entertainment afterward. She said it would be a "good show" with lots of singin' and pickin' by guitar and banjo players; even dancing if folks wanted to strut their stuff.

Jesse said the boxing match would get underway in the cool of the evening; probably around 6:00 p.m. Everyone knew there was only going to be one challenger when Jake Dalton stepped into the ring and that was going to be Dean Banfield.

*   *   *   *

The Banfield Social had taken on the atmosphere of a long awaited family reunion. It had only been a month since area families had their last outing together, but the spirit of kinship and the sharing of hardships associated with rural living was plainly evident in the smiles, handshakes and hugs everyone were receiving.

Families selected their tables at random. I was disappointed that the Gibson's didn't occupy a table near ours. I watched them come in and set up on the other side of the picnic area where we were located.

After Mrs. Gibson and her daughter, Natalie, had arranged the table settings, I watched her look around until she saw me and Jimmy standing by our table. My heart skipped a beat or two when she moved toward us.

"Maybe we could picnic together after all," I thought. Instead, she asked where Bob was and Jimmy pointed over to where the boxing ring was located. He and Dean were fussing with the ring ropes and they didn't see Natalie approaching them. Dean greeting her with a smile and welcomed her to the Banfield social. He then left her and Bob to themselves and joined us at our table.

After chatting and giggling for a minute or two, we saw Bob suddenly turn and point toward the corn field behind the milking barn while motioning for Natalie to follow him.

As they disappeared, we wondered if they were going for a romp in the corn stalks or to just run about and play a game of hide and seek. Jimmy just shook his head and laughed. I had suddenly lost my appetite for food. I wanted to do that with Natalie but I had known all along that she had eyes for Bob and not me.

The picnic was almost over by the time they emerged from the corn field. Bob seemed a bit embarrassed when his mother asked where he'd been. He just shrugged and said he had been showing Natalie around the ranch. Natalie was all smiles as she sat down beside us and began filling her plate up with the goodies that were on the table.

I remembered then the comment Natalie's mother had made to Vera at the Gibson's social last month. Natalie's shapely figure made her appear mature beyond her age and when the question came up at that time about how old she was, her mother had told Aunt Vera that her daughter was "14 going on 18."

Bob wouldn't fully discuss what went on—or came off...in that corn field, but Jimmy and me both thought some hanky panky had gone on in there. We teased him a bit afterward for being late for the picnic, but all he would say about his romp in the corn field was that it was "good, clean fun!" That was the last time I ever saw Natalie, but her pretty face and figure remained in my mind for a long time after that.

* * * *

We could hear one of the ranch hands softly strumming his guitar and singing a refrain from "Home, Home On The Range." He was soon joined by others, including Rich Henrihan who had broken out his favorite instruments; the guitar, harmonica and a five string banjo.

He was a pure Irish tenor and his soul mates, a collection of singing cowboys he had assembled for the social, entertained everyone for the first hour with variety of Western songs. In their final act, they sang a medley of Irish and American tunes; capped by Henrihan's stirring rendition of "My Wild Irish Rose."

That was a hard act to follow, Aunt Vera and Tess kept the crowd's attention by belting out a lusty version of "Alexander's Ragtime Band" as they played a duet on the piano. They then assembled a quartet of singing sisters, the wives of valley ranchers, who sang a variety of songs; concluding with "America the Beautiful." By the time they had finished, there wasn't a dry eye in the place.

Everyone congratulated Vera and Jesse for the heart stirring entertainment and they all agreed that it was the best Summer Social ever. There were no strangers in this crowd except for two sullen looking bystanders who stood apart from everyone else as they conversed with their own circle of friends whom we didn't know or recognize. Jake Dalton and Bernie McCoy were just biding their time until the big boxing match was to start.

Chapter 33

As they chatted by themselves toward the end of the social, Dalton and McCoy were joined by several others whose faces were unfamiliar to us. When Bob asked Hank Johnson who the strangers were he identified one of them as being Rusty Trudeau, the manager of Johnny Hayden's Diamond Bar saloon in downtown Fallon. Hank didn't know who the others were.

We heard one of the strangers asking Trudeau about Hayden's absence from the final Summer Social and the big boxing match that was about to get underway. Trudeau simply shrugged his shoulders and said his boss was "out of town on business."

Evidently Hayden was making himself scarce since one of his bartenders, Danny Forlani, had fingered Gino Morelli, a blackjack dealer from Harrah's casino in Reno, as the man responsible for killing Dalton's sister, Cheryl.

Morelli, in turn, had identified Hayden as the culprit behind the whole affair, but he had paid dearly for that confession when Dalton and McCoy dumped him in the well at Dalton's old farm house after he confessed to doing away with Cheryl under orders from Hayden.

Bob, Jimmy and I watched warily as Trudeau came to the ringside and slipped a large manila envelope into Jesse's hands. We later learned that it contained $1,000 in $10, $20 and $100 dollar bills.

Trudeau said it was Johnny Hayden's personal contribution in beefing up the purse. Hayden expected nothing in return, he said, only that it be matched by those who would be betting on Dean Banfield to beat his man, Jake Dalton. As he turned to leave, Trudeau added one more condition to the money he had just given Jesse:

"Remember, it's gotta' be a no holds barred, winner take all contest." Jesse couldn't agree fast enough.

"You can tell Johnny Hayden, he's got himself a bet."

It took only five minutes for Jesse and other area ranchers to match Hayden's $1,000 contribution and when he handed it off to Hoot Gibson for safe keeping, the envelope was bulging with loot from the betters on both sides.

Gibson then stepped into the ring and announced that the boxing match would get underway in ten minutes and that both boxers had agreed to the no holds barred, winner take all contest. Waiving the envelope above his head, he announced the purse and the conditions associated with it.

"This here's the $2,000 purse. Everything goes; no holds are barred and the last man standing gets it all!"

Cheers erupted from the gathering crowd when the purse was announced. It was the richest prize ever offered at the monthly Summer social boxing matches that had been held in the Fallon area for the past three years.

A frenzy of extra wagering was being made around the ring between the supporters of Banfield and Dalton as Dean and Jake chatted with friends and supporters.

Satisfied that Hayden's contribution had been matched, Trudeau exchanged pleasantries with Jesse and Hoot Gibson for a few moments. He waved a hand at Dean and Jake; wishing them good luck and he then he slipped back into the crowd. We didn't know whether it was sincere or not, but at least Trudeau appeared friendly and cordial to both sides.

Since Hayden had chosen not to be present, we wondered if Dalton and McCoy had already done away with him for having Jake's sister killed. Only Bob, Jimmy and myself knew what the real motive was behind Hayden's generous contribution. By sweetening the pot and setting conditions for the fight, Hayden figured Dalton would beat Dean and take home the $2,000. At the same time, he thought it would soothe Dalton's anger over his involvement in ordering Dalton's sister killed five years ago.

After cleaning up the picnic area, the wives began assembling in small conversational groups as the menfolk gathered a short distance away; waiting for the bell to ring while doing last minute wagering amongst themselves.

There was excitement in the air, but the frenzied atmosphere didn't set well with the ladies. Afterall, a Summer Social should be just that; not a hyped up confrontation between two antagonists in a boxing ring and wild betting among the onlookers.

Cousin Bob suggested that Hayden and his bar patrons may have been trying to influence the outcome of the fight by contributing such a large amount of money to the purse.

"That guy Hayden is trying to intimidate Dean," he said. Jimmy thought otherwise. "All the more for Dean's pocket," he added confidently.

I was wishing that I had a few dollars to bet on the match, but with less than five dollars to my name, I wouldn't be considered a serious better. Only bets of ten dollars and above were being wagered at ringside.

*   *   *   *

The bout had even attracted the attention of the Washoe County sheriff, Jeb Harrington, who had come out from Fallon to enjoy the picnic and see the fight. He had also talked to Dalton and McCoy before the fight began about the mysterious disappearance of a blackjack dealer from Reno named Gino Morelli.

The sheriff told Trudeau and his group of friends that Reno authorities had called him to report that Morelli hadn't shown up for work the past few days.

"He's just vanished into thin air and no one knows where'n hell he is," Harrington reported.

Trudeau and his friends somehow knew that Morelli had been a friend of Hayden's, and Hayden had grown up with our notorious ranch hands, Jake Dalton and Bernie McCoy; so Harrington thought the ex-cons could perhaps shed some light on the whereabouts of Morelli.

Had Harrington known what we knew about Dalton's sister being murdered by Morelli, at Hayden's behest, he would have immediately taken the ex-cons into custody and issued a warrant for Hayden's arrest.

But he had no clue or knowledge about the crimes that had been committed and we had been silenced by fear and threats of bodily harm at the hands of Dalton and McCoy if we had disclosed what we knew about that crime.

Dalton and McCoy both denied ever knowing Morelli. The Sheriff let it go at that, but he was still wary of the two and warned them both that if they came under suspicion, serious consequences could occur in the future.

We would have been more than happy to share our secret about Dalton and McCoy's sordid past, but we weren't entirely privy to what they were discussing as quiet words were being said between that group and the sheriff.

Besides, we really wanted to see Dean knock Dalton's block off inside the ring before we turned the criminals in. A couple of more days, we thought, wouldn't matter. As Harrington glanced around the restive crowd of ringsiders, he approached Dalton and McCoy with a warning:

"Remember, you fellers are still on probation, so watch your step and stay out of trouble."

In a parting gesture, he said he would get back with them when he had more information about the Morelli case.

Dalton and McCoy exchanged concerned looks. Both now knew that time was running out in their determination to avenge Cheryl's death. They had dropped Gino Morelli down the well after he confessed to killing Cheryl, but they were determined to do away with Johnny Hayden before they bailed out of town for good.

Dalton hadn't yet determined just how and when he and McCoy would do it but Dalton figured he first wanted to get his hands on some traveling money that would come to him if he won the big boxing match between himself and Dean Banfield.

When it was announced that it was finally time for the boxing match to start, no other ranch hands appeared eager to toss their hats into the ring. They all wanted to see Dalton and Banfield mix it up.

The scene was electric.

The gathering crowd couldn't wait for the fight to get underway. Final bets had been placed around the ring and the women were oblivious to what was going on.

As Dean and Jake stepped into the ring and went to their respective corners and began shadow boxing, Bob, Jimmy and I scurried about, telling everybody who would listen that Dean was going to trounce Dalton. With the wagering cut off, the menfolk were shouting that it was time to get the fight started.

Valley residents had been waiting weeks for this boxing match between their home grown parolee, Jake Dalton, and a two time Intermountain Light heavyweight champion from Utah, Dean Banfield. They didn't want to wait any longer.

It was going to be a classic, no holds barred, encounter. Good versus evil. A white hat against a black hat; a Katie-bar-the-door slugfest that would leave only one man standing at the end of the fight. It had also taken on an aura of a grudge match since Dalton had called out Dean after he (Dalton) had severely punished Rich Henrihan at last month's fight.

Dalton later called Dean a chicken livered pussy cat and Dean, incensed at such an unflattering remark, promptly accepted the challenge earlier in the week by delivering a one-punch message to the ex-con in—of all places—the milking barn.

Dean had backed up Dalton against the wall and punched him in the gut so hard it doubled him over for a few seconds. The big fight might have taken place right then and there but cooler heads prevailed and they were told to settle their differences in the ring. Dalton hadn't forgotten that wicked blow and he was determined to get even. Quickly.

*   *   *   *

Jesse stepped into the center of the ring and, as a formality, inquired if anyone present wanted to challenge Jake Dalton, the winner of last month's King of the Hill fight at the Gibson's social.

No hats were tossed in the ring so he announced that Dean had accepted Dalton's challenge to box for three rounds. There would be no referee, which surprised the crowd. Each round would last for three minutes and if one of the boxers got knocked down, the other one was to go to a neutral corner until the one that was knocked down either got up or stayed down.

In the latter situation, Jesse said the fight would be declared over and the man standing up would be declared the winner. It would be a "no holds barred, winner take all contest" and he told fighters that the winner would get $2,000 just as soon as the match was over. Bernie McCoy was in Dalton's corner and Rich Henrihan and cousin Bob were Dean's handlers.

The two boxers had stripped down to their waists and were standing in their corners waiting for the bell to ring. Prior to the fight, Dean had wanted to lace on 9-ounce gloves, but Jesse wouldn't go for it; saying it was going to be a boxing match, not a grudge match. But he knew all along that it would be just that; a knock-down, drag-out contest even though Dean and Dalton would be wearing 13-ounce gloves. Supposedly, the kind that could sting; not hurt an opponent.

Jesse beckoned the two boxers to the center of the ring for last minute instructions; telling them to fight fair and listen to the bell that would signal the beginning of the fight and the start and finish of each three minute round.

"Now, go back to your corners—and when the bell rings, come out fighting," he said.

Dean and Dalton eyed each other with contempt for a brief instant. While waiting for the bell to ring, McCoy told Dalton to "put him away quick" with his bolo punch and Henrihan cautioned Dean to keep his guard up and watch for any low blows that Dalton surely intended to deliver.

Chapter 34

The bell clanged and both boxers danced into the center of the ring where feints and jabs were exchanged. They stalked each other for a full minute; bobbing and weaving and waiting for an opening as the crowd yelled for more action.

"Mix it up—mix it up," they pleaded. But Dean and Jake were being patient. They didn't want to be goaded into making a mistake so early in the fight and being knocked down, or out, despite the powder puff, 13-ounce gloves they had on.

Dean glided into his classic "Joe Louis shuffle" and then, after a series of head and body fakes by Dalton, he saw the opening he was looking for. He moved in closer to Dalton. Three quick left jabs snapped the ex-con's back and a right hand crashed into Dalton's rib cage. That one hurt and both boxers clinched for a moment as Dalton tried to regain his breath.

The crowd was shouting and screaming for blood as both boxers traded blows. Over the din of the crowd, Jimmy and I were jumping up and down and hollering for Dean to finish Dalton off.

Both fighters got in some good blows toward the end of the first round when a stinging left jab, then another, by Dalton caught Dean by surprise. Both jabs landed flush on his jaw, but it was the powerful right hand to the side of his face that caused Dean to shake his head and clear his vision as the bell ended the first round.

"The guy's got a fast pair of hands," Dean commented as Henrihan doused him with some water while again telling him to keep his guard up and punish Dalton from the inside.

"Stick him in the ribs a few more times and he'll go down," the Irishman said. Bob toweled his brother off and also had some words of advice:

"He's out of shape and after you've worked him over with some good body blows, plant one on his kisser and he'll fold like an accordion." Dean just nodded in agreement.

On the other side of the ring, McCoy was urging Dalton to "take him out" in the next round.

"You've got his number now. Swarm him and then drop him with your bolo punch. He'll be finished after that."

Dalton sneered at Dean across the ring and as the bell sounded for the second round, he leaped off his stool and flew into Dean like a savage animal going for the kill. Dean had barely gotten off his stool when Dalton sent a flurry of blows to his head and body. He covered up and bounced off the ropes hoping to keep Dalton off balance as he shuffled into the center of the ring. The sudden blows caught Dean by surprise and he didn't see the bolo punch coming until it was too late.

After peppering Dean with quick left jabs, Dalton suddenly raised his right hand much like a softball pitcher does when winding up. Then in a whirling motion he swiftly delivered a paralyzing blow to Dean's groin. A sickening pain engulfed him and he staggered around in the middle of the ring; doubled over and barely able to stay on his feet. The ringsiders were on their feet; booing at Dalton for delivering a low blow while hollering encouragement to Dean.

The intentional low blow was meant to maim Dean and render him incapable of defending himself. We had warned Dean beforehand that Dalton was going to hit him with a low blow in order to end the fight as soon as possible, but it happened so fast Dean was only able to slightly deflect it with his left glove.

Sensing the kill, Dalton delivered a crushing one-two punch to Dean's head, sending him slumping to the ground and groaning with pain. As Dean lay in the middle of the ring, barely able to move, Dalton hovered over him instead of going to a neutral corner as he was supposed to do.

Henrihan stuck his head inside the ropes and pointing to the neutral corner, he told Dalton to "get over there," but Dalton refused. The crowd was going crazy by now, shouting and booing Dalton for not fighting fair.

* * * *

Hearing the commotion, the women disbanded and came over to the ring to see what was going on. Tess was shocked to see Dean lying face down in the ring with Dalton hovering nearby and taunting him. Bob kept imploring Dean to get up, but he couldn't and Henrihan kept yelling at Dalton and telling him to go to a neutral corner.

"Go to hell," Dalton shouted back, "this is a no-holds-barred fight and you keep your damned nose out of it."

That was too much for Henrihan to hear. At six feet three inches tall and 265 pounds, he was a formidable figure. Like an enraged bull, he jumped through the ropes and grabbed Dalton in a crushing bear hug. Then lifting him up like a sack of flour, he carried the struggling ex-con across the ring to a neutral corner; telling him he would "crush him like a grape" if he kept up his dirty tactics. "You'll be dead man if you keep it up," Henrihan growled into Dalton's ear.

With that he smashed Dalton up against the corner ring post and told him to stay there until the fight resumed. That move stunned Dalton for a moment and he just stood there with his arms draped over the ropes; completely dumbfounded at what had just happened.

Upon seeing his fighter neutralized, McCoy jumped into the ring and started after Henrihan when Bob climbed into the ring and tackled McCoy. The chaotic scene prompted the county sheriff, Jeb Harrington, to go to the ringside where Jesse was getting ready to ring the bell to end the second round.

"Things are getting out of hand in there, Jesse. I think we'd better end this fight here and now or we're gonna' have a riot inside and outside the ring." Jesse cautioned the sheriff not to intervene.

"It ain't over yet, Jeb; not by a long shot. The round's coming to an end, anyway, so let's see what kind of shape Dean's in before we go off half cocked."

By now, McCoy had struggled free of Bob's tackle and was heading toward Henrihan. Dean had somehow managed to sit up, but he was only vaguely aware of the bedlam going on in the ring.

When Henrihan saw McCoy approaching, he swung his arm and swiped McCoy across the side of his head; sending him stumbling across the ring and into the ropes near Dalton. A fierce look from Henrihan froze McCoy momentarily and left him wondering what his next move should be. Henrihan and Bob then turned their attention to Dean who by now had staggered to his feet and was holding onto the ropes just as the bell sounded to end the second round.

As they worked feverishly to revive Dean, Tess's anguished voice could be heard above the din of the crowd; pleading for Jesse to stop the fight.

"He's hurt—he's hurt, Jesse. Can't you see that?"

Jesse paid no heed and kept his eye on the time clock and his son at the same time.

"Thirty more seconds to go," he thought, "and the rest period would be up."

If Dean could answer the bell for the final round, he reasoned, he would let the fight to go on; otherwise the bout would be over.

Even Vera wanted to see the fight ended. She had never seen Dean knocked down before, let alone virtually knocked senseless, but she was worried that he was too hurt to continue. She saw the county sheriff, Jeb Harrington, standing nearby and asked him to intervene.

"Can't you stop it for heaven's sake? Everyone's supposed to be having fun, not fighting."

Even though Harrington thought things had gotten out of hand in the ring and the boisterous crowd was screaming for blood, he simply shook his head and declined.

"I'm just a guest here this evenin'. It's a little worrisome right now, but the crowd seems to be quieting down a bit. If it gets out of hand again, I'll put a stop to it in the interests of public safety."

*   *   *   *

Before the fight, Jesse had explained the rules of engagement. There would be three rounds; each three minutes long with a one minute interval between rounds. While they weren't fighting under the Marquis de Queensbury Rules, he knew if a boxer suffered an injury, like a cut above the eye or a low blow, the stricken fighter should be given sufficient time to recover before continuing the bout even though it was supposed to be a no holds barred fight.

The one minute rest period was up, but Uncle Jesse didn't ring the bell; declaring a one minute injury time out. He motioned for Dalton to remain in a neutral corner, cautioning him again about hitting below the belt, while Dean continued to recover.

"Fight fair and square, Dalton, or don't fight at all," he shouted across the ring to the ex-con. Dalton just ignored the command and told Jesse to have Dean either answer the bell or give up.

"Time's up, Jesse. Let's get on with it."

Jesse checked with Henrihan to see if Dean was capable of answering the bell for the third and final round.

"He's comin' around, Jesse. He'll be ready to go in a few more seconds."

Dean's eyes had begun to refocus and his head was clearing to the point where he could stand up rather than sitting on his stool, but he was still sickened by the low blow to the groin. Henrihan kept asking him if he wanted to keep fighting.

"Are you gonna' be okay?—look at me," he commanded, "so I can look into your eyes."

Dean waived the big Irishman off and said he wanted to continue even though things around him seemed to be in a blur. He remembered a boxer's time honored method of recovering from a low blow or a near knock out punch. "Hang on," he told himself; just hang on and tie Dalton up in clinches for a little while."

He then began dancing around to get his feet underneath him and motioned for Jesse to ring the bell to start the final round. The crowd came alive again and began shouting encouragement when they saw that Dean was ready to fight despite the brutal low blow to his groin and the head butts he had taken. Still, there were many doubters in the crowd that Dean could survive the next onslaught by Dalton.

They didn't realize that Dean was one tough fellow. He'd taken some hard blows in his boxing career and he had the smarts to survive by clinching and holding until he could regain his senses. That's exactly what he intended to do against Dalton.

The bell sounded and Dalton again bounded across the ring intent on putting his unsteady opponent away for good. Dean just saw a blur coming toward him and he instinctively stepped into a clinch as Dalton attempted to free himself. They struggled into the middle of the ring and Dalton hissed a warning:

"You're going down real hard this time, pussy cat!"

With that, he broke free of Dean's clinch and poked three quick left jabs to the side of Dean's head. The blows actually cleared Dean's vision and for the first time he saw Dalton's wicked sneer and a look of triumph on his face. He also saw the ex-con again launch another wicked bolo punch. Thereafter, everything seemed to go in slow motion. When delivering the blow, Dalton committed the sin of exposing his chin as his looping right hand first had to be raised, then lowered in a whirling, upward thrust that seemed to gain momentum as it got closer to the groin.

Only this time Dean could see it coming. He deftly blocked it with his left hand and before Dalton could raise his guard up, Dean had lashed out with two swift left jabs to the chin and a crunching right hand blow to his kidneys. A thunderous right hand to Dalton's chin sent him sprawling in the dirt where he lay stunned for a few seconds before staggering to his feet.

The crowd was in a frenzy now; screaming for Dean to finish Dalton off. Bob was pounding on the ring post and Jimmy and I were jumping up and down trying to see over everyone in front of us. I'd never been so excited in my life!

"Kill him! Kill him!" came shouts from Jesse's ranch hands. Even Hank Johnson, was pumped up; raising his fist in the air and hollering encouragement to Dean. Vera and Tess were holding on to each other for dear life; hoping it would finally end. Jesse looked at his stop watch. There was a little over a minute left.

The ex-con was the one in distress now, but he was not through. He lunged at Dean and began a furious barrage of blows to Dean's head and body.

Dean warded most of them off and when he finally saw that Dalton was tiring, he straightened him up with a vicious uppercut to the chin. Dalton's knees buckled. A stinging left hook and another thunderbolt from Dean's right hand crashed against Dalton's jaw.

An awful crack followed and the ex-con went down like a ton of bricks. For good. He was out cold. Those 13-ounce gloves couldn't soften the crushing blows Dalton had just suffered at the hands of the Intermountain Light Heavyweight Champion.

Blood began oozing from the corner of his Dalton's mouth before McCoy could reach his side, but he knew the fight was over. The crowd knew it, too. Jesse raised Dean's hand and declared him the winner as most of the crowd cheered wildly, then began breaking up and going home.

Hoot Gibson handed Uncle Jesse the large brown envelope with $2,000 in it and he gave it to his weary son, who in turn handed it to his wife, Tess. Dean gave her a big hug and a wisp of a smile crossed his face as everyone gathered around to congratulate him on his victory.

It was an exciting end to a day that had started off so well with food, music and laughter only to conclude with a savage fight that challenged the endurance and skills of both boxers.

For Bob, Jimmy and myself, it was, so far, the highlight of our Summer vacation. Long into the night, we talked about how Dean had flattened Dalton, but we still had not shared the terrible secret of the ex-cons' past with anyone for fear of their threatened reprisals against us, as well as the Banfields. We'd promised ourselves we would tell all after the sheep drive was over which was just two days away.

Chapter 35

Sunday was normally a day of rest around the Banfield ranch. We went to church, as we did every Sunday morning, but upon returning, Vera let it be known that she wanted the place cleaned up right away; especially the area in front of the bunkhouse where the boxing ring was located.

There were bad memories there and it disgusted her to even look at it. We were eager to grant her wish and went to work dismantling the ring right after lunch.

Within a couple of hours, Jesse, Hank and Dean had taken the ring down. They did the heavy stuff; removing the posts and rolling up the ring ropes. Bob, Jimmy and I pitched in by stowing everything away in a small equipment shed next to the milking barn while Aunt Vera and Tess engaged themselves in women talk from the quiet solitude of the ranch house porch.

We almost knew what they were thinking as the ring was being dismantled and the benches and chairs that had once encircled the ring were put away: "Out of site, out of mind and good riddance," was probably their thoughts as they watched us perform that chore.

They were still upset about how their well planned Summer Social had ended up; two men slugging it out, trying to knock each other down, if not out, while a loud and raucous crowd cheered on the gladiators.

Just thinking about it made them recoil in disgust. The day that had started out so full of excitement, with good food and entertainment; had again ended up violently. Both were deeply embarrassed about what had happened and we over-heard them apologizing to the ladies as they left the Banfield ranch Saturday evening.

The menfolk, though, viewed it in a different light. In their mind's eye, they saw good triumph over evil. It was exciting. The good guys won over the bad guys and they had nothing but praise for Dean's boxing skills and the courage he displayed in going up against an ex-con who didn't fight fair and square.

The few hands that remained at the ranch talked freely about it throughout the day since Dalton and McCoy weren't around. They had disappeared shortly after the fight; presumably to spend the night in Fallon where they could sulk and drink away their sorrows.

* * * *

Monday morning's breakfast was a bit tense for all hands. Dalton and McCoy didn't even sit down to eat. Instead, they loitered about with a cup of coffee in their hand, staying to themselves, and snacking on pieces of toast as Hank Johnson announced the work schedule for the day.

We were sitting across the table from our jovial Irish friend, Rich Henrihan, when Hank was issuing his orders. Henrihan was kidding Dean about the shiner he was sporting after his boxing match with Dalton.

"Forgot to duck, eh?" Henrihan kidded when Dalton and McCoy were out of hearing range.

"Good thing I planted Jake against that ol' ring post or you would've been history."

Dean just laughed and acknowledged that he was, indeed, in deep trouble at that time. He had escaped with a headache, a cut lip and a black eye. Other than that, he looked fit and trim as usual.

Dalton appeared to be in far worse shape. We noticed that both of his eyes were still puffy and one was nearly swollen shut. He was moving about rather stiffly and had indicated to a couple of ranch hands during breakfast that his ribs were really hurting and his jaw was swollen on the left side of his face; probably from that lethal right hand punch Dean had delivered in the third round. That one punch had ended the fight.

Following breakfast Uncle Jesse informed everyone that the big sheep drive to the North ranch would get underway early tomorrow morning. Then Hank dropped a bombshell on us; saying that Dalton and McCoy were going to herd the sheep to the North ranch instead of Bob, Jimmy and myself carrying out that assignment. Disappointment showed on our faces!

"How could they do that to us?" Bob wondered out loud.

We were to have been the shepherds on that drive and had held out hope all Summer long that we would be the ones herding those sheep. We viewed it as an epic, Summer's end journey; a thrilling adventure, across an arid desert and under a boiling hot sun just like the pioneers had encountered when they began settling the West nearly one hundred years ago.

Vera and Tess had apparently convinced Jesse and Hank that it would be too difficult for us to walk across some nine miles of hot, desert terrain with the temperature over 100 degrees and only the Banfield's sheepherder, Charlie Hartwell, and Nellie, their aging sheep dog, to help us. We let everyone know right away that we were real unhappy about being taken off that assignment, but our complaints fell on deaf ears.

We figured Jesse and Hank had probably assigned the sheep herding task to Dalton and McCoy to keep them away from the rest of the ranch hands as well as ourselves. They were going to be let go after the drive anyway and it was good riddance as far as we were concerned.

We should have told everyone about those ex-cons before now, but Uncle Jesse was critically short of help and both Dalton and McCoy were good workers. Also, we had been terrified into silence by threats of bodily harm if we disclosed our dirty little secrets.

But come Wednesday morning, after the sheep drive, we were determined to tell everyone what we knew about those two bad men so Jeb Harrington, the county sheriff, could pick them up.

They absolutely terrified me every time I looked at them, and after committing murder and mayhem, they deserved to go back to prison.

*   *   *   *

Dalton and McCoy had already hatched their departure plans and it didn't include herding a bunch of sheep all day long under a blazing hot sun. They decided they would not make the sheep run because of the beating Jake had suffered at the hands of Dean three days ago.

Their excuse was legitimate. Dalton was hurting and his ribs were indeed tender from the pounding Dean had given him. They both begged off on that assignment to Hank who, by now, had grown weary of their antics and sullen behavior.

Although they were unaware they were going to be let go in a couple of days, Dalton knew that time was running out for himself and his running mate, Bernie McCoy, if they were going to avenge the killing of his sister, Cheryl Dalton. Successful or not, they would have to flee the area or face more time in prison as their past was fast catching up with them.

Further troubling them was the fact that they knew we knew more about their sordid activities than we should have; especially how they did away with Gino Morelli, the blackjack dealer from Reno. After discovering we had been listening to their bunkhouse chatter, they also knew we would eventually squeal on them even though they had threatened to throw us down some mysterious well like they did Morelli if we spilled the beans about them.

But, we theorized, who would believe three young teenage boys about a body being thrown into a well? There was no evidence to prove it. It was our word against theirs that they had forced a confession out of Morelli for killing Jake's sister; then silencing him forever by tossing him down a well.

Before cutting him loose and letting him tumble head first into the well, Morrelli had fingered their long time friend, Johnny Hayden, as the one who had ordered the killing because Cheryl had betrayed Hayden's trust while they were living together in Las Vegas years ago.

Dalton was determined to take down Hayden and then he and Bernie were going to disappear; probably to Canada where Dalton had a friend in Vancouver, British Columbia, who could provide a safe haven for them with forged ID cards and new driver's licenses.

But getting assigned to make the sheep run was fouling up their plans to capture Hayden. They couldn't go into town this evening as they had to pack their meager belongings and sneak them into McCoy's car after everyone had gone to sleep.

That left only tomorrow night, but by the time they made the run to the North ranch and had secured the sheep for the night, it would be too late to nail Hayden. They had to do it tonight.

When drinking at the Diamond Bar saloon after the fight, they learned from a friend that Hayden always left early in the evening when he was in town. Hayden didn't hang around on weekends and they didn't know where he lived and they couldn't make that sheep run if they were going to carry out their deadly mission.

*   *   *   *

We were really bummed because we weren't going to be allowed to make the sheep run to the North ranch, so we helped Jesse's old sheepherder, Charley Hartwell, and a couple of other ranch hands make the final sheep count in the afternoon. Three hundred and seven was the final number after the culling process had been completed.

Nellie was on hand to help us. Her ability to separate ailing sheep from the rest of the herd was uncanny. She performed that task by command from Uncle Jesse. In quick order, she culled out five sheep from the herd that appeared to be the weakest ones. Those selections assured us that we would have ample servings of lamb chops in the days ahead. Fifteen others were culled from the herd and sent back to the outer pasture.

By late afternoon all preparations had been completed for the sheep drive when Jesse's foreman, Hank Johnson, announced just before dinner time that Dalton and McCoy would not be driving the sheep to the North ranch afterall.

It was a stunning bit of news.

At first, we thought Jesse or Hank had fired them on the spot. Hank didn't elaborate too much, but he appeared to be upset when informing everyone of the change of plans. Jesse wasn't too happy either.

Bob immediately volunteered our services; saying he, Jimmy and myself deserved to make that sheep run anyway.

"Hank," he pleaded, " we're strong enough to make that run. Besides, we'll have little ol' Nellie to help us, and if you'll make sure Charley Hartwell comes along we can make the trip without any problems at all." Bob was just warming up.

"Charley knows the way to the North ranch better than we do," he pointed out "and when we get hungry, he'll feed us. That'll free up a couple of other ranch hands to help you and dad around the ranch if you let us make that trip."

Bob was persuasive beyond his years. Jesse gave his grudging approval. He was impressed with his son's growing maturity and seemed convinced that we would be good shepherds. Hank did, too. Vera and Tess seemed dubious.

Jesse said his faithful old sheepherder could follow the herd and supply provisions to us throughout the day from his specially outfitted covered wagon which he reverently referred to as his Castle on the Plains. For good reason.

Charley carried everything from soup to nuts in it, but woe be unto the person who invaded his space. That wagon was his home on wheels and no friend or foe was permitted inside it; not even Jesse or Hank.

Confined as it was, Nellie had the run of the place, though. She could jump in and out of the wagon any time she wanted to, with a little help from Charley, of course. And she could even sleep at the foot of his bed whenever she spent time in the field with Charley.

When asked how he liked living the life of a nomad and in such tight quarters. Charley would simply say:

"All the conveniences of home and I've got a lot of company around me so I'm not lonely at all."

He said he would serve us hot meals at lunch and dinner time and make sure the sheep had ample feed and water.

"The laddies won't go hungry," he promised Jesse and Hank. "Neither will my little sweethearts," he laughed as he waved toward his flock of sheep. That comment brought a chuckle from everyone at the dinner table.

In preparation for the sheep drive, Hank said some milestone markers had been placed along the trail to guide us to the North ranch. In addition, he told us, water troughs for the sheep and our food supplies would be in place early the next morning at the second, fourth, sixth and eight milestone markers. Those provisions would sustain us so we (and the sheep) wouldn't be too distressed before reaching the North ranch.

Our provisions would be placed in four milk cans that had been washed out so food and water could be stored in them. Vera and Tess indicated they would fashion little wire baskets that could be affixed to the top, inside of the milk cans. The baskets would hold sandwiches, apples and cookies and they could be lifted out so water could be drawn from the milk cans at each stop.

Hartwell said he would also mount two other large barrels of water on the sides of his wagon for emergency purposes. After Bob's eloquent plea, and reassurances from Hartwell, Hank turned to Jesse for final approval. Jesse turned to Vera who, in turn, looked at Dean and Tess. It was Dean who finally convinced everyone that we could make the drive.

"Let the boys make the run, dad," he said. "They're up to it and Charley will be there to help them." They all grinned and shrugged in resignation. Vera and Tess knew they had lost this battle.

"Okay, boys, you've got it!" Jesse grinned.

Then pausing to measure his words, he told us to "eat a good meal and get a good night's rest.

"Come the 'morrow," he said, "you're gonna' need all the energy you can muster up."

A slight smile creased his leathered features as he finished his supper. He knew from past sheep drives that we faced a difficult journey, but with Hartwell and Nellie coming along he felt comfortable in giving us that assignment.

We began jumping for joy, then we realized that we were among mature folks so we should be acting a little more grown up. Still, it was hard to contain our enthusiasm for making the sheep run to the North ranch. We were boys that were going to be doing men's work and we felt good about it. I asked Hank what caused the change of plans.

"Dalton's still in rough shape after the Saturday night fight, so I'm sendin' him and McCoy up to the North ranch tomorrow mornin' to make sure everything is ready for the herd.

"If there's fencin' to repair, they'll do it. If they have to expand the pasture to accommodate the herd, they'll do that, too. They're also going to make sure there is plenty of feed and water at the ranch when the herd arrives there tomorrow evenin'."

With that, he turned and walked away. At the far end of the dinner table, Dalton and McCoy merely smirked at such suggestions. They had no intention of doing any of those things.

Later in the evening after everyone had gone to bed, they plotted their final strategy on how to take down Johnny Hayden.

Their hateful "get even" attitude toward Dean for the beating he administered to Jake last Saturday evening, and to Bob, Jimmy and myself for spying on them and knowing of the crimes they had committed, had already begun to cloud their vengeful minds.

Chapter 36

We were awake long before sunrise. The challenge of herding 307 sheep on an all-day trek to the North ranch was so exciting that we hardly slept a wink during the night.

Nellie, the Banfield's faithful sheep dog, must have known something was going to happen, too, as she began scratching on our bedroom door at four o' clock in the morning. It was pitch black and not a soul was stirring about.

Even Ol' Red never started crowing that early. The raucous rooster had ruled the barnyard until last month when he was given a swift kick into oblivion by Jake Dalton.

Uncle Jesse and Aunt Vera weren't even awake yet. Neither was Dean and Tess. Hank Johnson had yet to appear. Bob was the first one out of bed and as he opened the door, Nellie burst into the room. She wasn't as agile as she used to be. Still, at 14 years old, she managed to jump up on my bed and give me a little bark and a nudge; then she bolted over to Jimmy's bed and began nipping at his ears and licking his face.

"What a way to wake up," I thought!

Nellie would be a life saver this day in more ways than one!

We didn't know at that time what lay ahead and the magnitude of the task didn't really dawn on us until we gazed out upon a sea of wooly sheep following an early morning breakfast.

The herd actually looked much larger than that in the early dawn even though Nellie had bunched the sheep together like grapes on a vine. She didn't want to be rounding up strays before the drive got underway so she kept tirelessly circling the herd; nipping legs and butts here and there just to let the sheep know who was the boss.

Three hundred and seven of those little critters would be in our charge. They were baaing and growing restless and the tinkling of a bell could be heard above the bleating herd as Charley Hartwell and his covered wagon hove into view.

Since Dalton and McCoy had backed out of the sheep herding chore to the North Ranch, Hank and Jesse had decided that Charley should accompany us on the trip. That decision comforted everybody and we welcomed it as well. Charley was a feisty old character and he loved being with his "sweethearts," as he often referred to his precious flock.

Shortly after we had been awakened by Nellie, the rest of the household started stirring about. Vera and Tess were busy in the kitchen, preparing the provision-laden milk cans that Dean and Rich Henrihan were going to drop off at each rest stop.

Sealed inside each of the four milk cans was a small wire basket containing some apples and cookies as well as some sandwiches that had been wrapped in wax paper by Vera and Tess. Below the wire basket was several gallons of water and keeping the water cool was a small block of ice. We were well provisioned, but they would now become supplemental rations since Charley Hartwell would be accompanying us on the trip. Uncle Jesse assigned his son, Dean, and Rich Henrihan to go out ahead of us and drop off the milk cans at the milestone markers along the trail.

Aunt Vera had told Charley the evening before we left that she and Tess would have the day's provisions ready for him by the time we got ready to leave. He was right on schedule, but he first had to make a run over to the Southwest pasture where the remaining sheep, mostly Spring lambs, were grazing. He would check the remaining herd and pick up one of the young lambs. This would assure us of having tender lamb chops for supper later in the day.

Hartwell told Aunt Vera that he would return shortly to pick up the provisions and that he would catch up with us at midmorning, possibly at the third milestone marker.

He guessed it would be around 9:00 a.m. By that time the temperature would be a 100 degrees and rising. We had planned to stop at the second milestone marker where we could rest the sheep as well ourselves.

He indicated that milestone would be easily identifiable by a jumble of rocks on the left and a deep chasm a little further up the trail on the right that Mother Nature had somehow managed to carve out of an otherwise flat and desolate plain.

That chasm, he said, was "probably an old meteor pit" and it was the only place we had to be careful as the trail narrowed precipitously for about fifty yards at that point.

"Just be careful there, laddies—after you leave that second milestone, go slow for a little ways and don't let my little sweethearts get bunched up or they'll panic. Just spread 'em out—follow Nellie's lead and you'll get through there okay. I'll probably catch up with you near the third milestone marker."

With a wave of his hand, and saying he would see us shortly, he was off to the Southwest pasture.

Prior to Charley's departure, Vera provisioned us with a dozen oranges, a loaf of bread and a canteen of water. It was a curious mix of food and we wondered if that was enough for three always hungry boys, but we trusted her judgement since Hartwell would be joining us in a couple of hours.

"That ought to keep you going 'til Charley reaches you," she said while wishing us well and patting her sons, Bob and Jimmy on the back. She then gave us a big hug and told us to be careful along the way.

Her wistful look betrayed the concern she felt over a journey that might be too taxing for us even though we would have an experienced trail guide in Charley Hartwell backing us up and a faithful sheep dog leading the way. Nellie's uncanny, if not amazing, directional sense would be severally tested this day despite those milestone markers along the trail.

*　　　　　*　　　　　*　　　　　*

All the ranch hands had gathered to send us off; even Jake Dalton and Bernie McCoy. They had listened in to all of the preparations that were going on and were now standing behind everyone else and just observing the scene. They had spent half the night plotting what they were going to do and how they were going to do it. Timing would be crucial for them on this, their getaway day.

Hank Johnson, who had saddled up at the crack of dawn, was also watching the proceedings from atop his favorite mount; a sorrel-tipped beauty he had raised from a colt. The horse kept snorting and swiping its head back and forth until Johnson began gently patting him on the side of the neck with his right hand while loosely holding the reins with his left hand.

Hank told Jesse that he would be tracking us out to the first milestone marker to make sure we were safely on our way. He then planned to return to the ranch where he and Dean were going to repair a tractor and a wheat combine.

Hank had given Dalton and McCoy some chores to do up at the North ranch simply to get them off the Banfield ranch. They were just biding their time before heading up to the North ranch where they were supposed to spend the day making sure the fencing was secure and there was sufficient water and feed available for the herd once we reached the ranch in the early evening.

Unbeknownst to them, this would be their last day on the Banfield payroll. Aunt Vera and Uncle Jesse would be happy to see them gone. So would Tess and Dean. Bob, Jimmy and myself were going to tell everything we knew about those two ex-cons just as soon as the sheep drive was over. They had made everyone feel uncomfortable from the first day they were hired and it would be a big relief to have them gone and finally out of our lives.

After Dean had beat the stuffing out of Dalton at the Saturday Social, they had hardly spoken to one another. Dalton and McCoy were in a vengeful mood as a result of that beating and they intended to create some havoc before leaving the area for good.

Our favorite ranch hand, Rich Henrihan, was joking with us as we made final preparations to leave. Now, he and Dean and the other workers were on their way over to the milking barn.

We had been excused from that chore this morning, but thirty eight cows still had to be milked and Henrihan said he wanted to send us off on a cheery note by giving us his energy supplement; a squirt of milk in our faces for good luck. He had managed to nail us at least a dozen times since we had arrived and now he wanted to give us a parting shot.

"You boys oughta' drop by before leavin'," he laughed while cuffing us as round a bit and knowing we wouldn't accept his invitation.

"A squirt or two of warm milk will get you off to a good start." He then gave us a big bear hug and told us to be "good shepherds."

We had learned to like the big Irishman. His humorous remarks and quick wit always kept everyone loose around the ranch house. You couldn't be too serious with him and he would sing a misty-eyed Irish ballad at the drop of a hat.

*   *   *   *

The decision to have Charley Hartwell accompany us on the sheep drive to the North ranch was a welcome one for everyone concerned about our welfare. Uncle Jesse, with the blessing of Hank Johnson, had made that decision after hearing Dean and Bob make their pitch about having us make the sheep drive.

Hartwell's presence, they thought, would give us an extra sense of security and lessen our anxiety if we encountered problems along the trail. We would also be well fed as he loved to display his culinary skills for anyone at any time. For this trip, he told Jesse and Hank, he was going to prepare a special treat for us at the end of the day.

*   *   *   *

Sensing that the drive was going to get underway, Nellie rushed over to Jesse. Placing her paws on his knees, she began barking and wagging her tail furiously as if asking him to get the show on the road. He put his knarly hands on each side of her head and gently kissed her on the forehead. Then, with a sharp whistle and a final pat on the head he gave the order she was waiting for:

"Let's go, Nellie."

With that, his faithful old sheep dog gave three sharp barks and the drive to the North ranch was finally underway. Hank Johnson reined his horse around and headed toward the front gate to follow us for a little while to make sure we got off to a good start.

Nellie followed; barking commands that the herd seemed to understand. The bell sheep took the lead and the rest of the herd quickly fell into line.

This wasn't exactly the start of the Oklahoma Land Rush, but it felt like it to Bob, Jimmy and myself. A real surge of excitement came over us as we moved out and within minutes, Nellie had the herd moving at a good pace along the trail leading to the North ranch.

To conserve energy for the long, hot day ahead, she managed to slow the pace by planting herself in front of the bell sheep and barking out commands like an Army drill sergeant. By her actions, she let it be known that it was going to be a walk to the North ranch, not a run.

Our fateful trek across a remote stretch of desert had gotten off to a good start thanks to Nellie.

Chapter 37

Dalton and McCoy had no intention of spending the entire day at the North ranch as they had been told to do by Hank Johnson. As we disappeared out the front gate in the early dawn with Nellie and our flock of sheep in tow, they found themselves performing menial chores around the barnyard.

Those chores, which included slopping the pigs, feeding the chickens and pitching hay into the outside feeding troughs, were normally ours or the responsibility of less experienced ranch hands. When given those work assignments by Hank Johnson earlier in the morning, the ex-cons had looked at each other with mock surprise. Even disgust.

"Was this," Dalton asked McCoy, "an act of reprisal for refusing to drive the sheep up to the North ranch as originally planned, or was it merely a way to isolate us from normal ranching activities and get us away from everyone else so we couldn't cause trouble?"

Both Dalton and McCoy felt a message had been sent that they were no longer needed, or wanted, around the Banfield ranch. Whatever the reasons were, they had a deadly mission planned this day and herding sheep and working at the North ranch wasn't in those plans.

A final killing chore was on their minds and nothing was going to deter them from it. And if they could also victimize us along the trail, it would give them even greater satisfaction.

* * * *

By the time we had reached the first milestone, Hank saw that we had everything under control but the weather. We had left in the cool of the morning when it was a mere 69 degrees according to the temperature gauge on the side of the ranch house. Now, under a cloudless blue sky and with a gentle wind beginning to blow, the rising temperature suddenly struck down its first victim.

One of the sheep stumbled out of the herd and began to fall back as Nellie tried to nudge it along. After a few halting steps, it stopped; then fell over on its side. Nellie nudged and nipped, and for a moment, the stricken animal raised its head in a plaintive cry for help. Then it lay still. We had our first casualty, apparently from heat prostration…and we had barely begun our journey!

Hank Johnson joined us as we rushed to the stricken sheep's side. Slipping backwards out of the saddle and still holding the reins, he asked us to lift it up and into the saddle so he could take it back to the ranch.

He unstrapped his lariat; tying one end to his saddle horn while asking us to secure the sheep's feet and head by looping the remaining rope under the belly of his horse. He then cinched the end of the rope around the saddle horn so the sheep wouldn't slip out of the saddle when returning to the ranch house.

At least the meat could be salvaged, he said while cautioning us about the rising temperature that was swiftly approaching the 100 degree mark.

"You boys are gonna' have to be careful from now on. It's hotter than hell already, so don't move the herd along too fast. If you see some mesquite shade, put 'em down for a little while." He then gave us some reassuring words.

"Charley'll be joining you shortly and will give you some help as you move the herd along."

With a waive of his hand he reined his horse around and headed back to the ranch with a dead sheep in his saddle and a worried look on his face.

"Damn, he thought to himself, "we picked the hottest day of the year to move those sheep."

*   *   *   *

Hank hadn't expected trouble so early in the run. His big sorrel went into an easy gait on the trail that ran parallel to the main ranch road. In the distance he could see a car coming toward him. It was Dalton and McCoy heading to the

North ranch. McCoy slowed his car momentarily; then Hank waived them to a stop.

"You fellows headed up North?"

Jake leaned out the car window to deliver his answer.

"Yeah. We'll make sure everything's secure when the boys bring in the herd." Both Dalton and McCoy noticed the carcass of a dead sheep laying across Hank's saddle.

"The boys havin' a little trouble already?" Dalton inquired. Hank nodded before speaking.

"Yeah, they lost this one—the heat got to it early," he said, patting the dead carcass in front of him.

"It's kinda' hot to be movin' a big herd like that around," Dalton replied. Hank agreed while voicing his concern about another element.

"The damn wind's pickin' up a bit too—not a good time to be out here in the desert; especially under these conditions."

Hank was anxious to get back to the ranch house, but he had a final order for Dalton and McCoy.

"When you fellas get back this evenin', come'n see me. I wanna' know how things went up there."

With that, he reined his horse around and headed back to the ranch at a slow trot with the reins held high with his left hand and his right holding down the limp form of the dead sheep that lay astride his saddle.

As they pulled away and headed North, the two renegades both laughed at Hank's order.

"Hell, we're not reportin' back to him or anybody else," McCoy retorted. Dalton agreed.

"You better believe it. We're gonna' be our own bosses from now on and we don't need anybody tellin' us what to do."

Jesse's stern-looking foreman fully intended to terminate the two scoundrels when they returned to the ranch house in the evening. What Johnson didn't know was that Dalton and McCoy had no intention of coming back to the ranch. They were on a mission of no return and their utter disregard for human life would soon become evident.

The road and the trail leading from the Banfield ranch divided after a mile with the left fork of the road going in a Northwesterly direction toward Fallon while the trail we were on swung in a more Northeasterly direction to where the second milestone marker was located. We stopped there to rest. It took awhile for the entire herd to access the two water troughs and eat some of the hay that had been scattered about for them.

We also retrieved the provisions from the milk can and gulped down the sandwiches, apples and cookies that were in the little wire basket inside the can.

We had already emptied our canteen of water and eaten all the oranges and the loaf of bread that Aunt Vera had given us. The new provisions were a welcome treat. We expected that Charley would catch up with us within the hour or so. By that time we would be hungry and thirsty again. So would the sheep.

We had been cautioned that beyond the second milestone the trail would begin to narrow for a short distance. At that point, Jesse had advised us that we should spread the herd out into a long, thin line so they wouldn't bunch up and panic and fall off into the a deep gully that was on the right side of the trail. He had told us before leaving, that the gully appeared to be an old meteor crater.

Up to that point we had been moving the herd along at a good pace even though it was becoming unbearably hot. A brisk wind had begun swirling around us. Bob was the leading shepherd. Jimmy was on the left flank and I was on the right flank. Nellie kept circling the herd; keeping a wary eye out for stray sheep that would occasionally wander off by themselves.

After losing one sheep from our flock we had been keeping a careful watch on the rest of the herd. None seemed to be in distress; so after a 45-minute rest stop at the second milestone marker we continued on our way. I glanced at my pocket watch and noted the time. It was nearly 8:30 a.m. Within minutes we came upon that yawning, rock-filled gully off to our right that Jesse had spoken about.

Chapter 38

After inspecting his flock in the Southwest pasture and picking up one of his little "sweethearts, a tender young lamb that would become the staple for our evening meal, Charley Hartwell stopped by the ranch house to pick up the additional provisions that Aunt Vera and Tess had prepared for us.

"You watch out for our boys, Charley," Vera cautioned as the old sheepherder pulled away. "Feed them good and make sure they rest up along the way."

"Will do, ma'am. You can count on it."

The old sheepherder whacked the back of his horses with his reins. A "giddup" command followed and his fidgety team headed North for the rendezvous with us.

Just beyond the entrance to the Banfield ranch, he saw Hank Johnson coming toward him with a dead sheep strapped to his saddle. Sensing trouble, he reined his team to a stop and waited for Johnson to pull up alongside his wagon. What he saw didn't please him.

"What happened up there, Hank, did we lose some of the herd already?" Charley knew what the problem was before asking. Heat prostration.

"Only this one so far, Charley. We picked one hell of a hot day to put sheep on the trail. You'd better hustle up there and join the boys as soon as possible."

With a waive of his hand, Hank set off toward the ranch house; yelling back to his worried sheepherder that he would see him at the North ranch tomorrow morning. Charley was completely unaware of the danger that lay ahead. Not from the fierce heat, but from the lurking presence of two vindictive ex-convicts who were laying in wait for him behind the mound of rocks that were just beyond the second milestone.

Hartwell wasn't even supposed to accompany us, but Uncle Jesse, probably at the urging of Vera, as well as Tess and Dean, had decided that Charley should travel with us on the trip to the North ranch.

*   *   *   *

Putting Charley on the trail had fouled up Dalton and McCoy's plan to play havoc with us on their way up to the North ranch. Jesse's aging sheep-herder was not only going to be our guardian, but cook for us as well. Now, they knew Charley would be getting in the way and had to be taken care of so they could carry out their evil plans against us.

Their vengeful goal was to do us in—send us on a wayward journey in the desert…and make it look like an accident if we failed to survive. And if that didn't work, they had a shocking surprise awaiting us at the end of the trail.

The ex-cons had parked their car inside a cove in the rocks a short distance up from the second milestone marker where they couldn't be seen from the road or the trail. They had watched us at that rest stop and later on as we delicately negotiated our way past the only danger point on the trail—a deep gully on the right where the trail narrowed and, at times, was only eight or nine feet wide.

After they saw us make our way safely past that hazardous part of the trail, they knew Charley Hartwell would not be too far behind. A canteen of water slaked their thirst while they waited for him to appear.

Nearly an hour went by before Charley finally came into view. He stopped momentarily to let his team have a drink in the near empty water trough at the second milestone marker before cautiously moving onto the narrow trail ahead.

Halfway through that narrow access, he caught a glimpse of two shadowy figures approaching from the left and behind his wagon. He was surprised to see Dalton and McCoy.

"What're you fellers doin' out here," Charley inquired. "I thought you were supposed to be up at the North…"

His voice tailed off in a panic as he saw what was going to happen. He didn't even have time to whip his team into action and pull away before Dalton grabbed the reins and gave a violent tug on the right one as McCoy struck the left horse on the rear end with a tire iron.

Instinctively, feeling the pull of the reins, the team bolted to the right. Then seeing the yawning gully below them, they reared back; snorting and bucking as they attempted to scramble back onto the trail while struggling mightily to keep from tumbling down the steep slope.

Charley reached out and tried to grab the reins out of Dalton's hands, but it was too late. The wagon had lurched too far to the right. The wheels on the right side of the wagon slipped over the edge of the chasm and the heavily laden wagon suddenly lurched sideways and tipped over; sending it and the horses cartwheeling into the rocky terrain below.

Charley didn't have a chance. He was thrown clear and then crushed to death by the wagon as it tumbled into the chasm. Dalton and McCoy watched in grim silence at the carnage they had just created; knowing they had made it appear that an accident had happened rather than it being caused by their own callous deeds. They had just committed an unspeakable act of violence that had killed a faithful sheepherder, a valuable team of horses and a young lamb.

Their efforts to get even with everyone had begun to take a merciless toll and they intended to make us their next victims.

Up ahead, we had just past the third milestone and were looking forward to the next one where we knew there would be food and water for us. We kept looking back to see if Charley Hartwell was in sight and hoped he would be along soon.

The heat had already began taking a toll on us as we had quickly drank all of our water since leaving the second milestone. We were hungry. Some of the sheep were bleating mournfully; a telltale sign that they were as distressed as we were at the moment.

Since our trail was about a half mile East of the main road, we hadn't noticed a speeding northbound car whiz by us. It was Dalton and McCoy racing ahead of us. Unbeknownst to us, they were on their way to the next milestone markers where they were going to tip over the water troughs and destroy the provisions that had been stored in the milk cans for us. They were also going to rearrange the remaining markers that would be directing us to the North ranch.

We were alone in the desert with no provisions to sustain us for the rest of the journey and a herd of sheep that was already showing signs of extreme distress. We had no way of knowing that Charley Hartwell, his team of horses and a little lamb lay dead in a gully behind us. It was only mid-morning and our ordeal in the desert was just beginning.

Chapter 39

Vengeance had virtually consumed Jake Dalton and Bernie McCoy since learning that their boyhood chum, Johnny Hayden, had arranged the killing of Dalton's sister, Cheryl, five years ago. Now, it was effecting their ability to clearly think of the consequences if they failed in their deadly mission to do away with him.

This would be their last act of reprisal before leaving Fallon forever. They had no family ties to the area and no one cared a hoot about them; except possibly the county sheriff, Jeb Harrington, who would relish the chance to put them behind bars once again if he knew they had violated the terms of their parole.

The ex-cons couldn't have gotten away with harming Dean for the beating he administered to Dalton. That would be too evident to everyone. So they picked on us in an environment so hostile that even the hardiest humans would have difficulty surviving without food and water—in the hot, wind-whipped desert of Western Nevada.

Having three young shepherds wandering about in that environment with a herd of sheep and lost in a maze of misdirected milestone markers was an amusing game for Dalton and McCoy, but cruel punishment for us. We were mere minnows in their quest to catch a bigger fish—Johnny Hayden!

They had begged off doing the sheep drive, claiming Dalton was too beat up after his boxing match with Dean; but they reasoned to themselves, the drive to the North ranch would be a perfect cover for carrying out a little mayhem at our expense while hiding a crime that no one could ever prove they had committed—the tragic and senseless killing of Charley Hartwell along a lonely and desolate desert trail.

An unrelenting heat wave and lack of food and water was serving as their devils in disguise and, so far, their plan was working to perfection. Now, they were about to commit another murder in their crime filled careers.

Their old boyhood buddy, Johnny Hayden, would be their next, and last, victim for arranging to have Dalton's sister, Cheryl, killed at the hands of a Reno hit man, Gino Morelli. Through their brazen behavior and reckless disregard for human life, they had managed to kill two people and wreck havoc along our trail to the North Ranch.

Now, their timing had to be perfect if they were going to complete their vengeful journey. If everything came off as planned, they would be driving up highway 395 on their way to Vancouver, British Columbia, by late tonight. But, if their efforts were foiled in some way, they would be back in prison within a matter of hours; perhaps for the rest of their lives.

Dalton felt it was worth a gamble, desperate as it would be, to finally avenge his sister's death.

On their way to committing this fiendish act, they would also cause us trouble for spying on them and learning of their sordid activities in the past. Their bizarre scheme would also be a payback for the severe beating Dean had given Dalton at last Saturday's social gathering at the Banfield ranch.

Their plan was to change the remaining arrow-shaped milestone markers pointing to the North ranch; thereby taking us on a zigzag route across a barren, windswept desert; made even harsher by the fierce heat of a late Summer sun.

Such nonsense would not only severely lengthen our trip, but those misdirected markers would have devastating consequences for us and our beleaguered herd of sheep as we moved along the premarked trail.

More misery would be heaped on us by dumping over the waterfilled troughs that had been put out for the sheep earlier in the morning. They would also carry off our food provisions; leaving us in desperate straits and struggling for survival.

Although we had a faithful little sheep dog as a guide, Dalton and McCoy reasoned their cruel scheme would not only confuse us, but going without food and water for 10 or 12 hours would be enough to do us in by nightfall. By that time, they would be long gone.

*   *   *   *

Realizing he had little time to spare if he and Dalton were going to disrupt our journey, McCoy turned off the road and began following some wagon tracks that apparently led to the North ranch. They knew we would be coming along the trail shortly, so they had to act swiftly and get out of there.

"You know this area better'n I do, Jake—where d'ya think those other markers are?" Dalton pondered the question for a moment.

"The boys are probably moving past the third marker now. They must've stopped there to rest the herd, so the next one should be up ahead some place," Dalton responded.

A half a mile further up the trail and not far off the main road leading to Fallon, they spotted the fourth milestone marker where food and water had been placed for us. Small stones in the shape of an arrow were pointing due North toward our ultimate destination.

After looking around for a moment, Dalton changed the stones so they now were pointing in a Northeasterly direction so as not arouse too much suspicion about the true direction we should take. Next to the stone markers were two large water-filled troughs for the sheep. Beside the troughs was a milk can containing fresh water and some food provisions that would sustain us on the drive.

A quick look to the South told Dalton and McCoy that we were no where in site, so they quickly up-ended the troughs; spilling the precious liquid on the desert floor.

After flipping the lid off the milk can, Dalton retrieved our mid-morning snacks from the wire basket that was hanging inside the can and tossed them to McCoy who put them in his car. Dalton then tipped the can upside down and splashed our water on the ground.

They then jumped back into their car and drove North along the trail where they re-routed each of the remaining markers in zig-zagging patterns across the desert floor. They also destroyed our water and provisions that had been placed at the six and eighth milestone markers. Surveying the mayhem they had caused, a gleeful Dalton couldn't contain himself while thinking of our upcoming plight.

"Those little bastards are gonna' be real thirsty by the time this day's over," he gloated.

"Yeah," McCoy grinned, "and hungry as hell, too.

*   *   *   *

We couldn't wait to reach the fourth milestone marker up ahead of us. We were thirsty and hungry and the sheep were showing signs of extreme distress. Charley Hartwell hadn't come into view as yet and we were getting anxious about that. He was to have met us before the third marker; yet neither Bob, Jimmy or myself could see his wagon as we looked back on the trail.

"Charley's awful slow in gettin' here," Jimmy mumbled through parched lips.

"He'll be along shortly," Bob said confidently. "He's pretty reliable."

Still, doubt began to creep into our minds that Charley had either changed his mind about joining us or he had run into trouble somewhere behind us.

As we moved the sheep slowly along the trail, I once again began wondering how I had managed to get myself in this situation. I had laid awake almost every night since arriving at the Banfield ranch; thinking of a Summer lost and not being able to play tennis or hang out with my buddies. At this point on the trail, I could only hope this hellish day would soon be over.

"Right now," I thought, "I would give anything to be working as a carpenter's helper back home; making good money and even putting up with the likes of dad's grumpy old foreman, John Froman. It would be a picnic in the park compared to the situation we were in at the moment," I rationalized.

I just knew it couldn't be this hot and miserable back home and I certainly couldn't bring myself to believe that the worst was yet to come.

Two sharp barks from Nellie brought me back to reality. She was standing beside another sheep that had fallen down behind the herd. We rushed over to see what was the matter and quickly saw that heat prostration had again taken its toll.

The stricken animal was bleeding from its nostrils and was frothing at the mouth. It didn't even attempt to regain its feet and within minutes it had quit breathing. We began wondering how many more would fall before we reached our destination. I remembered what Hank Johnson had told us about putting the sheep down if the herd appeared too stressed.

"Shouldn't we stop for awhile to rest the sheep and let Charley catch up with us?" I asked Bob. He just shook his head and urged us to keep going.

Clumps of mesquite bushes were a distance away and could possibly offer some shade to the herd, but he felt we should press on to the next milestone which was a half mile or so up the trail. He figured that we should reach that marker within the hour.

Even Nellie sensed that was the right decision. When Bob waived his hand and told her to "keep 'em moving," she began running and barking commands only the sheep apparently understood. For the first time, I noticed a hint of discouragement in Bob's voice.

"I hope Charley's isn't too far behind us," he said in a voice weary with fatigue while hoping our next milestone marker would provide us with sufficient food and water to continue our journey.

"We can eat and rest the herd there and wait for Charley to catch up. He can't be too far behind us."

Nellie nudged the Bell Sheep out of the pack, which signaled the rest of the sheep to follow her lead. But Uncle Jesse's beloved canine companion was clearly in distress herself. She was moving more slowly now and only her instincts kept her going.

While a noticeable limp and arthritic legs were making it difficult for her to run around and through the herd as quickly as she did in years past, she still managed to keep the flock moving.

Distressed sheep have a tendency to bunch together, so Nellie kept disappearing into the herd and spreading them out so air could circulate among them more easily. Old sheepherder lore dictated that maneuver for the sake of their survival.

It was slow going due to the sweltering heat. A hot wind had once again began whipping up murky dust clouds and small whirl winds danced across the desert floor beating us into submission and clouding our vision. It took us almost two hours, instead of one, to reach the fourth milestone marker. Along the way, we had lost three more sheep from heat prostration and the scene that greeted us was demoralizing.

There wasn't a drop of water or a morsel of food to be found. The water troughs were empty and the provisions that had been placed in the milk can for us had disappeared, too. Nellie sniffed the damp ground where the water had been spilled and then lay down to cool off her tired body.

Even the next milestone marker seemed to be pointing in the wrong direction. The arrow indicated that we should take a Northeasterly route while the well worn trail we were following seemed to run in a Northerly direction.

What to do we asked ourselves? It was past noontime now. We hadn't had any water to drink or food to eat since reaching the second milestone marker early this morning. There wasn't a sliver of shade anywhere and the Sun had now become our unrelenting adversary, too; searing our souls and numbing our senses to the dangers that we were now facing. We knew that the temperature was well over the 100 degree mark, but we couldn't turn anywhere for relief. It was a helpless, futile feeling.

We slumped dejectedly to the ground; bewildered over what was happening to us and wondering why Charley Hartwell hadn't arrived to help us on our wayward journey.

Chapter 40

In our wildest dreams, it would have been difficult to make ourselves believe that Charley lay dead in a gulch a couple of miles behind us; a victim of a cruel hoax perpetrated at the hands of two ex-convicts who had absolutely no regard for human life.

We simply kept believing that he would be joining us at any minute; that he had been delayed for some reason or another, or that his plans had been changed by Jesse or Hank Johnson and that someone would soon be coming to our rescue.

For a moment, Bob thought about going back down the trail to see where Charley was; even walking all the way back to the ranch, if need be, to see if Dean, his dad or Hank could come and rescue us from our nightmarish ordeal.

We talked about it, as well as what to do next, and since it was getting late, we agreed that we should stick together and keep moving on.

We were puzzled, too, why the milestone marker was now directing us to go in an Easterly direction when the trail we were on was leading Northward.

In our dazed and confused state, we decided to follow the marker rather than the trail. It was a disastrous decision.

Nellie had been over this trail several times with Charley earlier in the Spring and she had the good sense to resist, but we didn't know any better. Nellie kept barking and running a few short steps Northward before returning to the herd. We should have followed her lead, but we didn't.

It was at this juncture of the trip that we began to realize that something had gone terribly wrong behind us and someone was deliberately playing a deadly serious game ahead of us.

We wondered who would think of pulling such dirty tricks on us? The answer was evident: With their twisted minds and hateful attitudes, it had to be Jake Dalton and Bernie McCoy. Their devilish handiwork was scattered about the desert—in misdirected markers, empty water troughs, spilled drinking water and stolen food. I was as angry as I was frustrated.

"Those guys are trying to do away with us," I told Bob and Jimmy.

"They've done a good job of it so far," Jimmy lamented. Bob tried to bolster our spirits, but he, too, was becoming discouraged.

"I know we've got to have some help soon, but we just can't lay down and quit now. That's probably what those two bad guys expected us to do…just lay down and die along with the sheep we're herding."

We knew Dalton and McCoy were supposed to be up at the North ranch, but along the way they had created all sorts of havoc just to torment us on a frightfully hot day.

By now, we were in such dazed stupors that we could hardly move or think rationally. Unobstructed by clouds, the sun's rays kept beating down at us; drying out our mouths and swelling our tongues so it was becoming difficult to communicate with one another.

Even Nellie was having trouble moving about. The sheep were suffering terribly, too. We kept prodding them with our staffs and they would bleat out in weak protest, but the urgency to keep them moving won out over simply standing still or falling down and not being able to get up again.

Strewn along the trail were nine more stricken sheep that we had to abandon. In our hazy minds we didn't know if they were alive or dead, but looking skyward, a tell-tale sign told us the grim truth: Vultures had suddenly appeared out of nowhere and were circling high above us. We knew, those winged scavengers didn't attack live animals; just dead ones.

We watched them circle for a few minutes; slowly descending in a downward spiral. Then, swooping in low to the ground, they finally landed less than a 100 feet from us and began to feast on the carcasses of the dead sheep.

*   *   *   *

As we began making our way toward the sixth milestone marker where, we hoped food and water would be available, I wondered if we were going to be their next victims. Then a tantalizing scene came into view. A huge lake appeared in front of us.

In a frantic effort to survive, we suddenly quickened our pace when we saw the water shimmering in the distance. It kept luring us on; tempting and teasing us until we realized we had become victims of an illusion.

The illusive rays from a blazing afternoon sun were bouncing off the desert floor; creating a mirage effect and making it appear that the lake was virtually at our finger tips. The closer we moved toward the lake, the more it kept moving away from us. As we staggered forward, our hearts sank when we finally realized that Mother nature was playing a cruel Summer trick on us.

"I can't take much more of this," I thought to myself.

A feeling of helplessness engulfed us once again and if it hadn't been for our staffs to lean on, we would have keeled over from sheer disappointment and exhaustion.

"Geez," Jimmy's whispered out of cracked lips and a parched throat, "I can't go much further." Bob offered encouragement.

"Don't give up now, brother. There's food and water up ahead—c'mon, suck it up and keep on moving."

We were both concerned about Jimmy's plight. He was a pitiful sight. He had gradually fallen behind us and was barely moving as he held onto his staff with both hands. Seeing his younger brother in distress, Bob dropped back and again urged him to keep going and telling him we were nearly there. He then took him by the arm and began helping him along the trail. His encouraging words also gave me the inner strength to keep going for a little while longer.

Bob was big for his age, a sturdy six-footer, even though he was only 15 years old and his stamina and will to survive was amazing. He gave us hope even though we were stranded in a barren, wind blown, desert and almost out of our minds with fatigue, fear and lack of water.

Poor Nellie was in distress, too. Our faithful guide was on wobbly, arthritic legs as she kept stumbling while trying to keep the sheep from straying too far from us. We didn't see how she could go another mile before tottering over for good. Still, we kept following her on a trail that appeared to be going nowhere.

Upon reaching the sixth milestone where we thought provisions awaited us, the scene looked similar to the one at the fourth milestone marker. Not a drop of water was available to quench our thirst; nor was there a morsel of food in sight that could sustain us for the rest of the drive. Complete despair now engulfed us.

By destroying our provisions, Jake Dalton and Bernie Mccoy had again dashed our hopes for relief from the fierce heat and wind that had been buffeting us all afternoon. Bob's earlier words had given us faint hope. Now there was no hope left in our weary bodies. Still, he urged us to keep moving.

"Hold on, guys," he said to Jimmy and myself as we slumped to the ground in complete despair. "I think we've only got about three miles to go."

That distance seemed beyond our endurance at the moment. Our parched throats were now so dry and tongues so swollen that we found it difficult to speak; so we only nodded our heads in silent reply.

*　　　*　　　*　　　*

It seemed like an eternity since we had left the Banfield ranch at dawn for the nine mile trek to the North ranch. We had no way of knowing just how hot it was, but in our muddled, heat seared minds we knew it was well over 110 degrees or so and it was showing no signs of cooling off.

We had been beaten into total submission by the blazing afternoon sun and the swirling winds that kept whipping up mini dust storms that clouded our vision and nearly choked us to death.

Somewhere along the trail I had lost my baseball cap that was supposed to provide shading for my face that was still tender from the radiator that had exploded when we were enroute to Fallon earlier in the Summer. After resting our frazzled herd for awhile, we somehow managed to find the strength to move on and follow the directional markers that seemed to be leading us to oblivion.

Toward evening and now totally exhausted after having gone without food and water for nearly 12 hours, we stopped once again to rest the herd. We had only traveled a little over a mile in the past three and a half hours. The fierce wind that had been beating on us all afternoon had quieted down, but an evening haze did little to ease the heat that still enveloped us.

Each halting step was an effort now, but we trudged on in an easterly, but wayward, path to the seventh marker; only to discover it pointing in a Northerly direction. At least we knew we would be nearing our destination if we could reach the eighth milestone marker.

When we signaled Nellie to get the sheep moving again, she continued to direct the herd further East. This wasn't the direction we were supposed to be going and Bob let her know it.

"No, no, Nellie," he whispered; waiving his arms and barely able to speak.

Then, he moved toward the front of the herd and grabbed the Bell Sheep by the collar and pointed her toward the North while gesturing to Nellie to re-route the sheep in that direction.

"We're going this way, Nellie," he said; again motioning for her to move the herd toward him and the Bell Sheep.

Nellie would have none of it.

Despite her weakened condition, she began barking furiously while racing far to the East as if to say:

"This is the direction we should be going; not where you're trying to take us."

We were in a real dilemma now. We had a lame, but gallant, sheep dog whose instincts told her earlier in the day to stay on the trail leading Northward. We had chosen to ignore her.

Instead, we had elected to follow the milestone markers Dalton and McCoy had rearranged and they had taken us on a near day-long, zig-zag course across a harsh desert landscape.

I reminded myself that if we had obeyed her earlier in the day that we would have already arrived at the North ranch.

"Was Nellie's instincts now telling her there was relief in that direction if we followed her on an Eastward path?" I wondered. A jumble of thoughts began racing through my mind.

"She's dis-oriented," I sadly concluded. "She's leading us astray—she's gone berserk—we can't rely on her anymore. Oh, dear Lord," I prayed silently, "what should we do now?"

I was in a panic; then a sudden calm came over me. It was an eerie feeling. The fear and despair that I had felt moments earlier gave way to a calmness that I had never experienced before. It was as if a still, small inner voice was telling me to have faith; follow Nellie—not to give up hope—and that we were going to rescued. But, my delusional thoughts gave way to reality when I looked around and saw our pitiful flock in dire straits and Bob and Jimmy on the verge of collapse.

*   *   *   *

Up to this point, Nellie had been our one beacon of hope and a faithful guide dog even though she, too, was near exhaustion from having to run around all day while keeping track of three weary shepherd boys and a stricken flock of sheep. Still, through sheer will, I was ready to go wherever she led us.

"We might as well follow Nellie," I whispered to Bob. "Maybe she really does know where she's going." Jimmy agreed.

"We've gotta' follow Nellie, Bob, she's been right so far," he pleaded deliriously.

Bob simply nodded his head in resignation and kept walking ahead. An unsteady gait and bowed head revealed his thoughts and state of mind. He had almost given up hope that we would be rescued. We couldn't go on much longer, given the distressed state we were in. Jimmy was practically out on his feet and I was on the verge of falling down and not being able to get up.

Despite our faith in Nellie, we had lingering doubts that she had perhaps lost her directional compass and that she could no longer be relied upon to lead us to the North ranch. Yet she was resolute in nudging our distressed herd in an Easterly direction. We followed reluctantly; being totally oblivious to what lay ahead of us.

As the evening shadows darkened the Western sky, Nellie kept running forward; sometimes 20 or 30 yards, and barking incessantly as she returned to the herd. She kept repeating the process until it became obvious that she was on to something. But what? Jimmy saw it first and he began frantically motioning us to look ahead.

In the late evening haze we could see a farm house in the distance; shadowed by a grove of trees and looking invitingly close. It couldn't have been more than a quarter of a mile away.

We were finally going to get some relief for ourselves and our stricken herd of sheep who had suffered terribly during our journey across the desert. At last count, we had lost 23 sheep to heat prostration.

"If anyone would ever come out to rescue us, I thought, "they wouldn't have trouble finding us. All they would have to do is follow carcasses of the dead and dying sheep that were strewn along the trail we had mistakenly taken."

We quickened our pace and as we drew near the house, we noticed there was no activity at all; no humans or animals or even a barking dog to scare us away. We had reached an old farm house that looked like it hadn't been lived in for years.

"Geez, why did Nellie bring us here?" Jimmy asked in a plaintiff cry. Noboby's gonna' rescue us this far out in the boondocks." I wondered, too, and was at rope's end trying to hold on until help arrived.

"Surely," I mumbled out loud, "somebody must be living here, or why would Nellie take us so far off the beaten path?" Bob nor Jimmy didn't have an answer to that question.

Upon closer inspection, our worst fears were confirmed. No one was living there. The windows were all shattered, the front door was missing and a screen door sagged loosely on one hinge. The inside of the house was in shambles. Broken glass and brown beer bottles littered the floor. We didn't want to look at that mess any more.

A feeling of anxiety swept over us again and we felt sure Nellie's instincts had finally led us astray.

Chapter 41

In the late afternoon, Dalton and McCoy left the North ranch and had driven to a roadside diner on the outskirts of Fallon. As they entered the diner Jake noticed a temperature gauge hanging on the side of the doorway. It read 109 degrees.

"Look at that, pal, it's still hot as hell around here. Still got some daylight left." Then his thoughts turned momentarily to our plight in the desert.

"I'll bet those little bastards got their butts scorched today," he said to McCoy.

"Yeah, if they're still alive, 'n kickin'" McCoy replied.

"We probably zig-zagged them to death if they followed our milestone markers."

The ex-cons laughed out loud at their callous remarks. They knew they wouldn't be recognized in that dimly lit diner so they hoisted a few beers and had a quiet supper after determining how they were going to capture Johnny Hayden and what they were going to do with him after they waylaid him. They then drove into Fallon and checked out the alley behind the Diamond Bar saloon.

McCoy parked his car in an obscure place where they could observe the back door exit of the saloon. Hayden drove a '39 Cadillac and it was in his personal parking stall. They knew he was inside then. They also knew that he usually left work about 9:00 p.m.

The oppressive heat stifled any conversation between them, so they just sat for awhile; each thinking their own thoughts and wondering if their pursuit of Hayden would be successful.

They hoped they could snatch Hayden after dark so they wouldn't be seen, so they had arrived early to make sure they wouldn't miss him if he left before dark. It was 6:25 p.m.

There were over two and a half hours of daylight left and subduing the Diamond Bar saloon owner before dark would involve a huge risk of being seen or getting caught. Still, they had to take that chance if Hayden left while it was still daylight. And that is exactly what happened.

They had only been parked about 30 minutes when the back door of the saloon opened. Out came Hayden with a pretty young lady at his side. Both were laughing and talking over something one of them had said. McCoy couldn't believe their bad luck.

"Holy Hell, he's got some broad with him. What're we gonna' do now?" he cursed in a whisper. Dalton wasn't about to let his prey go at this stage of the game.

"We'll hav'ta' follow 'em and see where they go," Dalton replied. As Hayden and his girl friend came nearer, they turned and walked down the alley toward a row of parked cars.

Hayden helped the lady into her car while they continued chatting for a few minutes. As she drove down the alley and out of sight, he looked after her for a moment and then he walked back to his own car.

Dalton and McCoy moved quietly into place. In the fading sunlight, they glanced in all directions to see if anyone was watching them. They were in luck. No one was in sight. Using the cars that were parked on each side of Hayden's Cadillac for cover, they crept up on the unsuspecting saloon owner as he prepared to unlock his car.

Dalton couldn't wait to see the look on his old pal's face when confronted with the fact that he had ordered his sister, Cheryl, to be killed five years ago.

Hayden saw them coming and, at first, assumed they had just parked their car and were going to enter the saloon via the back entrance. He put out his hand in a friendly, but cautious greeting, knowing his old buddies may have gotten wind of his involvement with Gino Morelli; the triggerman in Cheryl's death.

"Hi fellas—what's up?"

Dalton's smile turned into a wicked sneer as he grabbed Hayden's hand. Then, in a maneuver he had learned in prison, he spun Hayden around while twisting his arm behind his back and slammed him against the hood of the car. The violent shove caused Hayden to cry out in pain.

"What the hell are you guys up to, anyway?" he complained. Thinking they were about to rob him, he offered them a way out.

"You guys don't have to rob me. I'm your ol' buddy, remember? I'm sorry you lost the fight the other night to that Banfield fellow. If it's money you need, I'll give it to you, but you don't have to rough me up for a few lousy bucks."

"Shut up and be quiet," hissed Dalton as he looked around to make sure no one had spotted them.

McCoy moved swiftly to the other side of Hayden and sucker punched him twice in the kidneys; buckling Hayden's knees and sending him groaning in pain to the ground. His assailants quickly bound and gagged him. Then they dragged him down the alley to McCoy's car where they dumped him into the trunk and sped off.

* * * *

In the gathering twilight, on a lonely stretch of road outside Fallon, McCoy pulled his car off the road and opened the trunk. Groggy and terrified, Hayden struggled to stay on his feet after Dalton and McCoy had lifted him out of the car and took the gag out of his mouth.

They wanted some answers from the smooth talking saloon owner. Now sensing that his life was in danger, he began pleading to his captors to spare him further pain and agony.

"What do you want from me? he pleaded. I haven't done anything to you guys. It it's money you want, I've got $500 in my pocket. Take it and I won't ever say a word to anyone about what you've done to me."

The hatred Dalton felt toward Hayden for having his sister killed spilled out in a raging torrent of words that caught the owner of the Diamond Bar saloon completely by surprise.

"You son of a bitch, you had my sister, Cheryl, killed five years ago and now you're gonna pay for it." Hayden wouldn't confess to having that done.

"I didn't do it fellas; I swear I didn't do it."

McCoy then knocked Hayden down with a blow to the side of the head and Dalton began kicking him in the ribs while shouting at his stricken victim.

"You chicken shit bastard, we know you didn't have the guts to pull the trigger yourself—you had one of your lackeys do the dirty work for you."

Then to refresh Hayden's memory, Dalton kicked him in the ribs again while asking him a question he didn't want to answer.

"Does the name Gino Morelli ring a bell?" Dalton growled.

That query shocked Hayden into realizing he was in real trouble. Still, he shook his head in denial. McCoy delivered another swift kick to freshen his memory as Dalton continued his tirade.

"Morelli fingered you before we did away with him and that's what we're gonna' do with you, ol' buddy."

Hayden's assailants continued their assault on him until he was beaten to a pulp. Then they gagged him again, shoved their unconscious victim back in the trunk and headed down the road as the evening shadows deepened into darkness.

Chapter 42

Vera's motherly intuition told her that something had gone wrong on the trail. She had never felt comfortable letting us make that trip in the first place and had fretted silently all day about it. Even though she believed Charley Hartwell was shepherding us to the North ranch, she still worried about how we were doing.

"Someone should be checking on Charley and the boys," she kept telling herself throughout the day. "At least," she thought, "someone could have taken an hour out of their work schedule to see how we were getting along."

Jesse and Dean had spent most of the day repairing some machinery under a leanto outside the milking barn. Hank Johnson had been in the field with his ranch hands and they were now heading back to the barn to begin their milking chores before supper was served.

They were all oblivious to our plight and no one seemed concerned about us except Vera and Tess. Afterall, the men folk assumed, Charley Hartwell was with us so why worry?

Vera had managed to keep her feelings to herself until just before supper time when anxiety almost overwhelmed her. Finally, she told Tess how she felt as they set the table for the evening meal.

"I've been worried sick all day about the boys. I know Charley's been with them most of the way, but it's been so darned hot, they must be suffering in this heat." Tess quickly agreed.

"I've felt all along that the men should have made that sheep drive," she replied; thinking of the nine mile journey to the North ranch. "That's a long trip for three young boys to make in such hot weather."

Their prophetic feelings were on the mark. We were suffering. Nellie and the sheep were, too! And, unbeknownst to everyone, poor Charley lay dead at the bottom of a gully; the victim of two brazen criminals who had again shown an utter disregard for human life.

* * * *

The milking chores were over and the ranch hands began cleaning up after working in the fields all day. When Tess rang the supper bell that was hanging on the porch, she noticed the time. It was exactly 6:25 p.m. After everyone had sat down to eat, Aunt Vera raised the question about having someone go out to check on us following supper. Jesse scoffed at the idea.

"Vera, for pete's sake, the boys are okay. No use goin' out there now. They've still got a couple of hours or so to go before they finish the drive. I told the boys before they left that we'd would pick 'em up about sundown and that's what I intend to do." Then, reflecting on his comments, he added:

"Besides, Charley's probably fixing 'em a good meal right now; so stop fretting about 'em."

Jesse's insensitive remarks about our welfare brought a shake of the head and a cold stare from Vera. Dean defused the tension between his mom and dad by telling them that he would go check on us following supper.

The original plan was to bring us back in the morning in Uncle Jesse's pickup truck, but at Vera's insistence, she now wanted us brought back to the ranch as soon as possible.

"I'll be leaving in a little while," Dean said. "Dad and I have to first finish some work on the tractor we're repairing. As soon as we do that, I'll be on my way."

As an afterthought, he asked if anybody want to go with him to the North ranch. Hank Johnson said he would ride along. With their chores done for the day, he and the other ranch hands went over to the bunkhouse for a smoke. It was now 8:20 p.m.

* * * *

Just as Dean and Uncle Jesse were finishing their repair work on the tractor, a black, four-door sedan pulled into the yard. A grim faced Jeb Harrington stepped from the car and knocked on the back door of the Banfield ranch house.

Another deputy emerged from the other side of the car and posted himself as a lookout.

When Aunt Vera glanced out the window and saw Harrington's car in the yard, her heart sank.

"What are they doing here?" she wondered to herself. For a brief moment she was engulfed in fear. "The deputy sheriff of Washoe County doesn't normally make social calls this late in the evening," she thought, "especially when he brings along another deputy to back him up." She opened the door, gave Harrington a cordial greeting and invited him in.

"What brings you out here, Jeb?" she asked anxiously. "Has something gone wrong on the trail?" "I hope the boys are alright!" she quickly added.

The questions perplexed the sheriff. He wasn't aware that we were driving a herd of sheep up to the North ranch.

"I don't know what you're talkin' about ma'am," he said, doffing his hat. "I'm here about a different matter." Harrington then asked if Jesse was around.

"I'd like to visit with him before talkin' to those two renegades he's got workin' for him—Jake Dalton and Bernie McCoy."

Brandishing a piece of paper in the air, Harrington said: "I've got a missing person's report here that I want to talk to them about."

As if to emphasize the seriousness of his late evening visit, the sheriff told Vera that if he wasn't satisfied with the answers he got from the two ex-cons, and based on the information he had in hand about their activities over the past month, he was going to arrest them.

"That's why I brought one of my deputies with me. I need some backup in case things get out of hand. Those two characters are bad news and the sooner you get rid of them the better off you'll be around here."

Anxiety was clearly showing on Aunt Vera's face now. Then, believing we were safe, she gave a noticeable sigh of relief and motioned toward the barn, saying that Jesse was "out there" fixing a tractor with Dean. She said she would fetch him right away.

"You might as well bring in Dean and Hank, too," Harrington told Aunt Vera as she hurried toward the barn. "Everybody needs to know what we're here for."

Harrington obviously thought that Dalton and McCoy were doing chores or were in the bunk house when he came calling at the Banfield ranch house. He had no idea, nor did anyone else, that Dalton and McCoy had embarked on a day long spree of mayhem along the sheep trail to the North ranch.

After exchanging greetings with Jesse, Dean and Tess, as well as Hank, Harrington told them he had received a teletype report from the Reno police early yesterday morning about the mysterious disappearance of a fellow named Gino Morelli, a blackjack dealer from Harrah's casino in Reno.

They all listened in rapt silence as the sheriff recounted his investigative efforts over the past few hours.

"According to the police in Reno, this guy was a friend of Johnny Hayden's," Harrington revealed.

"I talked to Hayden yesterday afternoon and again today. He said he hadn't seen Morelli for a awhile and expressed surprise that he was missing."

As an after thought, Harrington said Hayden had provided him a valuable tip that could possibly implicate Dalton and McCoy in Morelli's disappearance. That's why he was anxious to talk to them.

*   *   *   *

What the wily Hayden hadn't told the sheriff was that he was the one who arranged for Morelli to put a hit on Cheryl Dalton years before for being unfaithful to him while they were living together in Las Vegas.

In the last two or three weeks, he had begun to feel that the two ex-cons may have found out about his past relationship with Cheryl. His trusted bar manager, Rusty Trudeau, told him they had been nosing around his saloon lately and inquiring about her activities when she worked at the Diamond Bar years ago.

He had begun to feel the heat from their inquiries; that they were about to entrap him, so he saw an opportunity to finger the ex-cons and get them out of his life forever.

Harrington told the Banfields and Hank Johnson that when he had questioned Hayden about Morrelli's sudden disappearance, Hayden had put the blame squarely on Dalton and McCoy.

"Hayden's a slick character himself, but some of his comments about those guys made sense to me. He even gave me the name of an eye witness to Morelli's abduction.

"That was a bombshell disclosure. I didn't know about that until this morning when I got a call from a fellow in Reno. He ID'd himself as being Frank Torrance—said he was a friend of Morelli's and lives in the same apartment complex as Morelli does.

"Torrance told me he also works at Harrah's. He said he'd seen Morelli being shoved into a car outside their apartment complex a few days ago in Reno—said he happened to be standing on his balcony taking a smoke when he saw two strangers confront Morelli.

"The guy said it was dark outside and the parking lot wasn't too well lit. He told me he could see some scuffling going on and that the strangers worked Morelli over pretty good before tossing him in their car and driving off in a big hurry.

"He also told me that Morelli was always getting in scrapes around town and didn't think anything about it until Morelli failed to show up for work three or four days in as row. He said he called Morelli's boss, Chet Rivera, at Harrah's who reported him absence from work without permission. When Torrance told Rivera what he had seen, Rivera advised him to call the Reno police right away. Rivera also told Torrance to call me since he knew that Morelli was a long-time friend of Johnny Hayden's and that Hayden might know who wanted to harm Morelli. Since Hayden is in my jurisdiction, he thought Hayden could shed some light on Morelli's disappearance.

"When Torrance got through telling me what he had witnessed, I asked him if he could identify the culprits who had kidnapped Morelli. He said it would be difficult, but that one of the guys, the taller of the two, had on a red checkered shirt and that they had driven away in an older model car; possibly a Chevy. He said it was a four door sedan and had a missing hubcap on the left front wheel."

*   *   *   *

After Harrington had finished recounting his discussions with Torrance and his meetings with Johnny Hayden, he told everyone present that was all he could say about that matter at the moment.

Believing that Dalton and Mccoy were in the bunkhouse or nearby, the sheriff growled out an inquiry as he headed for the door:

"Where's Dalton and McCoy right now?" he inquired. "I need to talk with them as soon as possible."

"Hold on, Jeb," Uncle Jesse cautioned. "They haven't been here all day. Our boys made a sheep run up to the North ranch this morning and I sent Dalton and McCoy up ahead to make sure everything was ready for their arrival. They should've been back here by now. There wasn't that much to do up there except to check fencing and put out some water and feed."

The sheriff shook his head in disbelief.

"You mean you put your boys at the mercy of those two hardened criminals?" Uncle Jesse was quick to defend his decision.

"No! no! Jeb. Charley Hartwell went along with the boys, so they're okay. Matter of fact, Dean and Hank were about to go pick 'em up when you arrived." Harrington still expressed concern.

"You could've sent an armed guard along with your boys and they would've still been in harm's way," the sheriff lamented. As far as I'm concerned, you never should have hired those guys in the first place. They've been trouble makers all their lives and they're not about to stop now."

Aunt Vera had heard enough. Her day-long fears for our safety jolted her into action. She had never wanted us to make that trip in the first place. Now, her heart was pounding and she was angry and upset.

"I'm not waiting for you men any longer," she said angrily. Me and Tess will go pick up the boys."

Motioning to the sheriff, she wanted to know if he wanted to follow her or should she follow him.

"You'd better follow me, mam. I know where the North ranch is so I'm gonna' be traveling pretty fast. I'll have my spotlights on, too."

With that Vera flung off her apron and told the sheriff that she and Tess would be right behind him.

Jesse realized Vera had exhausted her patience and she was not to be trifled with on this matter, so he said he would drive them up. He also had some words of advice for Dean and Hank.

"On your way up, check the trail and see how things went along the way. We'll meet you at the ranch." Dean nodded his approval as a sense of foreboding came over him for the first time.

"Could the boys have been victimized by Dalton and McCoy?" he asked himself as he and Hank Johnson sped toward the trail leading to the North ranch.

Chapter 43

As they drove away from the ranch house in Jesse's pickup truck, Dean asked Hank Johnson where they should drop off the main road and pick up the trail that led to the North ranch.

Dean knew that Charley Hartwell had been assigned to guide us along the trail and that Hank had followed us for a while to make sure we had gotten off to a good start.

Still, he wanted to drive over our entire route in order to track our whereabouts while Uncle Jesse, Aunt Vera, Tess and the county sheriff, Jeb Harrington and his deputy, drove up to the North ranch in separate cars. Dean was especially interested in checking the milestone markers where he and Rich Henrihan had left provisions for us earlier in the day.

Starting at the second milestone, they had stashed those provisions at every other marker and even though the trail was bumpy and rutted he felt they could make a quick inspection and meet everyone at the North ranch within the next 20 to 30 minutes. He was anxious to see what the county sheriff, Jeb Harrington, was going to do with Dalton and McCoy when they arrived there.

Dalton and McCoy were supposed to have returned to the Banfield ranch by late afternoon and Hank was going to terminate them at that time. Even though they hadn't shown up, there was little concern for their whereabouts. They were trouble makers and everyone ranch would be glad to have them out of their sights.

As they sped up the highway, Hank told Dean they were getting close to where the second milestone marker was located. Hank was more familiar with the trail and where the best access roads were along the way.

"Take the next dirt road coming up on the right. We'll hook onto the trail there. The second marker's just up the road a ways."

The empty water troughs and milk can indicated that we had been there earlier that morning. Even though a stiff wind had been blowing up dust clouds most of the day, Charley Hartwell's tracks were still visible in the rutted road. Dean kept driving along the trail until Hank told him to slow down.

"Better take it easy here—the road narrows by that gully comin' up on the right. Once we're past there, it won't take long to check the other markers."

As they slowly eased along the road leading to the third milestone marker, Hank happened to glance to his right. The sight that met his eyes horrified him.

"Oh, my hell, Dean—stop quick."

"Why? What's the matter?"

"Charley's down in the gully—looks like he's dead!"

Dean braked to a sudden stop and they both got out of the truck and gazed upon a scene of unimaginable horror.

In the boulder strewn gully below, they spotted Charley Hartwell's lifeless body wedged between two large rocks. Further down the slope, they saw what was left of his shattered wagon.

They scrambled down to where his body lay and quickly determined that he was dead. Probably killed, they thought, from striking his head on the rocks as he tumbled into the gully.

Charley's horses lay amongst the food and supplies that were scattered about. One of the horses was dead and the other one was barely breathing. It had lain there all day long; suffering in the heat with its two forelegs shattered and a serious head wound showing above the right eye.

Dean and Hank were shocked at the carnage about them. How could this have happened they both wondered? How could Charley have let his wagon slip off the path and into that gully below?

They knew he was never one to drive his team in a reckless manner and that he had managed to pick his way through that dangerous pass before without incident. So why, they kept asking themselves, could such an accident have happened?

They carried Charley's lifeless body up the slope and placed it in the back of Uncle Jesse's pickup truck. Then Hank retrieved a rifle from the gun rack in the cab of the truck and mercifully dispatched the injured horse.

They were both sickened over the tragedy and still in disbelief as they continued along the trail. At the fourth and sixth milestones, they noticed the water troughs had been up-ended as had the milk cans that had once stored our precious, lifesaving provisions. The milestone markers were taking them on a puzzling zig-zag route across the harsh and barren desert. Along the way, dead and dying sheep told another horrifying story: They quickly realized that we and our flock of sheep had been intentionally deprived of food and water the entire day.

Dean and Hank now knew that someone had purposely killed Hartwell so he couldn't accompany us on the sheep drive and that we had been led on a fruitless, day long trek to the North Ranch.

* * * *

Dean was growing more concerned by the minute. "These aren't the routes that me and Rich laid out for the boys early this morning, Hank." Uncle Jesse's foreman couldn't believe what he was seeing either.

"You're right, Dean. The boys got off the main trail. Someone's been out here messin' around with your markers. Looks to me like the boys haven't had any food or water since early this morning. I just hope they're still alive."

For a few moments, they silently wondered who would dare carry out such as fiendish scheme. Hank spoke first:

"This is the handiwork work of Dalton and McCoy. Why in hell would they pull such a stunt, anyway?" he asked Dean.

"I don't know, Hank—maybe in retaliation for the whipping I gave Dalton the other night. Whatever the reason, that's not important right now. We've got to find out what's happened to the boys."

Questions continued to come faster than answers as they continued their frantic search for us in the fading twilight.

They decided to follow the trail of stricken sheep to the East. Then, seeing headlights of a car on the main road off to the West and, believing it to be Uncle Jesse's, Dean quickly turned the car around and headed in that direction to see if we had been picked up at the North ranch.

By the time they reached the main road, the car had sped past them; apparently coming from Fallon and traveling North at a high rate of speed. Seconds later, it turned Eastward about a half mile up the road and disappeared as darkness settled around them.

Dean and Hank were disappointed, but a few seconds later, they saw headlights of two other cars coming toward them from the North. The lead car had spotlights glaring so they knew for sure it had to be the sheriff. Close behind was Jesse's car with Vera and Tess in it. They had been up to the North ranch and found no one there so they had decided to back track and try to find us.

When they saw Uncle Jesse's pickup truck coming toward them, they slowed for a moment; then they came to a stop in the middle of the road and hurriedly got out of their cars.

The look of anxiety on everyone's faces told the story. They hadn't found hide nor hair of us. No traces of the main sheep herd were evident at the North ranch either, Uncle Jesse said. And not a sign of Dalton and McCoy anywhere.

"We've got some bad news for you," Dean cautioned as he motioned toward the back of Jesse's truck.

"Charley's dead—I think Dalton and McCoy did him in; we don't know where the boys are right now and we've got a bunch of dead sheep on our hands."

Vera gasped and turned away; fearing the worst had happened to us as well. Tess embraced and comforted her. Jesse winced and cursed under his breath as he looked at Charley's lifeless body.

"I knew we should've got rid of those damn renegades long before now," he said to no one in particular.

Then turning to his son, Dean, he asked if he and Hank had seen any trace of us. Dean just shook his head. The worry lines deepened in Jesse's face; then he directed a question to his ranch foreman, Hank Johnson:

"Where'd you find Charley?" Hank quickly answered:

"In the gully aways back—along with his horses. One of the horses had been dead quite a while. I had to shoot the other one. The wagon was smashed to pieces on the rocks and his provisions were scattered everywhere."

The sheriff wanted more details and Dean and Hank recounted their grim findings along the trail. Dean weighed in first. "Somebody re-arranged the milestone markers we'd set out earlier this morning to guide the boys. They zig-zagged those markers all over the place. They also destroyed the provisions we had left along the way for the boys."

Hank Johnson interjected his thoughts:

"Truth be known, it looks like the sadistic work of Dalton and McCoy. After we recovered Charley's body from the gully, we began following the trail left by the dead sheep when we spotted a car coming down the road. We thought it was you folks at first, but by the time we got over here, it had gone up the road aways and turned East—didn't see it after that."

Everyone was getting nervous as they eyed the darkening shadows.

"We'd best get back on the trail left by the dead sheep," Hank urged. "I believe they'll lead us to where the boys are; maybe even Dalton and McCoy, too."

Chapter 44

I could see the despair in Bob and Jimmy's faces. Nellie had led us to an old abandoned farm house that, from appearances, hadn't been lived in for years. We were really stranded now.

There was only 15 or 20 minutes of twilight left and it had been nearly 12 hours since we had eaten any food and drank any water. Our throats were so parched and our tongues so swollen that we couldn't close our mouths. We could barely whisper to each other, the sheep herd was decimated and it taxed our strength to move about.

Panic stricken and crazed with thirst, we wondered what to do next. Nellie must have sensed our plight when Bob began scolding her for leading us to this God-forsaken place.

"Why'd you bring us here, Nellie?" he said in a rasping voice. This isn't where we're supposed to be."

He then reached down and patted her on the head as if to let her know that he had forgiven her for leading us astray. She was sitting on her haunches and watching the sheep mill around. It wasn't exactly dog talk that Bob spoke, but Jesse's faithful sheep dog knew what he was saying. She also knew something needed to be done. She suddenly bolted to the back of the house and seconds later began barking excitedly.

What's back there? we wondered.

Nellie stayed out of site while barking furiously. As we made our way through the bleating sheep and into the back yard in the fading twilight we saw Nellie perched on her hind legs with her front paws resting on a rickety, broken down bench that surrounded an old abandoned well. The bench had fallen into disrepair but the cobblestone exterior gave the well a sturdy look.

Nellie's plaintive bark turned to a whimper as if to say:

"Here's why I brought you here—there's water down there!"

We staggered over to the strange looking structure only to discover it was boarded up. It took all of our remaining strength to cast aside the heavy planks that lay atop the well.

We found ourselves peering into a huge dark hole that seemed twice as large as an ordinary well. The interior was inlaid with brick for a few feet. Further down, we could barely see some jagged pieces of rock jutting out from the sides of the well; then nothing but blackness after that. We were surprised to see a series of large iron handles leading down into the well, but they disappeared in the darkened hole.

We had to determine if there was water down there, so we found a couple of rocks nearby and, leaning over the thick wall, Bob dropped one into the depths below. Seconds later, we heard a faint splash. We also heard another peculiar noise…the sound of running water deep in the bowels of the well. I dropped another rock into the murky depths and we heard another splash.

"Geez," Jimmy mumbled as he collapsed on the bench beside us, "how're we gonna' get water out of there?"

"Maybe," I thought, "we could climb down into the well using those handles for support, but how far down do they go?"

Bob read my mind. He tested the handles to see if they would support my weight. They would, but in my weakened condition, he said it would be too dangerous for me to climb down inside it.

"One slip of the hand and you're a goner," he said; dismissing that idea for retrieving water.

*   *   *   *

We were in a panic now as we tried to figure out how we were going to draw some water out of the well. After looking around, we found a piece of tattered rope, a screwdriver and a rusty can in a pile of rubble inside an old shed that was nearby.

We punched a hole in the lid with the screwdriver, then we jabbed one end of the rope through the hole and secured it with a slip knot. We then lowered the can into the well.

It seemed forever before we felt the can sink into the water far below us. We then hauled it to top of the well where Bob cautioned that he would take the first drink to make sure it tasted okay before we took a drink. He lifted the can to his lips only to spit it out a moment later. The water smelled and tasted awful, but at least it was wet! He doused some of it on Jimmy's face to revive him.

Then, remembering his Boy Scout training that a person shouldn't drink too much water after a day long thirst, he let Jimmy and me drink just enough of the smelly liquid to wet our tonsils and to sooth our scorched tongues that by now were swollen nearly twice their normal size.

Our next concern were the sheep. They began crowding around us; perhaps sensing that we were going to help them. Their pitiful bleatings told us how distressed they were, but trying to provide water for the entire herd from out of a tin can wasn't going to work. If we were going to save the herd we had to have something larger than a small can to quench their thirst.

After again searching around, we found a large metal bucket with a handle on it lying alongside a nearby shed. Attaching the rope to the handle, we began lowering the bucket into the well when the sheep suddenly started bleating and moving frantically toward the front of the house. At first, we didn't pay much attention to what was going on until Nellie began barking excitedly.

"You guys go see what the fuss is all about while I'm drawing this water" Bob said anxiously.

*   *   *   *

As Jimmy and I made our way around the corner of the house I could see the headlights of an approaching car. We couldn't believe our eyes. We were finally going to be rescued!

Caught in the glare of the headlights and darkening shadows, it was difficult to make out whose car it was at first; Jesse's or Dean's. Our hearts were pounding and Nellie was barking frantically in anticipation of seeing our rescuers. A last bit of energy was mustered and as we waded through our bleating flock in the darkening twilight, the car came to a stop. Suddenly, the doors flew open and out jumped Jake Dalton and Bernie McCoy; sneering and cursing as they came toward us.

"What're you little bastards doin' on my property? Dalton growled. I was so terrified I couldn't answer. McCoy couldn't contain his glee.

"They sure know how to follow directions don't they?" McCoy gloated. "Those markers brought 'em right to us."

My heart sank as we turned and tried to run away, but in our frantic haste, we kept stumbling over sheep and falling down. Dalton quickly caught up with us.

Grabbing me by the arm and Jimmy by the scruff of his neck, he started shoving us toward the back yard. We kept struggling and kicking; trying to free ourselves from Dalton's steely grip. His hand was like a vice around Jimmy's neck and he had twisted my right arm up behind my back so roughly that it was hurting more with each halting step. He stopped momentarily to shout back at McCoy:

"Get Hayden out of the trunk and drag him back here. We'll throw him in the well first, then we'll dump these little bastards in there."

It was then that I finally realized we had stumbled onto Dalton's old farm house and the infamous well that we'd heard he and McCoy speak about so many times in the past.

Jimmy kept struggling and trying to get away. Twisting my arm further behind my back with one hand to keep me from getting away, Dalton suddenly let go of Jimmy and struck him with a savage forearm blow to the side of the head; knocking him senseless to the ground.

Jimmy lay still, but Nellie, who had been nervously watching the fracas, began growling and barking furiously at Dalton. Then she attacked the ex-con; biting him and pulling at his pant leg, but a swift kick sent her whimpering into the milling sheep. I was no match for Dalton's brutal strength and vice-like grip. Shouting above the bleating sheep, he cursed and threatened me.

"After we dump Hayden in the well, we're gonna' throw your sorry little ass down there, too, along with your buddies." Nobody'll ever know what happened to you—an' we won't be around to tell 'em 'cause we're bailin' outta' this place for good tonight."

Dalton continued his tirade; growling in the process and fully expecting to have the last laugh. Then in a smirking voice he sneered:

"You didn't have any trouble findin' my place did'ya kid?"

I could barely whisper an answer.

"We didn't know this was your place. Nellie led us here after you changed our markers and left us in the desert to die without food or water." I asked a question of my own:

"What'd you do with Charley Hartwell?" I inquired.

"Ol' Charley got hisself killed—went tumbling into the gully—now shut up kid—you're goin' in the well just like the others who've tried to screw us. Nobody'll ever know what happened to Hayden and you boys by the time we get through here tonight."

I struggled frantically to get out of Dalton's grasp as he pushed me into the back yard. McCoy was right behind us; dragging the near unconscious form of Johnny Hayden behind him.

As we neared the well, Dalton spun me around and made me look right at him. I was repulsed by what I saw. Evil was etched like stone in every pore and wrinkle of his ugly, unshaven face.

"Take a good look at that well, kiddo—it's gonna' be your permanent resting place," Dalton sneered. Then, just like he did to Jimmy, he sent a forearm crashing against my head. I fell to the ground; helpless and hurting from that cruel blow.

Bob had been standing by the well with the bucket of water he had just drawn from the well, but he froze in his tracks when he saw Dalton and McCoy coming toward him.

Spying Bob, Dalton shouted a warning:

"Get the hell out of the way—you little bastards are goin' in there, too, just as soon as we dump Hayden in there."

Bob fell back into the sheep that were milling about the well. He watched in horror as Dalton reached down and helped McCoy raise the struggling Hayden onto the well stoop. The saloon owner was still bound hand and foot and barely conscious from the severe beating that Dalton and McCoy had given him earlier in the evening.

In a vengeful voice, Dalton shouted at Hayden that it was finally payback time.

"You did away with my sis, now we're gonna' do away with you." Hayden screamed in protest.

"For God's sake, fellas, how can you do this to an old buddy? Please, I'll give you anything if you'll stop this nonsense. I'm sorry for the grief I've caused you."

Dalton and McCoy paid no heed.

"You should've thought about that when you hired Morelli to kill Cheryl," growled McCoy. "It's an eye for an eye and a tooth for a tooth as far as I'm concerned." A wicked grin spread across Dalton's face as he grabbed Hayden by the front of his shirt.

"That's for damn sure, partner. I'm sick of this guy's lies and apologies."

With that, Dalton and McCoy shoved the terror-stricken Hayden backward and sent him kicking and screaming into the dark depths of the well. Hayden's anguished screams echoed and re-echoed from its murky depths as he hurtled to the bottom. A splash was heard. Then silence.

McCoy ran over and knocked Bob to the ground just as Jimmy came around the corner of the house with a piece of two by four in his hand and Nellie at his side. I shouted for him and Bob to run, but they were no match for Dalton and McCoy. Upon seeing those two criminals again, Nellie began barking furiously, but that didn't deter Dalton.

I was practically lying at Dalton's feet when all this was going on. I heard him say: "you're next kid" as he reached down and grabbed me by the arms. Still groggy from being slugged by the wicked ex-con, I started to kick and struggle furiously with him. I knew that he was going to toss me into the well, too, but I was too weak to resist him.

He flung me atop the well stoop and began pushing me over the side. Suddenly, Jimmy managed to get behind McCoy who was busy restraining Bob. Jimmy smashed the burly ex-con on the back of the head with the two by four. McCoy staggered and went down to his knees. Bob grabbed the two by four from Jimmy and smashed McCoy again; this time fully in his face. Then Bob and Jimmy tried to rescue me from Dalton's clutches, but a swipe of his hand knocked Jimmy down and, while still holding on to me with one hand, he cuffed Bob with the other one; sending him sprawling to the ground with a blow to the side of his head.

I clawed frantically at the rough-hewn bricks that formed the perimeter of the well shaft and felt the flesh being ripped from my fingers as I desperately tried to keep from being shoved into the well.

I lost the struggle.

Chapter 45

After Dalton shoved me over the side, I managed to grab the top rung of the iron handles that led down into the well; only to have Dalton begin pounding on my fingers with his fists so that I was forced to loosen my grip on the top handle.

My fingers kept gradually slipping off each rung, but I managed to grab the next one; then the next one down until I was out of his reach. All the while he continued beating on my hands and I tried my best to keep moving them without loosening my grip; otherwise, I would go plunging down to a watery grave.

I was in such a panic that I hardly felt my feet touch something that prevented me from losing my balance and falling down the well shaft. My right foot had come to rest on a piece of ledge rock that was sticking out from the side of the well.

A sense of relief swept over me when I realized that Dalton couldn't get to me and that I wasn't going to drown. Still, I was terrified from being thrown into the well that was no longer a mystery to me.

In my weakened condition, I was trembling with fear and frightened half out of my mind. I wondered if the ledge rock I was standing on would break away and how much longer I could hold on before I would go tumbling down into the darkened shaft below me.

In quiet desperation, I gripped the last iron rung as tight as I could and listened to the sounds and the fury above me. Grunting and cursing continued to echo down into the well shaft. Suddenly, I heard a clang and then a loud whack. Dalton was no longer peering down at me in fiendish glee and forcing my fingers to let go of the iron rung.

* * * *

As they drove Eastward along the trail left by the dead sheep, the Banfields, with Uncle Jesse at the wheel, were being followed by Dean and Hank Johnson. Ahead of them, Jeb Harrington and his deputy, Earl Olsen, could see the grim tragedy that had befallen our stricken herd. Every hundred yards or so bodies of dead or dying sheep were strewn about.

A faint light in the distance caught Harrington's attention. Then a dark outline of a house came into view. Sheep were milling about everywhere, impeding their path. In the glare of their headlights they saw a parked car with its headlights on. Both doors were wide open and the engine was still running. Dean knew immediately that it was Bernie McCoy's car. But where was he and where was Dalton and the boys, he wondered.

As they drew closer, they spread out and formed a semi-circle around the car to prevent Dalton and McCoy from escaping. Dean parked his pickup truck on the left front bumper of McCoy's car; Uncle Jesse put his car on the right front bumper and Jeb Harrington pulled his car patrol car directly in the back of McCoy's vehicle. He and his deputy then turned both of their spotlights on to illuminate the area as everyone scrambled out of their cars and began looking anxiously around.

McCoy's headlights partially illuminated the left side of the house. No lights were on inside the dwelling and there was no sign of Dalton and McCoy or ourselves.

After briefly inspecting the inside of McCoy's car, Harrington saw that it was packed with clothes, boxes and two suit cases. From appearances, it looked like they were about to leave Fallon forever.

Harrington and his deputy sensed trouble in the making. Dean and Hank Johnson did, too, when they heard their faithful sheep dog barking up a storm. Nellie had heard them coming and she had darted toward the front of the house; then turned and disappeared into the back yard only to appear again.

Dean and Hank took off running toward the back of the house where they could hear shouting and barking going on.

The shouts and swearing grew louder. It was a chaotic scene and a whole lot of commotion was going on that I couldn't see.

Nellie was growling furiously as she tugged on Dalton's pant leg. Bob got off the ground and had hit the now-crazed criminal on the back of the head with the water bucket he had fashioned just minutes before.

As Dalton turned to see who his new antagonist was, Jimmy struck the ex-con flush in the face with the two-by-four he and Bob had used to put McCoy down. Both blows momentarily staggered Dalton. Now enraged and bleeding from his smashed nose and a cut on his cheekbone, he grabbed Jimmy and tried to throw him in the well just as Dean and Hank came running at him.

"Drop him Dalton or I'll kill you," an enraged Dean shouted to the ex-con.

Momentarily stunned to see Dean and Hank rushing toward him, Dalton instinctively bent down and tried to retrieve a weapon that was concealed in his boot. Hank grabbed Jimmy off the well stoop and carried him to safety knowing Dean could take care of Dalton by himself.

Dalton was still bent over when Dean pounced on him. A vicious left hook to the side of Dalton's head staggered Dalton. A thunderous right hand uppercut to the chin quickly followed. It straightened Dalton up and when Dean delivered another wicked left hook to Dalton's jaw, the ex-con was virtually out before he hit the ground. He fell backward against the side of the well as Dean grabbed his right leg and removed a .38 calibre pistol from his left boot.

Uncle Jesse, Aunt Vera and Tess rushed past him and into the back yard where they found Bob and Jimmy laying on the ground; too exhausted to stand and too dazed and shaken at the moment to recount what had happened to them.

Vera was clearly shocked at what she saw. How could we have survived such an ordeal, she wondered. As she knelt anxiously beside her ailing sons she wept and uttered a grateful prayer.

"Oh, dear God, thank you for saving my boys," she said as she propped them up in her arms and gave each one a motherly hug.

Uncle Jesse doused his sons with water and gave them a drink. Then realizing I was missing, he asked:

"Where's Danny?" Hardly able to speak, Bob motioned toward the well and whispered a reply.

"He's in there, dad. Dalton threw him in the well, but I think he grabbed hold of some of those iron rungs and held on for awhile. Dalton kept beating on Danny, thinking he would let go. I hope he's still hanging on."

Uncle Jesse sprang to the side of the well and peered down into the darkened shaft. I was never so glad to see someone's face in my life. Cautioning me to stay still, he reached down and grabbed me by the arm to make sure I wouldn't slip from his grasp. He then gently pulled me out and laid me on the ground.

My hands and arms ached after nearly being pulled out of their sockets from holding on so long after being tossed into the well. Had it not been for that small piece of ledge rock that broke my fall, and the heroic efforts of my cousins, Bob and Jimmy Banfield, who were able to bash Dalton and McCoy in the head and distract them long enough for help to arrive, I would have met the same terrible fate as the others who had been tossed into the well by Dalton and McCoy.

Harrington and his deputy put the handcuffs on Dalton and McCoy and shoved them in the back seat of their patrol car. With the wail of a police siren echoing in the distance, my Summer of Terror had finally come to an end in an old, abandoned well. The courage of my two cousins, Bob and Jimmy Banfield, and a brave little sheep dog named Nellie, undoubtedly saved my life. Our ordeal in the desert was finally over, but the memories from that terrible day would last me a lifetime.

That I survived was due to my Aunt Vera's motherly intuition and the fast, instinctive actions of the Washoe County Deputy Sheriff, Jeb Harrington, who sensed there was real trouble when Jake Dalton and Bernie McCoy, couldn't be found.

In an ironic twist of fate, those two hardened criminals, all ended up as they had done so many times in their younger days—together—but this time it was for life on that infamous "rock pile" at the back of the Nevada state prison in Carson City, Nevada.

Epilogue

In the ensuing days and months following my ordeal in the desert, I tried to put that stressful period out of my mind.

Unfortunately, I couldn't. Three days after my cousins and I were rescued, I became quite ill. A severe case of jaundice turned my skin, even my eyeballs, yellow and I developed a high fever. Apparently, the rancid water we drank at the well was contaminated. I must have swallowed more than my share as my cousins didn't become sick like I did.

After a short recovery period, I returned home to Midvale, Utah, in time to start school the first week of September, 1939, but the experience of being left to die in the desert and then being tossed into an abandoned old well had left me so traumatized that I could hardly function.

I became withdrawn and moody and school became a bore. My teachers wrote notes to my parents telling them I was failing in school and unless I began to improve, they were not going to pass me into the next grade. My frightening experiences caused me to stutter for two or three years afterward and I often dreamed of tumbling end over end down a darkened tunnel; only to wake up screaming and perspiring until my mother would come in to comfort and reassure me that everything was going to be alright.

Mother was a caring and loving person, but she had her hands full raising my other siblings, a brother and two sisters. My father was busy building homes around the Salt Lake valley and didn't seem to be interested in my activities. It was a lonely time in my life.

I had no one to turn to; no one that I could really confide in or talk to when my heart and soul yearned for help and attention. Finally, I turned to the one person that I knew could help me the most: myself.

Even as young as I was at the time, 13 and soon to be 14, I somehow knew that I had to change my attitude if I was to live a normal life. I wasn't the brightest kid in school, but I remember having a feeling that if I kept out of trouble and stayed on the right side of the law, I could be a good person; perhaps even make something of myself.

I had seen what happens when people break the law. The criminals that I met up with at the Banfield ranch were prime examples of youth gone astray and they suffered the consequences of their misdeeds later in life.

I was determined not to go down that road. This healthy respect for the law enabled me to take the high road through life instead of the low road and I never looked back even though it got pretty bumpy at times.

In my teenage years, I spent a lot of time in the library; reading books, lots of books, and I had a love of sports that bordered on fanaticism. Fortunately, that burning desire turned out to be a career path for me following service in World War II and Korea.

When World War II was winding down in 1945, a Navy buddy persuaded me to go with him to see a golf tournament at the Broadmoor Country Club in Seattle. It was a professional event and some of golf's greatest players at that time were competing for war bonds in lieu of prize money.

As we walked up the entryway to the club, we heard the announcer call Byron Nelson, Ray Mangrum and Ky Lafoon to the first tee. Nelson was the first golfer I ever saw hit a golf ball. He smashed it straight down the middle of the fairway and went on to win the tournament and set a new world record of 259 for the 72-hole tournament.

I was so impressed with the way he played that I later bought his instructional book, "Winning Golf." I taught myself how to play golf out of that book. Within six months I had broken eighty. Years later, on September 11, 1974, I had the great pleasure of inducting Nelson into the Original World Golf Hall of Fame in Pinehurst, North Carolina.

My keen interest in sports, first led me into tennis and then to a career in golf; my chosen profession. As a Life Member of the Professional Golfers' Association of America (PGA), I enjoyed moderate success; winning a number of local and regional events and playing in three U.S. Open tournaments and one PGA championship as a part time PGA Tour player.

The motivating factors in achieving those modest goals were perseverance and a burning desire to succeed.

My love of the game transcended my playing accomplishments. It enabled me to write several golf instruction books—"Chipping and Putting with Hall of Famer, Billy Casper, and "How To Master The Iron Game" with another Hall of Famer, Gene Littler. A third book on the ABC's of golf and the short game will be published in 2006. My instructional booklets, "The Secret of the repeating Swing" and "How To Get A Good Grip On Your Game" have been widely accepted as standard works for learning how to swing a golf club.

I have even managed to write a book of poetry about family life and the crazy, funny things we all did while living in such interesting places as Coronado, California, where I served as the head professional at the city-owned golf course for seven years; and in Houston, Texas, where I held a similar position at the Brae-Burn country club for six years. While in Houston in the late 1960's, I also founded and was the major stockholder in the 27-hole Inwood Forest country club.

All told, my company, Don Collett & Associates, has developed and/or managed 24 golf courses throughout the United States. But it was at Pinehurst where I reached the summit of my career. To have directed operations at that prestigious resort and while there to be given the opportunity to create and then serve as president of the Original World Golf Hall of Fame in the mid-seventies was truly an experience of a lifetime.

On September 11, 1974, as I hosted the President of the United States, Gerald R. Ford, and listened to him dedicate the Hall of Fame, I had a brief flashback to 1939.

I silently recalled my summer of terror in the western Nevada desert and I thanked the good Lord God for guiding me safely through some perilous times so that I could enjoy the proceedings that were unfolding before me at that very moment.

It was a historic, surreal-like setting to say the least; one that I wished I could have frozen in time, for on the stage with the president and myself, as well as some invited dignitaries, were eight of the greatest golfers of all time whom I was about to induct into the Hall of Fame: Arnold Palmer, Jack Nicklaus, Gary Player, Ben Hogan, Byron Nelson, Sam Snead, Gene Sarazen and Patty Berg. Relatives of the five deceased Hall of Famers, Robert T. (Bobby) Jones, Harry Vardon, Babe Zaharias, Walter Hagen and Francis Ouimet, were also in attendance.

I was wearing four hats at the time; serving as president of the famed, 10,000 acre Pinehurst resort; president of the World Golf Hall of Fame, which is now located in St. Augustine, Florida; tournament chairman of the World Open, a PGA Tour event; and mayor of Pinehurst.

Each was a major responsibility, but combined, those duties were too much even for a sturdy, athletic heart like mine. Two days later, on Friday, September 13th, I collapsed with a heart ailment and exhaustion. I was only 48 years old.

While recovering, I had plenty of time to think about the life I had lived up until then. Even though I did not see combat, I served as a radioman during World War II; then I changed my rate to journalist; rising in rate to Chief Petty Officer (journalist). The disciplines learned while serving in the U. S. Navy during World War II and the Korea War were meaningful experiences which shaped my career path in golf; not only as a player and an instructor, but later, as a successful golf course developer.

*   *   *   *

What prompted me to write this novel? Perhaps I felt a compelling need to tell the story of my youth—to clear my soul of that frightful time in my life when terror seemed to be my constant companion. The memories of that long ago summer had haunted me for years and I had kept my emotions bottled up inside me until I started to write my memoirs several years ago.

My experiences of that era taught me some valuable lessons that helped shape my life and character in later years.

It made me realize how valuable a human life really is and that I should be careful in my dealings with people; especially strangers. I learned to enjoy the great outdoors, the beauty of nature and all living things. The great golf hall of famer, Walter Hagen, said it best:

"Don't hurry, don't worry, and be sure to stop and smell the roses along the way."

We should all enjoy the passing of time that way.

I also learned to trust my instincts and to be patient and persevering in everything I did later in life; whether as a husband, a father or a participant in a particular sport. I also learned how to deal with adversity and to handle stress under the most intense competitive conditions.

More importantly, I learned how to love and express that love to my family and friends; something that was lacking in my own family when I was growing up. My mother was my great comforter and she always encouraged me to do my best whenever I competed in a sport, but she could only do so much.

She was not only a good mother and a wife, but she contributed to the war effort in WWII by working at a Remington arms factory in West Salt Lake; making 50 caliber machine gun bullets.

I always remember her telling me that I was going to do something great in my lifetime, but I can never remember my father even hugging me or telling me that he loved me.

I vowed early on that if I was ever fortunate enough to marry and raise a family that I would not withhold my true feelings from them. Hopefully, I haven't.

We live in a truly wonderful country where choices are made by us; not for us, as frequently occurs in other lands. I still get goose bumps when I salute the flag; when I hear the Star Spangled Banner or God Bless America sung or when I hear a stirring patriotic speech.

We do, indeed, live in a very special place on planet Earth, but I sometimes wonder if we really appreciate what we have and what has been given to us by those who came before us. And we don't seem to hear much good news anymore. Why is that? With the world rife with conflict and brazen, unpatriotic behavior, our way of life is being threatened as never before. That greatly concerns me.

But there is a solution. If we stay the course, take the high road, rather than the low road down the pathway of life, we can make good things happen in our own lives and in America as well. But, it must start and be nurtured in the home; not in the classroom.

Parents are the *early teachers* in life and it is in the home where that educational process should begin in earnest; where our young people are taught to be respectful of others, to obey the laws of the land and to appreciate the freedoms we enjoy.

There is much to be gained if we do—and much to be lost if we don't.

DON COLLETT

World Golf Hall of Fame
Pinehurst, N.C.

In 1971, Don Collett undertook a feasibility study to create a Golf Hall of Fame to honor the game's outstanding players and contributors of the sport. He raised the first $1 Million to build the shrine in Pinehurst, North Carolina. Construction got underway in 1972 and it was completed on September 11, 1974.

He inducted the first 13 honorees into the Hall of Fame consisting of eight living inductees along with representatives of the five deceased Hall of Famers. Mr. Collett served as the Hall's first President and arranged for the shrine to be put into a non-profit foundation in 1979 prior to it being turned over to the PGA of America.

As a result of his creation of the World Golf Hall of Fame, Mr. Collett was later honored by the state of North Carolina for his contributions to the growth and development of tourism in the State.

(Note: The World Golf Hall of Fame has been relocated to the World Golf Village in St. Augustine, Florida, along with all of the historical memorabilia Mr. Collett collected from throughout the world).

WORLD GOLF HALL OF FAME

INAUGURAL ENSHRINEMENT CEREMONIES

SEPTEMBER 11, 1974

1) Gary Player—one of golf's all-time greats.
2) Gene Sarazen—Enshrinee Acceptance.
3) Ben Hogan Accepts Enshirement.
4) Patty Berg, Byron Nelson, Sam Snead—on platform at Enshirement Ceremonies.
5) President Ford delivering Dedication Address.
6) Jack Nicklaus comments on his induction.
7) Arnold Palmer inducted into the Hall of Fame by Don Collett, President of the World Golf Hall of Fame.

A HISTORIC DAY IN GOLF

World Golf Hall of Fame Induction Ceremony at Pinehurst, North Carolina on September 11, 1974.

On the right, **Donald C. Collett**, President and Creator of the Hall of Fame, inducts one of the legends of the game, *Jack Nicklaus,* as a huge crowd looks on.

Nicklaus was one of the 13 original inductees that were enshrined in the inaugural ceremony.

ONE OF GOLF'S MOST HISTORIC DAYS

PINEHURST, NORTH CAROLINA—SEPTEMBER 11, 1974
WORLD GOLF HALL OF FAME INDUCTION CEREMONIES

Don Collett (right), President of the World Golf Hall of Fame, pauses for a moment after inducting one of golf's greatest players, Arnold Palmer, into the Hall of Fame. Collett, also a PGA Professional and creator of the Hall of Fame, inducted the original 13 enshrinees into the Hall, including, in addition to Palmer, Ben Hogan, Jack Nicklaus, Sam Snead, Byron Nelson, Gary Player, Gene Sarazen and Patty Berg.

OVAL OFFICE, THE WHITE HOUSE—1974

PGA Life Member Don Collett (right), president of the World Golf Hall of Fame in Pinehurst, North Carolina, presents a scrapbook to President Gerald R. Ford in December 1974 in The White House Oval Office. Three months earlier, Collett was alongside and played golf with the 38th President of the United States, who dedicated the Hall of Fame and participated in the induction ceremonies honoring the original 13 inductees into the Hall of Fame.
(Photo courtesy of The Office of Gerald R. Ford & Don Collett)

SYNOPSIS

The murky depths of an old abandoned well held many secrets, besides the bodies of past victims, but for 13-year-old Danny Collins, being thrown into that darkened shaft by a vicious ex-convict wasn't the way he expected his vacation to end in the Summer of 1939.

What was supposed to be a Summer of Fun ended up being a Summer of Terror for him. That he survived such an ordeal is a miracle in itself, but that nightmarish encounter with the ex-con didn't start at *The Well*. It was just the final confrontation between Danny and his antagonist, Jake Dalton, and his sidekick, Bernie McCoy.

There were other tense clashes with those two hardened criminals that left him in constant fear of his life, but none quite so harrowing as being thrown into an old abandoned well.

It's an action-packed novel, based on true events, that details life on a working ranch and the youthful courage of Danny Collins and his cousins, Bob and Jimmy Banfield, after they were left to die in the western Nevada desert.

978-0-595-36260-8
0-595-36260-5

To: Mark Figueroa ~
A scribe worth knowing ~

Best of luck in life
and in golf